Alan Bryden, Heiner Hänggi (Eds.)

Reform and Reconstruction of the Security Sector

Geneva Centre for the Democratic Control of Armed Forces (DCAF)

LIT

Alan Bryden, Heiner Hänggi (Eds.)

Reform and Reconstruction of the Security Sector

LIT

Gedruckt auf alterungsbeständigem Werkdruckpapier entsprechend
ANSI Z3948   DIN ISO 9706

Bibliographic information published by Die Deutsche Bibliothek
Die Deutsche Bibliothek lists this publication in the Deutsche
Nationalbibliografie; detailed bibliographic data are available in the
Internet at http://dnb.ddb.de.

ISBN 3-8258-7770-1

© LIT VERLAG Münster   2004
Grevener Str./Fresnostr. 2   48159 Münster
Tel. 0251-62 03 20   Fax 0251-23 19 72
e-Mail: lit@lit-verlag.de   http://www.lit-verlag.de

Distributed in North America by:

Transaction Publishers
New Brunswick (U.S.A.) and London (U.K.)

Transaction Publishers   Tel.: (732) 445 - 2280
Rutgers University   Fax: (732) 445 - 3138
35 Berrue Circle   for orders (U. S. only):
Piscataway, NJ 08854   toll free (888) 999 - 6778

Contents

IV. CONCLUSIONS

Preface

Theodor H. Winkler[*]

It is less than a decade ago that security sector reform (SSR) within the parameters of democratic governance was first identified as an important element of the international security and development debates. Today, SSR is widely recognized as key to conflict prevention, peace-building, sustainable development and democratisation.

The Geneva Centre for the Democratic Control of Armed Forces (DCAF) has been created in this context. Its mission is to promote the reform and democratic governance of the security sector in those states which are in need of it. As this volume shows, almost all states need to reform their security sectors to a greater or lesser extent, according to their specific security, political and socio-economic situations, as well as in response to the new security challenges resulting from the process of globalisation and post-9/11 developments.

In this vein, DCAF has decided to assess the progress made in pursuing SSR around the world on an annual basis – not by developing an SSR yearbook but by publishing an edited volume discussing specific issues that are relevant to practitioners and students of security sector governance. The first such book, relying on contributions from DCAF staff and experts drawn from partner institutions, was published in 2003 under the title 'Challenges of Security Sector Governance'. I am now most pleased to present the second volume, entitled 'Reform and Reconstruction of the Security Sector'.

This volume assesses the complex dynamics of SSR in key regions around the globe. It also looks at the particular challenges, in specific cases, of post-conflict reconstruction of the security sector. The regions and country case studies considered in this volume have been selected because they correspond to the priority geographical areas for DCAF's work programme. Contributions from academics and practitioners elaborate on both the conceptual underpinnings and the practical realities of security sector reform and – a crucial aspect of post-conflict peace-building – security sector reconstruction.

---

[*] Ambassador Theodor H. Winkler is Director of the Geneva Centre for the Democratic Control of Armed Forces (DCAF).

It is hoped that this book will contribute to the growing debate on security sector reform and good governance in the Euro-Atlantic region, West Africa and the Middle East. By bringing together the knowledge of both academics and practitioners the ultimate goal of this work is to contribute to meaningful results through better coordination, cooperation and implementation of projects by all those involved in this essential field.

Acknowledgements

In addition to the numerous publications resulting from its research and operational projects, the Geneva Centre for the Democratic Control of Armed Forces (DCAF) produces on an annual basis the results of ongoing research and analytical work on security sector governance by DCAF experts and our broader circle of collaborators. Without the efforts of a number of people we would not have succeeded in carrying this project to completion in the very tight timescales allotted. In particular, Karen Loehner, Jason Powers and Wendy Robinson provided invaluable administrative and editorial assistance. Tim Donais provided a great number of incisive comments and useful suggestions on earlier drafts of the manuscript while Eirin Mobekk proofread the final manuscript. Veit D. Hopf and Frank Weber of LIT Verlag steered us through the publication process with patience and encouragement. We would like to thank all of them and to express our special gratitude to the contributors to this book who did a wonderful job in meeting the great many demands the editors made on them.

The Editors
Geneva, 15 July 2004

PART I

INTRODUCTION

Chapter 1

Conceptualising Security Sector Reform and Reconstruction

Heiner Hänggi

Introduction

Since the late 1990s, security sector reform (SSR)[1] has emerged as a key concept, which has become widely accepted by development practitioners, security experts and, to a lesser extent, democracy advocates. It is a relatively ambiguous concept, which refers to a plethora of issues and activities related to the reform of the elements of the public sector charged with the provision of external and internal security. SSR is essentially aimed at the efficient and effective provision of state and human security within a framework of democratic governance.[2] Although SSR is still an evolving and, therefore, contested concept and lessons learned from practical experiences are still rather scarce, it increasingly shapes international programmes for development assistance, security cooperation and democracy promotion.

In practical terms, SSR varies substantially according to the specific reform context. There is general agreement that no common model of SSR exists and that, in principle, each country adopting SSR constitutes a special case and hence a different reform context. However, for analytical purposes, broad SSR contexts may be distinguished which contain a number of similar cases – depending on the criteria for categorisation. In this chapter, three such broad contexts of SSR will be discussed, each reflecting a different rationale for reform. First, SSR has been adopted by international development donors as an instrument to improve the efficiency and effectiveness of development assistance.[3] Second, SSR has become a tool to facilitate the practical coordination and conceptual integration of defence and internal security reforms in post-authoritarian states, particularly in post-communist states in Central and Eastern Europe and beyond.[4] Third, SSR has gained most practical relevance in the context of post-conflict reconstruction of so-called 'failed states' and states emerging from violent internal or inter-state conflict, as evidenced by a wide variety of cases such as Afghanistan and Iraq. In both cases, SSR is viewed by peacekeepers and development actors as key to success in the overall reconstruction effort. Security sector reconstruction, that is security sector reform in post-conflict contexts, exhibits a number of specific features which are distinct from other SSR settings.[5]

This volume traces the emergence of regional approaches to SSR in the post-9/11 era in the Euro-Atlantic area, particularly in the Western Balkans, West Africa and the Arab Middle East – regions in which the Geneva Centre for the Democratic Control of Armed Forces (DCAF) is active to a greater or lesser extent. It then looks at a series of specific post-conflict settings where security sector reform, or rather reconstruction, mostly under international auspices, has become a distinct feature – including Bosnia and Herzegovina, Kosovo, Liberia, Sierra Leone, Afghanistan and Iraq.

This chapter sets out to conceptualise security sector reform and security sector reconstruction as two closely interrelated concepts in order to provide a broad framework for analysis of the problems and challenges that are discussed in the following chapters. It starts with a broad definition of 'security sector' in the framework of a deepening and widening notion of security. This is followed by a discussion of what SSR means in general and in the specific reform contexts mentioned above. It will show that while security sector reform and security sector reconstruction can be distinguished for analytical purposes, overlaps are manifold. This chapter therefore suggests that security sector reconstruction is conceptualised as a variation of the theme – or a specific context – of security sector reform, which has become an important dimension of global security.

Security and the Security Sector

Since the end of the Cold War, we have witnessed a substantive widening and deepening of the concept of security. On one hand non-military security issues such as political, economic, societal and environmental aspects are now broadly accepted as component parts of a meaningful security agenda. Furthermore, military threats and the way states respond to them have changed, as illustrated by the events of 9/11 and its aftermath. Asymmetrical threats and warfare, as well as the blurring of the lines between different dimensions of traditional and new security issues, have emerged as characteristic features. The US-led 'war on terror' is particularly illustrative of the changing nature of military security as well as the increasing 'securitisation' of non-military issues. On the other hand, the primacy of national security has been undermined by the logic of globalisation and the corresponding changes in the role of the state. With the proliferation of intra-state wars and the privatisation of conflict in poorly governed and 'failing states' the inter-national community began to recognise that more often than not it is indi-viduals and social groups which need to be protected rather than the state whose dysfunctionality is often the primary cause of insecurity. This led to the emergence of new security concepts such as 'societal security' and 'hu-man security'. The latter, which has gained much recognition in the interna-tional arena, illustrates best the paradigmatic change from the primacy of national (and international) security to the growing importance of transna-tional, sub-national and individual security. Although still an ill-defined and contested concept, human security covers a wide range of threats to the secu-rity of individuals and social groups such as anti-personnel landmines, small arms and light weapons, child soldiers, trafficking in women as well as, in its wider notion, all aspects of human development such as economic, food, health and environmental insecurity. In sum, what makes these problems 'new' security issues, shaping a new or transformed international security agenda, is not that they are truly novel phenomena but rather that they are 'securitised', which means that they are explicitly characterised and treated as security concerns.[6]

As security is a contested concept, one might assume that the same holds true for the notion of the security sector. There are almost as many definitions as there are scholars and institutional actors trying to define what the 'security sector' comprises. This notwithstanding, there seems to be a certain convergence on a general definition which may vary in scope accord-ing to the perspective adopted (see Table 1.1.). Throughout the chapters in this book, however, a case is made for adoption of a broad definition of the security sector.

From a *security perspective*, the security sector reflects the broad no-tion of security (see above) because it does not cover the military alone, but acknowledges the importance and in some countries the predominant role of non-military security forces in the provision of public security, internal or external. Accordingly, the security sector encompasses all those state institu-tions, which have a formal mandate to ensure the safety of the state and its citizens against acts of violence and coercion such as the armed forces (do-mestic and foreign), the police, gendarmerie and paramilitary forces, the intelligence and secret services, border and customs guards as well as judicial and penal institutions. Given the prevalence of private and other non-statutory security actors in an increasing number of states, however, forces such as guerrilla and liberation armies, non-state paramilitary organisations as well as private military and security companies have to be considered either as part of the *de facto* security sector or at least as important actors shaping security sector governance. Thus, the security sector – as defined from a broad security perspective – would include statutory and non-statutory security forces.

Table 1.1: Definitions of the 'Security Sector'

Perspectives	Definition A[7]	Definition B[8]	Definition C[9]	Definition D[10]	Focus
Narrow	Security forces	Groups with a mandate to wield instruments of violence	Core security actors	Organisations authorised to use force	**State-centric**
	Civilian management and oversight bodies	Institutions with a role in managing and monitoring	Security management and oversight bodies	Civil management and oversight bodies	
Broader		Judiciary, penal system, human rights ombudsmen	Justice and law enforcement institutions	Justice and law enforcement institutions	
			Non-statutory security forces	Non-statutory security forces	**Human-centric**
				Non-statutory civil society groups	

From a *governance perspective*, the security sector covers the elements of the public sector responsible for the exercise of the state monopoly of coercive power and has traditionally been a key feature of the modern nation-state. This includes the elected and duly appointed civil authorities responsible for management and control of the security forces, such as the executive government, the relevant ministries (so-called 'power ministries', particularly the ministries of defence and of the interior), the parliament and its specialised committees. Like any other part of the public sector, the security sector should be subject to the principles of good governance such as accountability, transparency and democratic participation. Given the broad notion of security and the increasing importance of internal security issues, particularly in the wake of 9/11 and its aftermath, justice and law enforcement institutions are viewed as relevant actors for security sector governance. Thus, judiciary and ministries of justice, criminal investigation and prosecution services, prison regimes, ombudspersons and human rights commissions should be considered as a component part of the security sector if defined in the broad notion of the term. Given the importance of civil society for democratic governance, non-statutory civil society groups such as the media, research institutions and non-governmental organisations play, or should play, an important role in security sector governance. Thus, the security sector, as defined from a democratic governance perspective, would include a wide range of civil society actors in addition to the state institutions tasked with security sector management and oversight.

Considering civil society actors and non-statutory forces as component parts of the security sector in its broad sense helps to transcend the essentially state-centric nature of the concept which, in an increasing number of cases, wrongly assumes that the monopoly over the means of coercion rests solely with the state and its institutions. From a security and a governance perspective, one would assume that limited involvement by non-statutory security forces and a strong role of non-statutory civil society actors are more desirable than the contrary.

Not only is the essentially state-centric notion of the security sector transcended by the relevance of civil society and private security actors, but security sector governance also tends to have a regional and trans-regional dimension. Most countries are part of a regional security complex, and many security challenges are often transnational and therefore cannot be dealt with by national means alone. It thus makes sense to think in terms of sub-regional, regional and trans-regional security sectors, which are constituted by multilateral military, policing and intelligence capacity, intergovernmental security organisations, their inter-parliamentary assemblies and supranational judicial bodies. Even transnational private security forces such as international militia and terrorist groups as well as transnational civil society actors such as international non-governmental organisations (INGO) would find their place in a regionally or trans-regionally conceived security sector. The Euro-Atlantic region, particularly the European Union, may be viewed as the strongest expression of such a security sector beyond the national level (Chapter 2). Even in a conflict-prone area such as the Western Balkans,

elements of a sub-regional security sector are emerging, as illustrated by the
Ohrid process, which is intended to establish an integrated border security
management system for the region (Chapter 7). In West Africa, too, indications of an emerging sub-regional security sector can be witnessed – as evidenced by the growing security role of the Economic Community of West
African States (ECOWAS) and the creation of the ECOWAS Mechanism for
Conflict Prevention, Management and Resolution, Peacekeeping and Security in particular (Chapter 4). ECOWAS is playing a central role in the post-
conflict rehabilitation of two of its member states, Liberia and Sierra Leone
(Chapter 8). In this context, the Arab Middle East – plagued by serious democratic and security deficits – seems to constitute a strong counterfactual
argument though the nascent SSR debate tends to be framed in a regional
context (Chapter 5).

        In sum, the definition of what constitutes the security sector is multi-
faceted, evolving, and therefore debatable. However, in response to the new
security agenda resulting from post-Cold War and post-9/11 developments,
there seems to be a tendency to broaden the scope of the security sector beyond its state-centric core. This results in (1) the consideration of non-
statutory private security and civil society actors as parts of the security sector and (2) the conceptualisation of the security sector on regional and trans-
regional levels.

Security Sector Reform and Reconstruction

A dysfunctional security sector is the point of departure for security sector
reform (Chapter 2). A security sector can be considered as dysfunctional if it
does not provide security to the state and its people in an efficient and effective way or, even worse, if it is the cause of insecurity. Moreover, as a consequence of the aforementioned broad definition, a security sector cannot be
viewed as functional if it is deficient it terms of governance. Thus, SSR is
meant to reduce security deficits (inefficient and ineffective provision of
security or even provision of insecurity) as well as democratic deficits (lack
of oversight over the security sector) which result from dysfunctional security sectors. In other words, SSR is a means that serves the objective of providing 'security within the state in an effective and efficient manner, and in
the framework of democratic civilian control'.[11] In an address to the World
Bank staff in October 1999, UN Secretary-General Kofi Annan made a
strong case for security sector reform. Referring to the concept of good gov-

ernance, he noted that 'another very important aspect is the reform of public services – including the security sector, which should be subject to the same standards of efficiency, equity and accountability as any other service'.[12] A recent authoritative definition of SSR stems from the Development Assistance Committee (DAC) of the Organisation for Economic Co-operation and Development (OECD), which states that 'security system reform is another term used to describe the transformation of the security system – which includes all the actors, their roles, responsibilities and actions – working together to manage and operate the system in a manner that is more consistent with democratic norms and sound principles of good governance and this contributes to a well-functioning security framework'.[13] The SSR agenda favours a holistic approach to the provision of security in a double sense. First, it integrates all those partial reforms such as defence reform, police reform, intelligence reform and justice reform, which in the past were generally seen and conducted as separate efforts. Second, given its normative commitment to consolidation of democracy, promotion of human rights and implementation of the principles of good governance such as accountability and transparency, it aims at putting the security sector and its parts under democratic governance.[14]

What all these attempts at defining SSR have in common is that they contain two normative elements which constitute the core of the SSR concept, namely the development of (1) affordable security bodies capable of providing security (operational effectiveness and efficiency aspect) and (2) effective oversight mechanisms consistent with democratic norms (democratic governance aspect).[15] The task of providing both security (state and human security) and democratic governance is difficult, even for consolidated democracies, not to speak of developing, transition and post-conflict countries. In case of the latter, the challenge is even greater given the fact that SSR has to tackle a third objective, namely to address the legacies of past conflict including disarmament, demobilisation and reintegration (DDR) of former combatants, judicial reform in the form of transitional justice, the proliferation of small arms and light weapons, and anti-personnel landmines.[16] These two – and in the case of post-conflict environments – three objectives, are widely recognised as the core elements of SSR.[17]

As has been mentioned elsewhere, the SSR debate suffers from an imbalance between the broad acceptance of this rather recent concept and the relatively little consideration and investigation of specific reform contexts. In other words, it suffers from a 'conceptual-contextual divide',[18] which has

Table 1.2: Contexts of Security Sector Reform

	Developmental context	Post-authoritarian context	Post-conflict context
Key criteria	Level of economic development	Nature of political system	Specific security situation
Key problem	Development deficit	Democratic deficit	Security and democratic deficits
Key reform objective	Development	Democratisation	Peace-building / nation-building
General reform process	Transition from underdeveloped to developed economy	Transition from authoritarian to democratic system	Transition from violent conflict to peace
Nature of external involvement	Development assistance coupled with political conditionality	Accession to multilateral institutions as incentive for reform	Military intervention / occupation; mostly UN-led peace support operations
Key external actors	Development/financial actors: multilateral donors (e.g. OECD, UNDP, World Bank); bilateral donors; non-state actors	Security actors: international (e.g. EU, NATO, OSCE); governments; non-state actors (e.g. INGOs, PMCs)	Security actors: intervention forces; peacekeeping forces under international auspices; non-state actors (e.g. PMCs)
Specific security sector problems	Excessive military spending; poorly managed / governed security sector leads to ineffective provision of security, thereby diverting scarce resources from development	Oversized, over-resourced military-industrial complex; strong state, but weak civil society institutions; deficiencies in implementing SSR policies	Government and civil society institutions collapsed; displaced populations; privatisation of security; possibly pockets of armed resistance; abundance of small arms and anti-personnel mines
Possibilities for SSR	Mixed (depending on political commitment to reform, strength of state institutions, role and state of security forces, regional security environment, donor approach to SSR, etc.)	Rather good (strong state institutions, professional security forces, broader democratisation process), even better if external incentives available (e.g. accession to EU or NATO)	Rather poor (weak and contested state institutions, privatisation of security, dependence on peace support / intervention forces)

to be bridged if the study of SSR is to facilitate the design and implementation of SSR programmes. There is a widely held view that reform contexts matter, and that SSR differs from country to country in the sense that, in addition to specific historical conditions, the level of economic development, the nature of the political system and the security environment will heavily influence the pattern of the reform process. For analytical purposes, a number of very general reform contexts can be identified, which exhibit a degree of commonality depending on the criteria applied. If the level of economic development, the nature of the political system and the specific security situation are used as points of departure, three different SSR contexts may be distinguished each of which has contributed to shaping the SSR debate in its own way: (1) the developmental context, (2) the post-authoritarian (primarily post-communist) context and (3) the post-conflict context (see Table 1.2).[19]

Before discussing these three SSR contexts, it must be underlined that highly developed countries, consolidated democracies and states which are internally and externally secure, also face pressures to reform their security sectors, particularly in response to new security requirements accentuated by 9/11 and its aftermath[20] or to deficiencies in international security governance related to the effects of globalisation.[21] These pressures are not specific to a given reform context but ar more generally applicable. All states are challenged by this new security agenda, irrespectively if they are developed or developing countries, transition states or consolidated democracies, post-conflict societies or those countries which are part of the 'democratic peace' area.[22]

Developmental Context

As mentioned above, the origins of the SSR concept stem from the development community, who have increasingly acknowledged the importance of linking development with security, emphasising the crucial role a well governed, efficient security sector plays in the provision of security and as a precondition of sustainable economic development. Conversely, if poorly managed and governed, the security sector can act as a spoiler of development efforts. Initially concentrating on the reduction of excessive military expenditures, in the late 1990s the development community began to embrace the SSR concept permitting at least some donors to justify greater involvement in security-related issues.[23] Since then, the concept has gained much wider recognition, particularly in the debate about increasing the efficiency and effectiveness of development assistance.[24] In other words, SSR in a developmental context is an externally, particularly donor-driven process, which may be used as an incentive, or a political condition, for the provision of development assistance.

The SSR agenda pursued by the development donors makes the concept problematic from the perspective of recipient countries. Other than in post-conflict countries, SSR programmes are still quite the exception in developing countries which, although in principle in need of SSR, are not haunted by the legacy of recent violent conflict and therefore not forced to rely on external involvement for the provision of public security.

Post-Authoritarian Context

SSR has also become an issue for post-authoritarian states, who have embarked on a transition to democracy. This holds particularly true for post-communist states in Central and Eastern Europe and for post-Soviet states, which undertook or are still undertaking efforts to democratise their public sector, including the security sector. However, until recently, SSR has not been widely used as an operational concept within the Euro-Atlantic region. Earlier in the 1990s, SSR-related objectives such as good governance, efficiency and effectiveness were usually conceived by the transition states only in terms of democratic control of armed forces, defence reform and/or defence modernisation. Post-authoritarian experiences, however, and post-communist legacies in particular, such as continued authoritarian leadership, nepotism, corruption and unaccountable segments of the security apparatus, have led many analysts and practitioners to think more holistically about key aspects of security sector governance. External involvement also matters in the post-authoritarian SSR context as illustrated by the roles played by NATO and the EU in the transition of post-communist states in Central and Eastern Europe and beyond. Whereas NATO still exhibits a preference for the more traditional armed forces and defence reform agenda, the emergence of the EU as an, albeit constrained, security actor in the region, concentrating on various aspects of internal security reform (policing, border management, refugee and asylum policies), has been a key factor in broadening the debate to include all aspects of the SSR agenda. Still today, these two multilateral institutions shape the SSR agenda each according to their own statutory preferences – defence reform (NATO), internal security reform (EU). [25]

If SSR is viewed as having been more successful in European post-communist states than in developing states, then this is probably due to the significant leverage the EU and NATO have to encourage comprehensive SSR in candidate states. If states wish to accede to these Western institutions they have to meet a number of requirements, some of them related to democratic governance of the security sector. At the same time, however, the relatively rapid accession of a great number of former communist states – boosting NATO to twenty-six and the EU to twenty-five member states – might result in a loss of the leverage NATO and EU hold over these countries in the post-accession era.[26] Whether the policy of using engagement with and the option of accession to NATO and EU as an incentive for SSR-related transformation will work in the Western Balkans remains to be seen. It will most certainly turn out to be a more complex, time-consuming and resource-intensive process given the post-conflict setting that inhibits SSR in that sub-region (Chapter 7).

Post-Conflict Context

A third area where SSR has found growing acceptance are post-conflict societies emerging from internal or inter-state conflict, embarking on a process of reconstructing all parts of the public sector which had been destroyed or become dysfunctional during the past conflict (Chapter 6). Among the activities currently subsumed under the heading of SSR, most of them take place in post-conflict settings. Clearly, engaging in SSR in post-conflict environments poses special challenges, and also presents particular opportunities. One the one hand, SSR seems to be particularly difficult in an adverse environment such as a post-conflict setting, usually characterised by weak state institutions, a fragile inter-ethnic or political situation, with influential armed and other security forces, both statutory and non-statutory, and precarious economic conditions.[27] On the other hand, given the quite obvious need to 'rightsize' the security sector and reform or even reconstruct it after the end of the conflict, post-conflict situations represent 'windows of opportunity' for security sector reform or, in many cases, security sector reconstruction programmes.[28] Generally speaking, in such societies there is a strong will to accept external support for all kinds of reforms, even in the most sensitive areas such as the security sector. This holds true only for the cases of civil war and internal conflict prior to the post-conflict reconstruction efforts. In cases where an inter-state war such as a foreign military intervention aimed at regime change and resulting in a transitional occupation preceded post-conflict reconstruction efforts, the security environment may simply be too adverse to implement a comprehensive and effective SSR programme as evidenced in Afghanistan (Chapter 9) and particularly so in Iraq, where armed resistance means that SSR is taking place under combat conditions (Chapter 10). Even without armed resistance against the intervention troops, irrespectively if their presence is legitimised by a UN mandate or not, post-conflict contexts pose the most formidable challenges to SSR.

As mentioned above, SSR in post-conflict settings, or security sector reconstruction, follows the same two key principles as SSR in other contexts, namely (re-)establishing security forces which are able to provide public security in an effective and efficient manner and in the framework of democratic, civilian control. What makes security sector reconstruction different from security sector reform, however, is the fact that it has to deal with the specific legacy of past conflict. This may include oversized armed forces, both statutory and non-statutory, that need to be downsized, surplus weapons that need to be removed, anti-personnel landmines that need to be cleared, large numbers of perpetrators that need to be prosecuted. Thus, more often than not, disarmament, demobilisation and reintegration of former combatants, judicial capacity-building to permit for transitional justice, curbing the proliferation of small arms and light weapons, and clearance of anti-personnel landmines are viewed as key elements of security sector reconstruction, but not necessarily of security sector reform activities in developmental and post-authoritarian contexts.

Three further points may be added to make a case for an analytical distinction between security sector reconstruction and security sector reform. First, post-conflict settings are characterised by a need for the immediate provision of public security, which may undermine, or at least delay, the tackling of longer-term issues of security sector governance (Chapters 6 and 8). Second, the tensions between external imposition and local ownership of SSR has special relevance in the context of post-conflict security sector reconstruction because more often than not physical security will have to be provided by international actors while sufficient local capacity is gradually being built up – a process which may take a very long time. Finally, the need to provide immediate security through international means, to (re-)construct state security institutions and to establish effective and legitimate security governance mechanisms poses a difficult challenge in post-conflict settings where private security actors (or non-statutory security organisations) throw into question the state's or, in a transitional phase, the international authority's monopoly on the legitimate use of force. The role of non-statutory security forces in the Kosovo conflict (Chapter 7), the proliferation of irregular forces recruiting child soldiers in Liberia and Sierra Leone (Chapter 8), the continued authority of regional warlords in Afghanistan (Chapter 9), the existence of a variety of local militias in Iraq (Chapter 10) and the role of often unaccountable private military and security companies in conflict and post-conflict environments are good cases in point to illustrate the adverse implications of the privatisation of security.

What the developmental, post-authoritarian and post-conflict contexts have in common, is that SSR tends to be characterised by a greater or lesser involvement of external actors – not necessarily as principal actors of reform, but certainly as its initiators. In all three contexts, there are tensions between external imposition and local ownership of SSR. This seems to be a crucial issue, both because of questions around sustainability of reforms and because, in exporting Western reform models, there has been a 'missionary tendency' around Western approaches to SSR. The difficulties of finding a balance between international best practices in this area and domestic political cultures of reforming states are raised throughout the chapters of this volume although without necessarily leading to specific recommendations on how this could best be solved. This tension is inherent in the SSR concept itself and is thus not amenable to easy solutions.

Challenges of Security Sector Reform and Reconstruction

This volume sets out to improve our conceptual and empirical understanding of security sector reform and reconstruction, to identify major challenges in this policy field and to outline specific policy recommendations where appropriate. As developed in this chapter, security sector reconstruction is understood as a specific context of security sector reform – SSR in a post-conflict environment. For analytical purposes, a distinction is made in the structure of this book between security sector reform (part II) and security sector reconstruction (part III). This, however, does not preclude the contributors from using the terms 'security sector reform' and 'security sector reconstruction' in an interchangeable way – in the end, it is the reform context that matters and not the terms used for addressing context-specific issues. Part II addresses approaches to security sector reform in a regional context, with emphasis on the Euro-Atlantic area in general (Chapter 2) and Central and Eastern Europe in particular (Chapter 3), on West Africa (Chapter 4) and the Arab Middle East (Chapter 5). Part III looks into one of the three SSR contexts discussed earlier – that of post-conflict reconstruction. It starts with the development of an analytical framework for empirical research on post-conflict reconstruction of the security sector under the auspices of international institutions (Chapter 6). This is followed by four case studies with two chapters concentrating on a number of cases in two subregions, namely the Western Balkans (Chapter 7) and West Africa (Chapter 8), and two chapters focusing on more recent cases of security sector reconstruction, both resulting from post-9/11 military interventions, namely Afghanistan (Chapter 9) and Iraq (Chapter 10).

The volume concludes with a review of the main issues and challenges of security sector reform and reconstruction based on the findings of the previous chapters. While not particularly optimistic either of past experience or future prospects for SSR, this volume effectively lays out the complex challenges faced by both external and internal actors in this area, and in this sense it may make a useful contribution to the ongoing debate on SSR – standing for both security sector *reform* and security sector *reconstruction*.

Notes

[1]   'Security sector reform' is the term of choice in this chapter because it is most commonly used by practitioners as well as analysts. Reference is made, however, to alternative terms such as 'security system reform', used by the Development Assistance Committee (DAC) of the Organisation for Economic Co-operation and Development (OECD), 'justice and security sector reform', introduced by the United Nations Development Programme (UNDP) and 'security sector transformation', which is increasingly being used in the African context to underline the need for fundamental change in governance processes in the security sector (see Chapter 4).

[2]   On the concept of security sector reform see, for example, Born, H., Caparini, M., Fluri, P., (eds.), *Security Sector Reform and Democracy in Transitional Societies* (Nomos: Baden-Baden, 2002); Bryden, A., Fluri, P., (eds.), *Security Sector Reform: Institutions, Society and Good Governance* (Nomos: Baden-Baden, 2003); Brzoska, M., *Development Donors and the Concept of Security Sector Reform*, DCAF Occasional Paper no. 4 (Geneva Centre for the Democratic Control of Armed Forces: Geneva, 2003); Ball, N., *Enhancing Security Sector Governance: A Conceptual Framework for UNDP* (9 October 2002); Ball, N., Fayemi, K., Olonisakin, F., Williams, R., *Governance in the security sector*, in Van de Walle, N., Ball, N., Ramachandran, V., (eds.), *Beyond Structural Adjustment. The Institutional Context of African Development* (Palgrave MacMillan: New York, 2003), pp. 263-304; Chalmers, M., *Security Sector Reform in Developing Countries: An EU Perspective* (Saferworld and the Conflict Prevention Network: London, 2000); Chanaa, J., *Security Sector Reform: Issues, Challenges and Prospects*, Adelphi Papers, no. 344 (Oxford University Press: Oxford, 2002); Cooper, N., Pugh, M., *Security Sector Transformation in Post-Conflict Societies*, CDSG Working Paper no. , (King's College: London, 2002); Ed-

munds, T., *Security Sector Reform: Concepts and Implementation*, DCAF Working Paper no. 3 (Geneva Centre for the Democratic Control of Armed Forces: Geneva, 2002); Germann, W., Edmunds, T., (eds.), *Towards Security Sector Reform in Post Cold War Europe. A Framework for Assessment* (Nomos: Baden-Baden, 2003); Hendrickson, D., *A Review of Security-Sector Reform*, CSDG Working Paper no. 1 (Centre for Defence Studies, King's College: London, 1999); Hendrickson, D., Karkoszka, A., 'The Challenges of Security Sector Reform', *SIPRI Yearbook 2002: Armaments, Disarmament and International Security* (Oxford University Press: Oxford, 2002); Karkoszka, A., 'The Concept of Security Sector Reform', in *Security Sector Reform: Its Relevance for Conflict Prevention, Peace Building, and Development* (United Nations Office at Geneva and Geneva Centre for the Democratic Control of Armed Forces: Geneva, 2003), pp. 9-15; Lilly, D., Von Tangen Page, M., *The Privatisation of Security and Security Sector Reform* (International Alert: London, 2002); *Security System Reform and Governance: Policy and Good Practice. A DAC Reference Document* (Organisation for Economic Co-operation and Development [OECD]: Paris, 2004); Smith, C., 'Security Sector Reform: Developmental Breakthrough or Institutional Re-engineering', *Conflict, Security and Development*, vol. 1, no. 1 (2001); *Towards a Better Practice Framework in Security Sector Reform: Broadening the Debate,* Occasional SSR Paper no. 1 (Clingendael, International Alert, Saferworld: The Hague, London, August 2002); United Nations Development Programme (UNDP), 'Democratizing security to prevent conflict and build peace', *Human Development Report 2002: Deepening Democracy in a Fragmented World* (Oxford University Press: Oxford, 2002), pp. 85-100; United Nations Development Programme (UNDP), *Justice and Security Sector Reform: BCPR's Programmatic Approach* (UNDP; New York, 2002); Winkler, T., *Managing Change: The Reform and Democratic Control of the Security Sector and International Order*, DCAF Occasional Paper no. 1 (Geneva Centre for the Democratic Control of Armed Forces: Geneva, 2002); Wulf, H., *Security Sector Reform in Developing Countries* (Deutsche Gesellschaft für Technische Zuammenarbeit [GTZ]: Eschborn, 2000); Wulf, H., *Security Sector Reform in Developing and Transitional Countries*, paper prepared for the Berghof Handbook for Conflict Resolution (forthcoming).

[3] Brzoska, *Development Donors*.

[4] Cottey, A., Edmunds, T., Forster, A., 'The second generation problematic: rethinking democracy and civil-military relations', *Armed Forces and Society*, vol. 29, no. 1 (December 2002).

[5] Cooper/Pugh, *Security Sector Transformation*.

[6] Hänggi, H., 'Making Sense of Security Sector Governance', in Hänggi, H., Winkler, T., (eds.), *Challenges of Security Sector Governance* (LIT: Münster, 2003), pp. 5-6.

[7] Informal DAC Task Force on Conflict, Peace and Development Co-operation, *Security Issues and Development Co-operation: A Conceptual Framework for Enhancing Policy Coherence* (Organisation for Economic Co-operation and Development [OECD]: Paris, 2000), p. 8.

[8] Hendrickson, *A Review of Security-Sector Reform*, p. 29; Greene, O., 'Security Sector Reform, Conflict Prevention and Regional Perspectives', *Journal of Security Sector Management*, vol. 1, no. 1 (March 2003), p. 2.

[9] *Security System Reform*, pp. 16-17; Karkoszka/Hendrickson, *The Challenges*, p. 179.

[10] UNDP, *Democratizing Security*, p. 87; *Towards a Better Practice*, pp. 3-4.

[11] Edmunds, *Security Sector Reform*, pp. 3-4.

[12] Annan, K., 'Peace and Development – One Struggle, Two Fronts', Address of the United Nations Secretary-General to World Bank Staff, October 19, 1999, p. 5.

[13] *Security System Reform*, p. 16.

[14] Brzoska, *Development Donors*, p. 16.

[15] Ball, *Enhancing Security Sector Governance*, pp. ii, 5.

[16] *Security System Reform*, pp. 16, 17;

[17] Hänggi, *Making Sense*, pp. 17-18.

[18] Chanaa, *Security Sector Reform*, p. 61.

[19] There are a number of contexts in which SSR is problematic if not impossible and which, therefore, are not considered in this chapter: (1) lapsing or stalled democracies where there is no commitment to reform; (2) conflict-prone and war-torn societies or civil war settings where the legitimacy of the authorities is contested by armed insurgency or other forms of violent opposition, and (3) developing countries under authoritarian rule with the military or other security forces being key pillars of state power. See Brzoska, *Development Donors*, p. 40; Wulf, *Security Sector Reform*, p. 6.

[20] Reference is made to the increased salience after 9/11 of intelligence, police, law enforcement and border security, the blurring of lines between internal and external security, and the need to find a new balance between increased powers of the security sector and the existing oversight mechanisms. See Slocombe, W., 'Terrorism/Counter-Terrorism: Their Impact on Security Sector Reform and Basic Democratic Values', in Bryden/Fluri, *Security Sector Reform*, pp. 291-301.

[21] Reference is made to deficiencies in the accountability of national armed forces being deployed under the auspices of international institutions. See Born, H., Hänggi, H., (eds.), *The 'Double Democratic Deficit'. Parliamentary Accountability and the Use of Force Under International Auspices* (Ashgate: Aldershot, 2004).

[22] For the 'democratic peace' proposition, see Russett, B., *Grasping the Democratic Peace; Principles for a Post-Cold War World* (Princeton University Press: Princeton, NJ, 1993).

[23] Brzoska, *Development Donors*, pp. 20-22.

[24] Karkoszka, 'The Concept', pp. 10-11.

[25] Caparini, M., 'Security Sector Reform and NATO and EU Enlargement', in Hänggi/Winkler, *Challenges of Security Sector Governance*, pp. 55-84.

[26] Ibid, pp. 77-78.

[27] Karkoszka, 'The Concept', p. 11.

[28] Brzoska, *Development Donors*, p. 32, see also pp. 10-13.

PART II

SECURITY SECTOR REFORM

Chapter 2

Security Sector Reform in the Euro-Atlantic Region: Unfinished Business

David Law

Introduction[1]

Security sector reform in the Euro-Atlantic security region enjoys a number of important advantages. While many states in the Euro-Atlantic are in the throes of a post-communist transition, including several underdeveloped post-communist states that are among the world's poorest and most authoritarian, the region also counts nineteen of the world's twenty-four most affluent economies.[2] This is important for experience has shown that security sector reform requires significant resources over an extended period. The region also has the longest history of multilateral practice and the largest concentration of institutions involved in aspects of security sector reform, as well as a number of state-level and non-governmental actors that have played a leading role in this area, both within the Euro-Atlantic region and further afield. Together, they have amassed decades of experience in carrying out the reform of defence and public security institutions. This has instilled an appreciation within the region of the importance of embedding reform in a multilateral process where the political costs can be shared and lessons about best practices readily disseminated. Last but not least, the Euro-Atlantic region is the only one to enjoy a multilaterally approved, politically binding Code of Conduct on the Politico-Military Aspects of Security. Agreed by all Organisation for Security and Cooperation in Europe (OSCE) members in 1994, this document established a number of key guidelines for the security sector, thus establishing a framework for subsequent reform efforts in the Euro-Atlantic area.[3]

Notwithstanding these advantages, security sector reform in the Euro-Atlantic region has proceeded in a fragmented and uneven manner, and with largely unsatisfactory results. In several countries, serious reform efforts have yet to begin or are still only in their infancy, despite over a decade of national and international pressure for reform. This is a judgement that also applies to the developed democracies that have acted as the mentors of transition states in the reform process, as strategic change at the beginning of the twenty-first century has driven home the need for radical adjustments to the security sectors of all countries. The result is that the Euro-Atlantic region finds itself hard pressed to address either the peace support contingencies that were the hallmark of the 1990s or the 9/11 type of threats that characterise the current decade. In consequence, the Euro-Atlantic region runs the risk of being able neither to project stability beyond its borders nor to protect key assets within them.

This chapter will look at the reasons behind this situation and suggest steps that could help build momentum for a deeper, broader and more effective process of reform. The first section of the paper will review the factors that have shaped thinking about security sector reform in the Euro-Atlantic region. In the second section, we will examine the structure of the security sector in the region. Here we shall introduce the concept of a regional Euro-Atlantic security sector as a vital complement to the national security sectors of the region. The third section will focus on key institutional actors that are active in security sector reform activities in the region. Before concluding, the chapter will propose a number of policy approaches designed to reinforce and render more effective ongoing and future reform efforts.

The Evolution of Security Sector Perspectives in the Euro-Atlantic Region

The concept of security sector reform in the Euro-Atlantic region has been shaped by a number of policy experiences, some of which emerged well before the term, 'security sector reform' was first coined in 1998 by the then UK Development Minister Claire Short.[4] Formative experience with security sector reform in the Euro-Atlantic region dates back to the Cold War. During the East-West conflict, little attention was paid to how security sectors were structured or governed. The protagonists were above all interested in gathering allies and maintaining alliances for their ideological, political, socioeconomic and military competition. One major exception to this pattern was concern about inflated expenditure on the military and the resulting diversion of resources meant for development, an issue primarily championed by the United Nations and one that remains a concern today.[5] However, a sea change occurred after the end of the Cold War, as in third world conflict situations the constraining effect of the East-West struggle dissipated and local wars erupted with new energy. Western donors realised that unless they could ensure that the entire security sector – not just the military, but the paramilitary and other entities with a capacity to use force – were adequately resourced and trained, and at the same time subject to political control by governments accountable to their citizens, their efforts in support of development would likely prove moot.

The second experience shaping the concept of security sector reform came with the challenges of transition in the post-communist states of Europe and Eurasia. Initially, the focus of Western donors in the Euro-Atlantic region was on civil-military relations and the need for democratic control of the military. The experience with post-conflict reconstruction in Bosnia and Herzegovina made it evident that the prospects for successful post-conflict development were contingent on a major restructuring of the entire security sector and its subordination to rigorous criteria of transparency, accountability and good governance, under the conditions of inter-community reconciliation and ethnic tolerance. Similarly, it became clear that reform not only of the military, but also of customs and border guard regimes, paramilitary forces and intelligence services was the key to successful transition in Central and Eastern Europe (CEE), the Russian Federation and other post-Soviet states, regardless of whether they had experienced serious conflict after the USSR's dissolution or not. Accordingly, more and more practitioners came to accept that the prevailing focus on the military needed to give way to a more comprehensive approach that encompassed, in line with lessons learned in the developing world, the entire security sector.

The third experience shaping Euro-Atlantic approaches to security sector reform has come with the changes in the strategic environment at the beginning of the twenty-first century. September 11th 2001 (9/11) is often used as shorthand for this shift because of its enormous geo-political impact and the way it has highlighted how a non-state terrorist group can inflict catastrophic damage with unconventional weaponry. 9/11 has also drawn the attention of the world to the vulnerability of even the world's most powerful military actor to the machinations of a relatively small, non-territorialised network with modest resources, but with a revanchist agenda enjoying significant transnational resonance.

The 9/11 attacks affected countries throughout the Euro-Atlantic region, whether because of their strategic ties with the US, economic interdependence or the new patterns of politico-military cooperation later developed in the struggle against terrorism. However, if at first the impact of strategic terrorism on states other than the US may have appeared largely indirect, subsequent events have signalled that others can be directly at risk. 9/11 type terrorist attacks have now taken place in Madrid; al-Qaeda cells have been discovered in a series of countries, including those not participating in the US military campaign in Iraq; statements attributed to al-Qaeda leaders have underscored that the movement's targets include a wide range of countries, regardless of their Middle East policies.[6]

Irrespectively of how one assesses the importance of 9/11, it seems undeniable that a number of factors have come together in these first years of the twenty-first century to effect a paradigm shift in the international security environment. If several individual aspects of the new strategic paradigm are in themselves not new, their collective impact has been to create what might be called *a new quality of threat*. The world has entered an environment that is a different from that of the 1990s or the Cold War period as the latter was from World War II and the big power rivalries of the 1920 and 1930s.

As with the experience in first developing and then transition countries, changes in the strategic environment also point to the need for security sector reform, but this time on a much broader front. No longer can security sector reform be something that developed countries promote in only developing or transition countries. The onus is now on them to move beyond piecemeal reform efforts, mainly restricted to their armed forces, which they undertook in the 1990s and embrace a much more ambitious reform agenda.[7] The other side of this coin concerns the situation of the transition countries of the Euro-Atlantic region. At the bidding of their Western mentors, some of them have taken a broad approach to restructuring their security sectors and in the process made a number of the changes that developed countries now have to envisage. As the reform process continues in the Euro-Atlantic region, the previously hierarchical relationship in which Westerners showed the way should yield to one where advice on policy and lessons learned travel along a two-way street.

During the Cold War, the *leitmotif* was the external threat that faced all countries of the Euro-Atlantic area. During the 1990s, there was a shift to internal security considerations as new states emerging post-Cold War plunged into domestic conflict. In these conflicts, the developed democracies were involved through peace support activities, sometimes suffering serious losses. However, for most of the developed democracies, their involvement was on a sporadic or *à la carte* basis. The next progression combines the key characteristics of the two preceding ones. The risk has been 'democratised' as countries both rich and less so have felt themselves exposed in the same manner.

Notwithstanding the very different characteristics of the third policy experience, there are common threads running through all three. One is that there is an economic bottom line to dysfunctionality in the security sector, whether this is in a developing, transition or developed country. The economic disruption caused by the 9/11 attacks is a case in point.[8] Another is that certain kinds of pathologies (see Table 2.1) can afflict the security sector, irrespective of the level of development.

A dysfunctional security sector – one that is deficient in terms of governance or efficiency – can threaten the interests of a state and its citizens in several different, and sometimes interlocking, ways. The over-consumption of state resources by the state sector can have negative consequences for the transition countries of the Euro-Atlantic region where resources are particularly scarce. The opposite kind of problem can have adverse consequences as well. An under-resourced security sector can invite foreign invasion, subjugation and loss of sovereignty. This is a problem that has assumed special importance in many of the post-Soviet successor states where there is little or no tradition of state sovereignty in modern times and where military service has not been a mainstream career.

A related problem can occur when a country over-invests in certain dimensions of its security to the detriment of others. For example, the United States has attached enormous importance to building up its armed forces as opposed to developing other instruments to conduct its security policy. Resources for the military have increased exponentially while those for foreign policy have lagged far behind. This is bound to have repercussions for the kind of policies that are selected to deal with conflict and post-conflict situations, such as in Iraq.[9] In contrast, many traditional allies of the US have neglected their military capabilities over the years, favouring instead economic means, diplomacy and other soft security instruments. Again, this is bound to have repercussions for policy.

When the security sector is subject to little or almost no control this can generate a situation where a security sector actor becomes sufficiently influential to be able to impose its interests on the entire nation in the name of state security. A possible example concerns what has happened in Chechnya. The Russian military serving in the area and the general staff have developed approaches to the conflict that are not necessarily consistent with the security interests of the Russian Federation, and which its elected representatives may be relatively powerless to correct. Russia may be stuck in the throes of a problem from which Turkey is hopefully at long last emerging. Extreme versions of this kind of pathology can be found in states where democratic control has collapsed altogether or never been developed at all.

Table 2.1: SSR Pathologies

SSR Pathologies		Possible Consequences		Impact
Overconsumption of resources by SS	▶	Diversion of resources for growth & development		
Underinvestment of re-sources into SS	▶	Risk of foreign subjuga-tion & loss of sovereignty		Enhanced likelihood of:
Overemphasis on soft security instruments	▶	Insufficient scope for peace support operations	▶	• underdevelopment
Overemphasis on hard security instruments	▶	Inability to participate in peace support operations		• conflict
Too little democratic control of SS	▶	Inappropriate security sector influence on policy		• dedemocratisation
No democratic controls of SS	▶	Capture of state by secu-rity sector interests		

Ultimately, security sector dysfunctionality can mean that a country is denied the security essential for economic growth and civil peace, and can cause the failure of democratisation. As for the developed countries, the risk is that security sector dysfunctionality may provoke de-democratisation.

National and Regional Security Sectors in the Euro-Atlantic Region

In the Euro-Atlantic region, security sectors can be identified operating on a number of different levels. There are the national security sectors whose basic morphology is common to that found in other security regions, but whose characteristics may vary from country to country. There are also the sub-regional and regional security sectors through which the national sectors need to operate to address their security concerns and which have distinct features that differentiate them from those of other regions.

The National Security Sector in the Euro-Atlantic Region

The morphology of the national security sector can be considered to consist of five different dimensions (as shown in Figure 2.1). First, there are the actors that have the capacity to use force. This category includes both statutory and non-statutory security bodies. The statutory bodies are those jurisdictions with a mandate to provide security from a representative authority such as the armed forces, military reserves, the police, paramilitary forces, intelligence services, and border and customs guards. The non-statutory actors are of two types – there are the bodies that can legitimately contribute to the security of government, business and individuals, but lack a mandate from a representative authority. Here the reference is to the burgeoning number of private security operations, most of which operate in a legal limbo in most Euro-Atlantic countries. Then there are the outlaws – the groups involved in organised crime and terrorism.

The second dimension embraces the civil management bodies or those elements of the executive power that prepare and make decisions about the use of force and state security. This includes such executive institutions as the President or the Prime Minister, ministries of Defence, the Interior, Foreign Affairs, the National Security Council and similar coordinating bodies, as well as ministries not traditionally associated with security such as those responsible for agriculture, transport, health, immigration and financial management bodies. The third dimension consists of the legislature or those elected bodies that have a mandate to oversee the decisions of the civil management authorities and the actions of the security actors subordinated to them. The fourth dimension embraces the legal and constitutional framework governing the security sector and all those bodies involved in assessing the legality of security sector decision-making, defending the rights of those working within the security sector or whose rights are affected by their actions, and penalising or correcting behaviour that infringes national law.

Civil society bodies form the fifth dimension. NGOs, the media, think tanks, public opinion – all the non-governmental entities involved in monitoring the security sector, publicising them, providing training on security sector issues and so on. Special cases are constituted by two groups. Political parties can act like civil society bodies when they develop policy and shape political platforms, but normally not when they are involved in bringing out the vote or fund-raising activities. Similarly, there are corporate enterprises that assume substantial responsibilities for the protection of vital national infrastructure, a pattern that has taken on new significance with the shift in the strategic environment. They develop and manufacture equipment and systems for security sector actors at home or abroad, and assume humanitarian roles in support of security sector reform such as has occurred in Afghanistan.[10]

Figure 2.1: Morphology of the Security Sector[11]

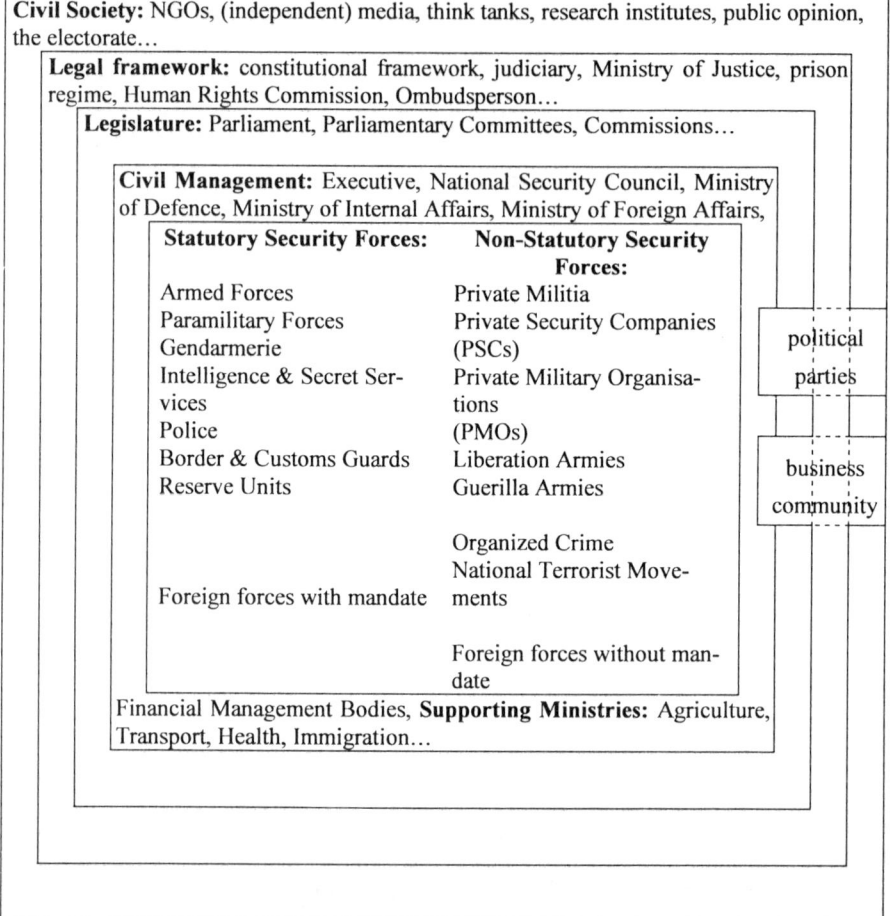

What all this means in practice can vary significantly. A country which has only recently become a sovereign state, will be likely to have underdeveloped civil society, judicial, legislative and civil management institutions, with the possible exception of an over-strong executive, as well as statutory security forces that are under-regulated or weak in comparison with both criminal groups and private security operations. This is the case, for example, of Ukraine, Belarus, Armenia, Azerbaijan and the states of Central Asia. New states whose emergence has been accompanied by conflict often have the additional challenge of contending with competing security sectors on their soil – the case of Moldova, Serbia-Montenegro, Georgia and Bosnia and Herzegovina. In all of these states, there is the further complication that part or all of the domestic security sector is controlled and managed by foreign troops whether operating under or without a UN mandate. Russia combines features of both 'new' and 'new post-conflict' states, namely, weak institutions across the board, with the arguable exception of the presidency and with the exception of the statutory security forces, which the country inherited from the Soviet Union and which, while weakened, are generally strong enough to deflect efforts to ensure their effective oversight. At the same time, Russia's security sector profile is overshadowed by the unrelenting insurgency in Chechnya, propelled by indigenous elements, but also supported from abroad.

The situation in most states of Central and Eastern Europe is different again. These are countries that emerged intact after the Cold War and that were faced not with the need to build their security sectors from scratch, but with the challenge of restructuring what was already in existence. The prospect, which had emerged by 1993-94, of joining the EU and NATO and the enormous incentive this has represented for carrying out reform further shaped their situation.

All transition countries now face the additional challenges associated with ensuring that their security sectors are a match for twenty-first century threats. As for the countries on the Western side of the erstwhile East-West divide, this is their main impetus for reform. Here, two broad categories can be identified. There are the countries that have a robust security sector, well resourced and well developed through the five dimensions described above. Here security sector reform is mainly about re-balancing resources among security sector actors, refocusing mandates, realigning relationships within the security sector and strengthening democratic oversight. This category typically includes countries with large defence establishments as well as a number of smaller countries accustomed to assuming a significant degree of responsibility for their own national defence, whether traditionally members of a security alliance or not. A second category typically includes countries who took advantage of the East-West stand-off during the Cold War to over-rely on neighbouring states and alliances for their security, and have discovered that such behaviour is no longer safe or politically acceptable. For such countries, security sector reform has both a qualitative and quantitative aspect.

For the sake of simplicity, it is probably useful to limit the number of different reform environments or modes to three. A formative mode where the security sector has to be built from scratch, as in a new state or one that has been devastated by conflict. A reconstruction mode where the challenge is to reinvigorate aspects of an existing security sector in parallel with systemic change such as the transition from totalitarianism, a process that has largely been completed in the countries that have recently acceded to NATO. A transformative mode, which faces all states as they seek to address the new security challenges that have emerged at the beginning of the twenty-first century. All three phases have also to contend with what might be called an operationalisation mode where the overriding task is to make a reformed framework work effectively (see Figure 2.2). For example, in a reconstructed security sector where the main constitution and framing documents such as a national security doctrine are in place, the challenge then becomes one of ensuring the requisite material and political capacities are available, a process that is often associated with the deepening democratisation of political life and institutions. Just as there are intermediate phases within these various modes, there are several Euro-Atlantic countries that find themselves coping with the exigencies of various reform modes at the same time.

Figure 2.2: Modes of Security Sector Reform[12]

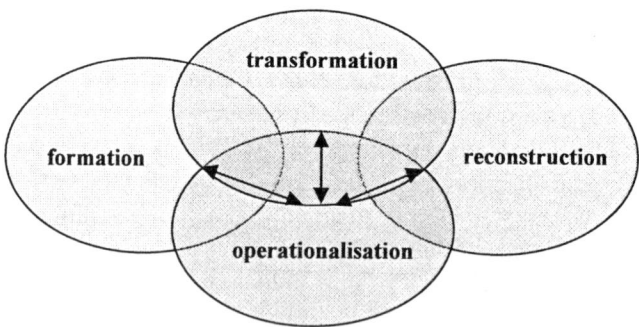

The Regional Security Sector in the Euro-Atlantic Security Region

Theorists and practitioners of security sector reform are accustomed to conceptualising the security sector on the level of the state. However, in a world where there is scarcely a security problem that can be dealt with by national means alone, it is essential to think in terms of regional security sectors. In the Euro-Atlantic region, there is both a regional security sector and three sub-regional security sectors of note.

The latter category includes the sub-regional security sector based on the bilateral and multilateral agreements in the security field that have been signed by members of the Commonwealth of Independent States. A second is in the process of being established as part of the process of European unification around the European Union. A third may be emerging in North America if, and as Canada, the United States and Mexico seek to intensify and multilateralise their cooperation, not only in the military area, but also across the security sector. All three are faced with the question of whether and to what extent they should see themselves as part of the larger construct that is constituted by the Euro-Atlantic security sector.

The Euro-Atlantic security sector, as depicted in Figure 2.3, is structurally similar to the generic security sector. The underdevelopment of this regional security sector, relative to the threats it has to contend with, is striking. The statutory security forces are generally too few in number and/or too uncoordinated to deal with the challenges at hand, whether at home or abroad. In particular multilateral military, policing and intelligence capacity is insufficient to cope with the peace support operations that Euro-Atlantic countries have assumed in places such as Afghanistan and Iraq, let alone in Africa with its frequent security crises. Multilateral-level resources for consequence management in the wake of 9/11-like disasters are similarly underdeveloped. Decision-making at the executive level in the main Euro-Atlantic security institutions remains essentially in national hands and takes place with little coordination among regional institutions. The regional assemblies, with the partial exception of the European Parliament, attempt to oversee the operations of the various institutions, but have no power of sanction and are composed of delegates appointed by the national parliaments. The underdevelopment of the judicial framework for the Euro-Atlantic security sector is underscored by the limited mandates of the various international and regional courts that adjudicate over legal issues in the region. Finally, while there are elements of a civil society and media that operate transnationally in the Euro-Atlantic region, these are still in an embryonic phase.

Figure 2.3: The Euro-Atlantic Security Sector

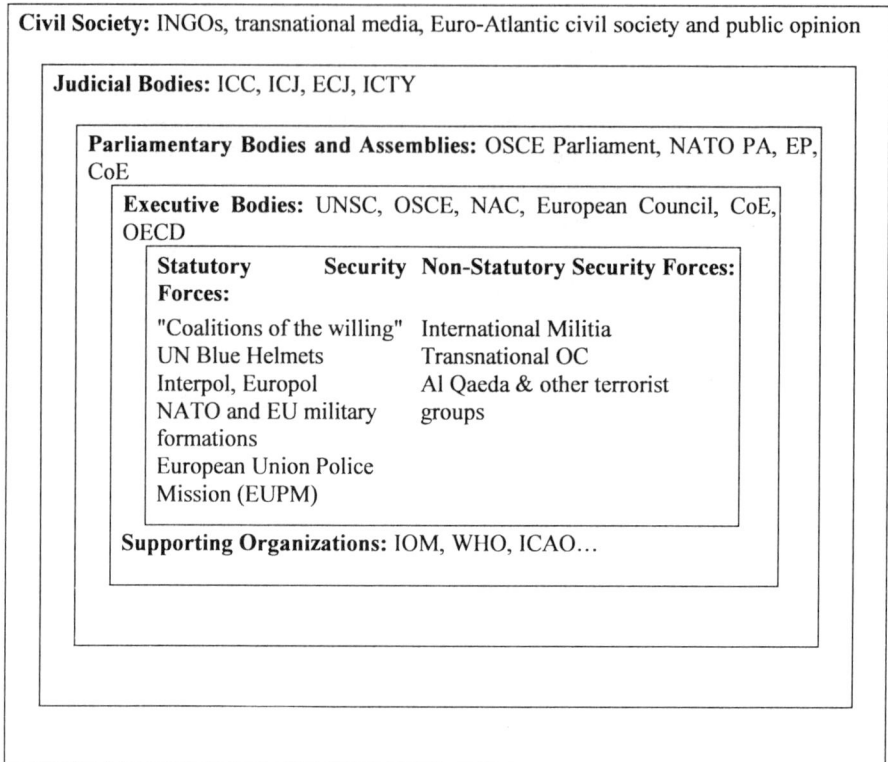

Civil Society: INGOs, transnational media, Euro-Atlantic civil society and public opinion

Judicial Bodies: ICC, ICJ, ECJ, ICTY

Parliamentary Bodies and Assemblies: OSCE Parliament, NATO PA, EP, CoE

Executive Bodies: UNSC, OSCE, NAC, European Council, CoE, OECD

Statutory Security Forces:	**Non-Statutory Security Forces:**
"Coalitions of the willing"	International Militia
UN Blue Helmets	Transnational OC
Interpol, Europol	Al Qaeda & other terrorist
NATO and EU military	groups
formations	
European Union Police	
Mission (EUPM)	

Supporting Organizations: IOM, WHO, ICAO...

Many of these shortcomings are understandable reflections of a process of regional security sector formation that is still much very much in progress. By the same token, there is much that has not yet been done, and could be done under existing conditions, to enhance good governance and operational efficiency at the Euro-Atlantic level. We return to this issue in the final section.

Who's Who in Euro-Atlantic Security Sector Reform

There are three principal actors in the security sector reform activity undertaken within and on behalf of the Euro-Atlantic region – national governments, non-state actors, and regional and international institutions. National governments have played a key role in putting security sector reform on the development agenda of developed countries, and it is largely their efforts that have determined whether and to what extent security sector reform has been undertaken in the countries of the Euro-Atlantic region. A second category is that of non-governmental organisations such as the Geneva Centre for the Democratic Control of Armed Forces (DCAF). Such bodies have been playing an increasingly important role in supporting security sector reform, both in standalone efforts and as part of bilateral and multilateral programmes sponsored by governments. They form an important part of the civil society dimension of what we have called the Euro-Atlantic security sector, as depicted above in Figure 2.3. Much national-level security sector reform is carried out through regional and international institutions and donors, the bodies that form the executive of the Euro-Atlantic security sector. It is on the activities and approaches of this third category of actor that this section will focus.

The regional and international bodies active in security sector reform cover a broad range of primary mandates. Bodies such as the United Nations Development Programme (UNDP), Organisation for Economic Co-operation and Development (OECD) and the World Bank have come to security sector reform with a growth and development perspective. There are bodies whose involvement has been prompted by their democracy vocation as in the case of the Council of Europe or their security vocation as in the case of NATO. Then there are bodies whose interest stems from their comprehensive approach to economic development, security and democracy – the case of the European Union, the Stability Pact and the OSCE. Whatever their primary mandate, all the institutions working in the area of security sector reform are sensitive to the need for just a such comprehensive approach.

A second point of differentiation concerns the main instruments that are used in security sector activities. Some bodies' involvement is restricted to norm development, the case of the OECD; others are primarily active in the financing or implementation of project activity, the case of NATO, the Stability Pact and the World Bank. The EU, the OSCE and the UNDP do both. A third point of differentiation is geographical focus, which ranges from the Balkans to Europe (without Central Asia), the Euro-Atlantic area and worldwide. Finally, there are different country foci, with organisations tending to restrict their activities to developing or transition countries, and in some cases to both.

Several aspects of this institutional line-up stand out. One is that none of the institutions work on security sector reform in the developed democracies. Another is that in neither North America nor in the Commonwealth of

Independent States (CIS) are there any multilateral security sector reform activities of note, nor is there a developed tradition of inter-institutional dialogue and cooperation. For example, representatives of the World Bank and UNDP participate in the OECD network on conflict, peace and development cooperation, but NATO, the main body involved in conflict prevention, management, resolution and reconstruction in the Euro-Atlantic area does not sit at this table. This has partly to do with the fact that the OECD and NATO have different core mandates and focus on different countries in their security-related activities. However, it also has to do with longstanding frictions between security and development practitioners, and the fact that until very recently the interconnections between the two fields were largely obscured. Whatever the reasons, the result is that NATO does not readily take advantage of the excellent work that the OECD has done in the area of setting norms for security sector reform, in terms of both donor practice and policy coherence in project development and implementation. By the same token, the OECD does not have ready access to NATO's plentiful and practical post-conflict experience. For interface between the two institutions, national ministries acting through their representations in the two institutions have to be relied on, a mechanism that is insufficient. What is true of the relationship between the OECD and NATO is also generally so of other institutions working on security sector reform.

The relations between NATO and the EU, arguably the most important relationship within the Euro-Atlantic region in terms of security sector reform, are a case in point. NATO and the EU are key players here for a number of reasons. First, NATO and EU members have the experience of several generations of multilateral reform in the security field. NATO, for example, has been through several strategic concepts in its fifty-five year history, each with its own implications for defence doctrines, command structures, field operations, and so on. This has spawned a culture of adaptation, which has been passed on to the EU, where eighteen of its twenty-five members are also NATO members. At the same time, this NATO and EU experience has stood members well in their efforts to promote defence and security reform in partner and prospective new member countries in CEE and the CIS. Second, this reform experience has taken place in a multilateral framework. This is important because multilateralism can be a great facilitator of reform. It can allow for a more rational use of resources – for example, because understandings reached with other countries in one's region means that it is not necessary to practice total defence of one's borders or that it is possible to pool certain border-guarding functions. It can allow for the political costs of reform to be more widely shared among different countries, which can also enhance the prospects for success of the entire endeavour. Multilateralism can furthermore facilitate the sharing of information about best reform practice. Third, notwithstanding the current budgetary difficulties of some members of NATO and the EU, they still represent the world's two richest clubs. If the requisite political will and leadership are forthcoming, they are certainly capable of meeting the costs of reform. Fourth, both bodies are committed to enhancing their cooperation in the fight against strategic terrorism and the proliferation of weapons of mass destruction. In view of such advantages, it is difficult not to conclude that if NATO and the EU do not succeed in leading a successful security sector reform effort, then it is not going to happen anywhere else.

Nevertheless, there are a number of obstacles standing in the way of NATO and EU playing this role. The first problem is one of policy fragmentation, which owes to the fact that both NATO and the EU tend to take a partial approach to security sector reform. NATO, as a collective defence and more recently also a collective security body, has tended to focus on defence reform and democratic control of the military. For many NATO members, security sector reform and the operations of security actors other than the military are not part of the Alliance's mainstream business. Yet, it has proven possible to include security sector reform as a legitimate activity in the special Partnership for Peace programme on terrorism set up after the events of 9/11 and for interested NATO members and partners to embrace a security sector reform agenda for specific countries – notably Ukraine.[13]

The EU is a political union with important stakes in economic and social policy and the free movement of people, but still only embryonic experience in dealing with military matters. It has tended to focus on border, policing and immigration issues in member and would-be member countries. It does not have a specific role in the reform of the armed forces of its own members, although the decision to set up the EU rapid reaction force does have significant repercussions for military reform. On balance, neither NATO nor the EU is inclined to take a holistic approach to security sector reform in their programmes. However, everything we know about the subject from the experience of the last decade or so underlines that a holistic approach is absolutely essential if reform is not going to create more problems that it resolves.

The fragmentation problem has its roots in the different agendas and expectations that NATO and EU members entertain with regard to their respective institutions. To take the EU, this translates into there existing several different bodies that deal with one or the other aspect of security sector reform, but without any coordination of these activities. At NATO, the problem is simpler, but there is also no single body that is responsible for shaping the security sector reform agenda.

The problems of conceptual fragmentation and internal organisation have been exacerbated by the fact that for NATO and the EU inter-institutional coordination has tended to be the exception, not the rule. This is a serious issue in two areas in particular. First, there has been little or no coordination on enlargement, which has meant that there have been no overarching requirements for the new members to adopt in the security field. As a result, states that have become members of both organisations have needed to cope with two different security packages, while those states that have become members of, for example, only the EU, have had to cope with a package which is different from that facing those that have only joined NATO. Second, there has been little coordination on partnership policies. Both NATO and the EU have developed new programmes for partnership with the regions that will not be part of the 2004 enlargement process, in particular Central Asia and the Caucasus. However, there is no coordination at the policy level, which can be a recipe for duplication, policy confusion, misuse of resources, and so on.

There is a risk that policy incoherence may be exacerbated now that the two enlargement processes of 2004 have been completed. The EU and NATO training systems for security sector actors are different as are the weapon systems and security sector technology in use. A further problem concerns the rapid reaction forces that both institutions are in the process of constituting. There appears to be considerable overlap in the forces earmarked for the two purposes. Moreover, arrangements for deciding which organisation would have first call over double-allocated resources in the event of a policy divergence appear unclear. Furthermore, as long as NATO and EU countries have not in their majority come to approach security sector reform as a requirement that has to be met in their own countries, progress among their memberships as a whole will remain limited. There is a double standard here which is in no party's interest, and which undermines the natural potential for the NATO and EU to show leadership on security sector reform. Yet, coordination is certainly workable as underlined by the *Berlin plus* arrangements, their activations for the handover of command arrangements from NATO to the EU in Macedonia and now Bosnia. Another case in point is the Ohrid Process where not only NATO and the EU, but also the OSCE and the Stability Pact were brought together with Western Balkans countries to work on border management reform. The increasing frequency and institutionalisation of staff-to-staff contacts is also promising. But there remains much more to be done. First and foremost, it will be necessary for leading members of NATO and the EU to come to understand and accept that these two bodies are fundamentally interdependent.

Policy Issues and Conclusions for Security Sector Reform in the Euro-Atlantic Region

As this chapter has argued, security sector reform in the Euro-Atlantic region remains unfinished business. The reform processes initiated in the 1990s in the transition countries are in various stages of implementation. Some countries, particularly those that have joined NATO and the EU have made significant strides in reconstructing their security sectors. Others, those with a weak tradition of state control and who suffered major conflict after the Cold War, have made less progress. Both groups have, however, a considerable way to go before their security sectors can be considered well governed and efficient in their operations and activities. Their task is complicated by the emergence of strategic challenges that place considerable new burdens on all security sector actors. With enlargement having brought NATO to twenty-six members and the EU to twenty-five, there is the further difficulty that reform may begin to appear an optional course and be relegated to the back of an, admittedly impressive, queue of reform challenges in other policy sectors. Much will depend, as this process goes forward, on the quality of leadership demonstrated by the developed democracies, the degree of cooperation among them and the examples they set as they too attempt to cope with the changes that are at play in the strategic environment. Overall, the objective of the key actors involved in developing and implementing the security sector agenda – national, intergovernmental and non-governmental – should be to make the national and regional security sectors of Euro-Atlantic space significantly more capable of addressing the changing strategic environment.

While the nature of reforms will differ from security sector to security sector, there are some common parameters that can be posited. Three critical issues stand out, each of which has to be approached in different, but largely interdependent, reform settings. The first issue concerns the functioning of individual security sector actors and the role of the civil management bodies that are responsible for their activities. The assignments, operations, capabilities, management and performance of such jurisdictions – their overall 'fitness'– need to be reviewed against the changed strategic requirements. Such a review should include actors that have not been traditionally associated with security concerns – those responsible for civil infrastructure protection, immigration, food chain security, combating pandemics, and the like – but which under contemporary circumstances can play a crucial role in crisis prevention and consequence management. Likewise, communities need to reflect on the role of actors such as private military organisations and private security companies, whose influence has increased significantly in recent years but whose activities remain largely unregulated. [14]

A second critical issue concerns the way that these different actors work together. The nature of inter-agency cooperation in the Euro-Atlantic region varies considerably. In some settings, security sector actors operate essentially on a stand-alone basis or are even adversaries. In others, cooperation is highly structured and ongoing. Then there are situations where security sector interface is *ad hoc* in nature, varying from casual to intensive in nature as a function of ongoing or anticipated events. Whatever the model, security sector actors need to be able share information, analysis and decision-making authority. New structures will sometimes be required, but their creation can often be disruptive, deflect energies from concrete tasks on the ground and be debilitating for basic functions. The onus should, therefore, be on seeking new synergies across traditional jurisdictional dividing lines rather than on creating new institutions.

A third issue relates to the actors and mechanisms that are supposed to ensure that security sectors operate efficiently, transparently, accountably and responsibly. Concerns about strategic terrorism, weapons of mass destruction (WMD) and arbitrary violence have led people throughout the Euro-Atlantic region to accept that governments should have greater powers of deterrence and retaliation. This is understandable. However, if abuse is to be prevented and public support for strengthened government mandates in this area maintained, this process needs to be flanked by enhanced oversight of the security sector at all levels. In particular, there is a need for improved legislative control over the executive, more independent ombudsperson mechanisms to provide recourse to citizens in the event of governmental misconduct, heightened activism by civil society and rigorous but also responsible involvement of the media.

The oversight question brings into play the oversight and monitoring functions of parliament, ombudsmen, the courts, the media and civil society. Concerns can range from the formal frameworks that govern the duties of legislatures in security sector decision-making to the material conditions and training programmes on which parliamentarians must rely if they are to perform effectively. Another example concerns whether legislation on the media or on non-governmental organisations allows them to play their role in disseminating security sector information and overseeing the performance of individual security sector actors. Also, in both Europe and North America, countries are faced with concerns about the democratic deficits that can occur when decisions affecting national security are taken by supranational entities whose transparency is limited and which are not always subject to effective democratic control.[15]

The three critical issues of fitness, interface capability and oversight need to be addressed for each of the security sectors referred to above. However, in addition to the national, sub-regional and regional environments, decision-makers also have to take into account developments on the sub-state and the global level (see Table 2.2). These environments are largely interdependent. Change in one will have implications for another; a failure to make the necessary changes in one setting can threaten the viability of the entire system. In other words, reform of the Euro-Atlantic security sector cannot proceed in isolation from the international system while national security sector reform that fails to integrate sub-state – provincial, municipal and the equivalent –actors in the national process will also suffer in terms of efficiency. Cumulatively, the critical issues and multiple reform environments described above can be visualised as providing a notional framework for a strategic audit of the security sector of and within the Euro-Atlantic area (see Table 2.2).

Table 2.2: Notional Framework for SSR in the Euro-Atlantic Region

Level Issues	Sub-state	State	Regional	Euro-Atlantic	Global
Individual actor fitness					
Actor interface capability					
Monitoring & oversight mechanisms					

Within this complex system, there are a number of points of priority importance. First and foremost, there is a need for a holistic approach to security sector reform. Police and military units need to be able to work together. Government departments need to be able to practice 'joined up government', the term developed in the United Kingdom at the end of the 1990s to underscore the need for clusters of government departments to work together on issues affecting the mandates of multiple actors. Similarly, the international governmental organisations to which this chapter has referred need to overcome their jurisdictional and political barriers, and find new synergies: 'joined up institutions' must be at a premium.

A second priority is to get the resources right. As we have argued above, some countries devote too few resources to their security sectors. Others earmark sufficient resources, but they are ineffectively used. A third category over-allocates resources to hard security instruments – military power – and downplays the importance of soft security tools such as foreign policy, outreach programmes, opportunities for immigration and free movement, and cultural openness.

A third priority is the need for more and better education and training for both those who are professionally involved in the security sector and those on whose behalf it is supposed to operate. In a very short space of time, security has become a globalised phenomenon, more transnational than national, less military and more broadly security-oriented, less the realm of the state and more that of a panoply of non-state and ultra-state actors. Education systems have not kept up with this progression. This has now to be repaired with broadly–based efforts to ensure that both decision-makers and the public are adequately informed.

A fourth and related priority concerns the need for the various partnership programmes developed by the Euro-Atlantic institutions to be reinforced and extended. This is especially important in view of the (almost) parallel enlargement of NATO and the EU. Partnership programmes need to be extended to other areas of the globe, where multilateral security institutions are weak or non-existent and where redoubled efforts to spur integration into the global community can make a decisive difference.

Finally, security sector reform has to be embedded in a coherent and comprehensive overall strategy for creating new poles of cooperation between the Euro-Atlantic region and other parts of the world. There is a requirement for a dual approach, one that relies both on soft and hard security means. During the Cold War, Western strategy relied on deterrence and dissuasion, on one hand, and dialogue on the other. In this new strategic era, this duality continues to be necessary, but its content has changed. Deterrence and defence have to be reframed as something that all security sector actors have to be able to deliver. As for dialogue, in the world of the early twenty-first century, the messages of the Euro-Atlantic institutions have to be able to convince not only elites, but also an ever more interconnected 'street level'. In particular, the strategy has to be designed with the objective of enlisting broad support within the wide community of state and non-state actors that have allied or associated themselves with the Euro-Atlantic community since the end of the Cold War. A last element concerns the overall credibility of the Western project. During the Cold War, Western strategy could not have ultimately been successful unless it had been seen as offering a superior societal model. Leading Euro-Atlantic states are far too often nowadays perceived as speaking with a forked tongue, following double standards in their policies or preaching the acceptance of democracy abroad while ignoring the causes for its dwindling credibility at home.[16]

At its core, the rationale for security sector reform in the Euro-Atlantic area could not be more straightforward. Without security, economies cannot develop, societies cannot flourish and countries and their people have to live in the fear or reality of conflict and war. Consequently, governments invest considerable resources into providing security. Yet these efforts often fall woefully short of the mark. The twentieth century was the bloodiest one on record. Much points to the likelihood that the twenty-first will be similar, or perhaps even worse. Hence, the need for comprehensive change in the way we think about our security and use the human and material assets at our disposal. Here, the Euro-Atlantic region not only has the responsibility, but also the opportunity to take the lead.

Notes

[1] This chapter has been prepared with the assistance of Oksana Myshlovska, research assistant at DCAF.
[2] As per the World Bank's economic indicators for 2003. See *World Development Indicators, 2003*, World Bank, Washington DC.
[3] The Code of Conduct forms part of the 1994 Budapest Summit Final Document entitled 'Towards A Genuine Partnership in a New Era', available at <http://www.osce.org/docs/english/1990-1999/summits/buda94e.htm#Anchor_COD_65130>. See also Ghébali, V.-Y. *The OSCE Code of Conduct on Politico-Military Aspects of Security (3 December 1994). A Paragraph-by-Paragraph Commentary. (Democratic Control and Use of Armed Forces* (DCAF, Geneva, 2003), available at <http://www.dcaf.ch/publications/DCAF_Documents/DOC3.pdf>.
     For a list of seminal documents of significance to security sector governance see Hänggi, H., 'Making Sense of Security Sector Governance', in Hänggi, H. and Winkler T.H., eds., *Challenges of Security Sector Governance* (LIT: Münster, 2003).

[4] Rt Hon Clare Short MP, 'Security, development and conflict prevention', statement to the Royal College of Defence Studies (13 May 1998), available at <http://www.dfid.gov.uk/News/Speeches/files/sp13may.html>.

[5] Brzoska, M. (November 2003), *Development Donors and the Concept of Security Sector Reform*, DCAF Occasional paper, # 4, (Geneva, November 2003), available at <http://www.dcaf.ch/publications/Occasional_Papers/4.pdf>.

[6] See 'USA – Intelligence Doubts Al-Qaida Nuke Claims', *Daily Defence News* (27 April 2004).

[7] See Law D., 'Security Sector Reform Comes to Canada', *On Track* (Journal of the Canadian Association of Defence Organizations), Vol. 8, no.3 (September 2003), pp 10-12.

[8] On the impact of 9/11 see Looney, R., 'Economic Costs to the United States Stemming From the 9/11 Attacks', *Strategic Insights*, Volume I, Issue 6, (August 2002), available at <http://www.ccc.nps.navy.mil/si/aug02/homeland.pdf> ; Dean A. and Yonah A, *Terrorism and Business: The Impact of September 11, 2001* (Transnational Publishers, Ardsley, NY. 2002).

[9] In 2002, USA military expenditure reached USD 335.7 billion, compared with USD 148 billion for NATO Europe altogether. See World Bank, *World Development Indicators, 2003*, (World Bank, Washington DC 2003) As an example of the divide in spending between hard and soft security instruments, the US plans to spend USD 450 billion in 2004 on the military and only USD 15 billion on official development assistance. See Sachs, J. 'America's Ignorance Is a Threat to Humanity', *International Herald Tribune* (8 June 2004).

[10] An example of such a business organisation is The Business-Humanitarian Forum (<http://www.bhforum.ch/>).

[11] This Figure is based on Ball, N., Bouta, T. and Van de Goor L., *Enhancing Democratic Governance of the Security Sector: An Institutional Assessment Framework*, Clingendael, (Netherlands Institute of International Relations, The Hague, 2003) available at <http://www.clingendael.nl/cru/pdf/2003_occasional_papers/SSGAF_publicatie.pdf >
A similar approach is taken in such OECD and UNDP documents as:
OECD, *The DAC Guidelines: Helping Prevent Violent Conflict. Policy Statement and Executive Summary* (2001); UNDP, *Justice and Security Sector Reform: BCPR's Programmatic Approach*, (November 2002) available at <http://www.undp.org/bcpr/jssr/docs/jssrprogramaticapproach.pdf>; UNDP, *Security Sector Reform and Transitional Justice. A Crisis Post-Conflict. Programmatic Approach*; OECD (2004), *Security System Reform and Governance: Policy and Good Practice*. DAC Guidelines and Reference Series, (March 2003), available at <http://www.oecd.org/dataoecd/8/39/31785288.pdf>.

[12] The modes approach is similar to Edmunds's generations approach outlined in his report '*Sector Reform: Concepts and Implementation*', but it differs in that it sees SSR as a process that is relevant to all countries; that is developed, developing and in transition, and observes that countries may have to address the demands of more than one mode at one time. See Edmunds, T., *Security Sector Reform: Concepts and Implementation*, Report for Geneva Centre for the Democratic Control of Armed Forces (2001).

[13] On the Ukraine-NATO partnership see: <http://www.nato.int/issues/nato-ukraine/> ; see also the NATO-Ukraine Action Plan, 2002, available at <http://www.nato.int/docu/basictxt/b021122a.htm> ; for the Charter on a Distinctive

Partnership between NATO and Ukraine, see:
<http://www.nato.int/docu/basictxt/ukrchrt.htm>.

[14] See DCAF *Private Military Firms. Fact Sheet,* (2004), available at
<http://www.dcaf.ch/pfpc-ssr-wg/PMCs_Caparini_Template.pdf>.

[15] See Born, H., Hänggi, H., (eds.), *The 'Double Democratic Deficit'. Parliamentary Accountability and the Use of Force Under International Auspices* (Ashgate: Aldershot, 2004).

[16] See for example Law, D., 'Democratic Deficits, North America, and Security', in *Connections*, Partnership for Peace Consortium, Volume 1 (September 2001).

Chapter 3

Learning from Security Sector Reform in Central and Eastern Europe

*Chris Donnelly**

Introduction

There is no wholly satisfactory way of assessing the success of a security sector reform process. One measure is to put the army (or police force, intelligence service, etc.) to the test against a competent opponent. Others include measuring financial efficiency in peacetime or studying the esteem in which the force is held, to measure the nature of its relationship with government and society, reflected, for example, in army recruiting figures or in complaints against police. However, all these measures can only provide a partial picture. What makes it difficult to arrive at an overall conclusion is that our evaluation, in the final analysis, must be based today on a subjective estimation of the likely nature, extent and imminence of a *future* threat. The key question – what will armed forces, police, border regimes, intelligence services etc., actually be needed for – cannot be answered with the degree of concrete certainty that characterised security and defence forces during the Cold War.

In pursuing this theme, therefore, this chapter will lay out two patterns, two frameworks of change, according to which each national effort can be measured. The first framework is that of the changing environment – the social, economic, political and security background within which the defence and security sector exists and must function. This, it should be said, is something, which applies not just to Central and Eastern Europe (CEE), but also to the whole continent and even further afield. It would be unfair to evaluate CEE efforts without reference to the wider context. What compli-

---

* Between 1989-2003 the author worked in NATO. He has served as Special Adviser for Central and Eastern European Affairs to four Secretary Generals of NATO. The views expressed in this chapter are his own.

cates this context is that, as is so often the case, so many things are changing at once that it is not easy to find some constant against which to measure progress.

The second framework is provided by the common experience of CEE countries – to establish which experiences of reform are common to all, so as to see how well a country might have done on any given issue in comparison to its peers. Viewing the security sector reform process from two such different perspectives allows some balance to be achieved by which a final judgement can be made as to, on the one hand, how well a country has been able to generate military and security forces to meet the real threats it faces today, and on the other hand, how well a country has done in terms of what could reasonably be expected of human beings and their imperfect institutions in the face of unforeseen and difficult circumstances.

The goals of this chapter are twofold. Firstly, to make an honest and objective assessment of capability. It is too easy to appreciate and praise effort rather than results. Countries can only live with an illusion of security and defence capability if it is not tested, and during the Cold War our defence and security establishments as a general rule were not tested. Secondly, an evaluation process should permit us to learn from our mistakes and from those of others – and to help others avoid the same mistakes. In this respect an external view – 'to see ourselves as others see us'– can be of real help, providing that it is handled with cultural sensitivity.

Security Sector Reform against a Changing Environment

Establishing the successes – and failures – of security sector reform efforts in Central and Eastern Europe is far more complicated today than would have been thought possible a decade ago. In the early 1990s the problem facing CEE countries, if difficult, appeared quite straightforward. It was to overcome the legacy of the Soviet system and convert the armed forces and policing forces of the countries of the former USSR and of its former Warsaw Pact allies to a model that would suit the newly emerging democracies and market economies of these countries.

Today that early optimistic evaluation seems naïve, as does the enthusiasm with which Western countries rushed to offer their advice and help to CEE countries in the firm belief that their problems would be solved if only they would adopt a 'Western model'. Furthermore, many of those Western countries now face their own very serious problems of defence reform for which there are no easy solutions.

The fact is that just about everyone grossly understated the magnitude of changes that the collapse of the Soviet system between 1989 and 1992 would usher in. As a result, reform initiatives commenced during the mid-1990s were soon overtaken by events. Notwithstanding the immense amount of effort that has gone into it, the history of defence reform in CEE over the past decade could be summed up as 'too little, too late'. The rapid pace of world events changed the security environment and dramatically compounded the effects of the resistance to change caused by institutional inertia, vested interest and governmental incompetence. No sooner had the objectives of reform been set during the post-Cold War decade than they became obsolete and had to be changed. It is little wonder that the rate and extent of change required has been beyond the capacity of many, especially small, European countries to manage. However, this process, it must be reiterated, did not just affect CEE countries. For example, the UK introduced a major defence reform programme in the late 1990s, but was forced to recognise that this had been overtaken by events after only three years and has had to institute revisions.

The simultaneous changes which, with the wisdom of hindsight, we can recognise as affecting Europe in the last decade, and which bore especially heavily on countries of CEE (which were least fit to withstand them), are fourfold. Had these changes come slightly more quickly, or with more internal violence in Europe, they would have been recognised as the revolution that they actually were. As it was, their cumulative effect was apparent only belatedly. Like a patient beset by four different ailments, it was difficult to diagnose the exact nature of the problems because of the confusion of symptoms. This problem of diagnosis has led, logically, to a problem of treatment. The required treatment is in some cases so radical that it cannot yet be applied. The changes affecting the region are dealt with from four perspectives:

- The interdependency of defence reform and societal reform;
- The fundamental change in the nature of conflict;
- The technological revolution;
- The information revolution.

The Interdependency of Defence Reform and Societal Reform

The first factor in the changing security equation was the truly *fundamental* nature of the social, political and economic reforms that CEE countries had to adopt. This demanded nothing less than a total change in the relationship between armed and security forces and their societies. Recruitment, funding, management and leadership, civil-military relations and democratic control – all the core business of an army or a police force – had to change completely. Attempts at reform – many of which failed – have improved our understanding of the interactive nature of the relationship between army and society. It is now clear, for example, that countries such as Norway and Germany cannot institute such radical military reform, as they perceive they need, without a correspondingly great reform of their social systems. As Germany abandons conscription in favour of professional regular forces, the national health-care system would be in danger of collapse, so much does it rely on the virtually free labour provided by young men who opt for civilian service rather than military conscription. Norway has so integrated its military role into its national social infrastructure – for very good historical reasons based on its unhappy experiences in 1940 – that to reform its army seriously will require a massive programme of social change and alternative mechanisms to support the national civilian infrastructure of this large, thinly populated country. It is the failure of repeated reform efforts in many countries which has reminded us that military and security sector reform goes hand in hand with social, economic and political reform. We cannot have one without the other and this is not just a problem of CEE. Perhaps the most extreme and evident example is Russia, where time and again military reform efforts have come to nothing because society itself has not found adequate new political, social and economic mechanisms. Russia, moreover, is also a good example of the fact that the greater role an army plays in national life, the more its failure to reform hinders national reform in general. Because of their resistance to change, the Russian armed forces and security forces are one of the major obstacles to societal reform. Changes there have been aplenty in the Russian Army, but of reform there has been precious little.

The Fundamental Change in the Nature of Conflict

The second factor complicating security sector reform has been the fundamental change in the nature of conflict and the corresponding changes in the roles of security forces, especially armed forces, intelligence services and, to a lesser extent, border regimes. The causes of this 'paradigm shift' are deep rooted and long standing. The collapse of the Soviet system was a catalyst for rather than a cause of the change. Equally, September 11, 2001 (9/11) and subsequent terrorist attacks have brought this paradigm shift to our notice, but only as the drastic symptoms of a deeper process.

The impact of this profound change is still not fully appreciated in many countries and their security institutions. Nowhere, not even in the US, have the full implications of this change and their complex interactions been realised. Events have changed the very definition of the term 'national security'. At the start of the 1990s this term was virtually synonymous with 'defence', particularly in CEE countries. Now it is recognised that 'defence' is only a small element of 'security', although there is no agreed boundary regarding what the term 'security' should encompass. Equally, the term 'deterrence' now needs re-definition. In the Cold War this was defined as conventional forces backed up by nuclear weapons – both for NATO and the Warsaw Pact. Today there is no agreement as to what constitutes deterrence against the new threats that the fundamental change in the nature of conflict has ushered in. Where the military does have a deterrent role, this today may be expressed by pre-emption or by a guarantee of drastic retribution. These are radically different functions for armed forces to perform than 'national defence', and demand very different kinds of military and societal organisation (and equipment and training).

By the same token, the change in the nature of conflict has destroyed, or at least seriously eroded, the traditional distinction between internal and external security and the institutional mechanisms for achieving these. Internal security can no longer be assured by police and counter espionage services alone; nor can external security be ensured solely by the traditional trio of diplomacy, armies and spying. Foreign aid programmes and government departments for international development are now also in the forefront of security. Armies are as likely to find themselves delivering, or securing the delivery of, foreign aid as they are to be fighting. Peacekeeping forces may have to fight to create peace. Having destroyed a country's resistance, a military force is likely to have to rebuild the damage and work with NGOs to do so. All these changes have placed new and extremely taxing demands on Europe's armed forces, against which their reform efforts must be measured.

It is this factor, the change in the nature of conflict itself, which has been the major cause of the growing gap between the US and many European countries. The roots of this gap are both conceptual and practical. Most mainland European countries have, within living memory, learned by bitter experience not to put their trust in military might to ensure national security. These countries (starting half a century ago with the core of the EEC) concluded that only political and economic integration would protect them from one another. Under the umbrella of a US nuclear guarantee, this allowed them to reduce defence preparations and defence expenditure to what amounted in practice to a third rate governmental activity, and to concentrate instead on economic and political integration. Defence became something that could be taken for granted; the defence portfolio in government was rarely a route to promotion; defence expenditure became more an element of social security – jobs and profit – rather than national security. Just as this was true of many European NATO members, so it was also true of many Central European countries in the Warsaw Pact, although for rather different reasons. Deprived as these countries were of true national control over their armed forces, their populations came to see them, at least in some measure, as agents of Russification or as an external imposition. With the dissolution of the Warsaw Pact, 'defence' has been a third rate concern in most Central European countries too. The defence institutions of most European countries, East and West, are now proving too weak and inflexible to respond to the dramatic new challenges that face them today.

However, the experiences of the US, the UK, Russia and Turkey in regard to the utility of military power have been very different. These countries in the twentieth century owed their creation, survival or position in the world to military power, and the general level of respect in which their armies came to be held by their populations reflected this (the US post-Vietnam experience was a temporary phenomenon). The readiness of these countries today to use force compared to the reticence of mainland European countries (with the sometime exception of France) in similar circumstances to do the same, is already posing a problem and is likely to be an even greater cause of friction in the future.

The practical result of this is that many European countries, both East and West, have been unwilling or unable to pursue defence reform as far or as fast as either logic or US/NATO pressure should have dictated. In the face of the new security threats which most, if not all, European nations today acknowledge, it would make sense for most countries to move away from armies based on territorial defence towards armies (and policing forces, intelligence services etc) which are able to go to where the threat is to be found and neutralise it there. This requires armed forces and other security agencies to be capable of being (a) deployed, (sent abroad), (b) employed (fighting or doing other difficult tasks) and (c) sustained (by rotation of troops, supply lines, popular support at home, defence infrastructure systems etc.). Many countries have concluded that this requires a regular professional force instead of a conscripted force, although in fact there has been little or no investigation of alternative reserve systems that could allow nations with good geographical or historical reasons for not putting their faith in small regular forces to hedge their bets.

Regardless of how much it might make sense, such a course of action has not been followed. For many European countries this has created a dilemma and has left them in an exceptionally difficult situation, resulting in the stalling of defence reform processes in many places. Many CEE countries have found it difficult to convince their population of the sense of abandoning conscript territorial forces. When combined with a military establishment wedded to maintaining a large Cold War conscript-based infrastructure (which, although worthless, is nevertheless very profitable), it allows reform to be halted completely. Smaller countries in Central Europe have found moving from a conscript force to a regular force to be so expensive that, were they to follow this course, they could no longer maintain a force capable of fulfilling the whole range of military activity desirable for the armed forces of a sovereign country.

This last conclusion has been so shocking for some CEE countries that they have shied away from it. Giving up national territorial defence is difficult not only for armed forces brought up to understand *only* this concept of force generation, but also for national populations of countries that history and geography have condemned to be close to a big neighbour which they do not yet fully trust – as they do not yet fully trust (or even fully understand the complex nature of) the Alliance which many of them have so recently joined. For CEE countries that have so recently regained their sovereignty, the idea of surrendering part of it by sharing military systems is still difficult to swallow. It has not helped matters that some of these countries, especially the Baltic republics, have received contradictory advice from the different countries helping them. Some of these have continued to advocate universal conscription and territorial defence as the basis for defence. Others have advised the opposite – to adopt small, professional armies. Trying to do both at once in a small country has proved impossible and has caused much confusion.

NATO, and the EU, do not yet have an answer to this problem. NATO asks for deliverable military capabilities and minimum defence expenditure (two per cent of GNP). However, NATO has as yet no mechanisms to broker the sharing of force capabilities in a way which would ensure the *guaranteed* delivery of a balanced force structure from a variety of different national components. A few CEE nations are exploring tentatively the idea of joint forces on the lines of the Belgian-Netherlands model of a combined Navy, but this process is just beginning. Another approach open to small CEE countries is to try for 'niche capabilities' where nations offer a small specialist military capability to a multi-national force or coalition. This is a good stop-gap idea, but it also runs the risk of being an excuse for not pushing for security sector reform.

On the whole, therefore, Central and Eastern European countries are maintaining fully national armed forces, which copy all the poor economies of scale that we have seen for decades in Western Europe. Like many Western armies today, only a tiny fraction of their current forces are useable in the context of any new security threat as these are currently envisaged. 'Lots of bucks, but not much bang' would sum up the result.

The Technological Revolution

The third factor, which compounds the above problem, is the pace of technological innovation. This means that the cost of an item of equipment is constantly rising relative to the whole defence budget, because the equipment is becoming more complex and technologically sophisticated. For example, the purchase cost of a new aircraft rises in real terms by about twelve to fifteen per cent per year, and associated training and maintenance costs rise even faster. Therefore, if a defence budget is pegged at a given level, rising only by the rate of inflation, then each year the force that can be maintained for this budget must either become smaller or more obsolete. In practice, CEE countries' armed forces have all become both smaller and more obsolete as they have struggled to maintain capabilities that they cannot afford. Many are currently faced with the problem of how to generate an effective military ethos for a force base which is so small that it cannot maintain effective *combat* capability. A recent complaint from one CEE defence chief was that soldiers should not be recruited just to be logisticians. It is hard not to sympathise with this sentiment. What is happening is striking at the very essence of traditional military practices. Only some really radical new ideas, and a very powerful political motive to implement them, will resolve this dilemma.

The problem of national defence industries in CEE further compounds the difficulties of defence reform. The Warsaw Pact and Soviet system rationalised defence production, allocating national (and in the USSR regional) specialisations and concentrating research and development (R&D) mostly in the Russian homeland. The break-up of the Soviet Union and Warsaw Pact fragmented this coherent industrial system, rendering most of the constituent parts non-viable. These factors – specialisation; the linkage to Soviet production standards; the collapse of demand in world arms markets and the absence of domestic markets – have all reduced the CEE defence industrial base to a fraction of its former self. Reform has proved impossible. Closure seems to be the only option for all but a small slice of the industry. Where factories have been subsidised or artificially converted (that is with no sound economic basis – quite a common situation in Russia) the result more resembles a day-care centre for the unemployed rather than a serious viable enterprise.

This third factor, like the two preceding factors, contributes to the overall drastic fall in European military capabilities that the past decade and a half has witnessed. When this is compared to the potential for a rise in capability that the proliferation of technology (coupled with the cleverness in using it) has provided to new 'enemy' – that is the likely sources of (asymmetric) threat that Europe will face in the next decade – the failure of reform in Europe is all the more striking.

The Information Revolution

The fourth factor which affects the evolution of security sector reform is actually a largely separate issue although the information revolution, in the sense of the growth of IT as a tool of Command and Control or as a weapon of electronic warfare, is really an aspect of factor number three above. The aspect of this information revolution which we are concerned with here is that which relates to today's universal availability of information. The media and information services are today uncontrollable in democratic countries (and, arguably, even in most non-democratic ones). This means that *every* action and *every* policy decision of a defence establishment and of armed forces is likely at best to be the subject of public scrutiny and at worst to be deliberately misrepresented, misused and subjected to downright disinformation.

The media and information networks today create a qualitatively new environment in which defence operates and which *must* be taken into account in everything that is done. This places a tremendous burden on the soldier and the defence administrator that few, especially in CEE, have been prepared to deal with. Even in major armies of established democracies this is an enormous problem. Images of US soldiers mistreating prisoners in Abu Ghraib gaol spring immediately to mind as a recent example of this problem.

Like the other factors affecting defence reform noted above, this is not amenable to a 'quick fix'. To deal with this new environment requires the introduction of a new culture in defence and security establishments from top to bottom. This is perhaps the most neglected element of security sector reform, but it is by no means the least significant.

Tracing Patterns in the Security Sector Reform Process

The factors discussed above are objective and widespread phenomena and applicable everywhere in Europe, not just in CEE. However, CEE countries faced the security sector reform problem first – before Western European countries were really aware of the need for such fundamental reform. There has in fact been a remarkable similarity between the paths followed by CEE countries as they came to grips with the problems of security sector reform. This tends to be the case even when there are marked differences in size, location and economic or social circumstances between the various countries, although 'local colour' gives different values to the common factors in this complex equation. However, what at first appears to be very evident differences are usually quantitative rather than qualitative, and more apparent than real. Establishing this 'common path', therefore, provides us with an alternative means of evaluation – one that should allow general lessons to be drawn.

Local circumstances will always continue to ensure that there will never be an exact model that can be copied *in toto*. Nevertheless, studying elements of other nations' experience can be of enormous value and save much time, effort and heartbreak. The value, therefore, of tracing the pattern of security sector reform in CEE and identifying, if only tentatively, the various stages of the process is that this could be of real use to countries – for example in Northern Africa and the Middle East (see Chapter 4) – which are now just beginning to face up to the problem of restructuring the relationship between their security forces and their society or government. In other words, having evaluated as best we can the progress of reform against the objective demands of the new security situation, it is useful to set the balance by looking realistically at how countries have generally coped in such circumstances. This will give us a much kinder evaluation because it recognises the extreme difficulties that *any* government has in coping with such deep seated and multi-faceted changes.

The first stage in the process after the CEE countries had re-established their independence was generally characterised by a crisis of values. This was occasioned by a loss of rationale and the de-legitimisation of ideology (which was stronger in some places than others). 'Patriotism' lost its meaning and was often replaced by an awkward combination of scepticism and nationalism. This moral crisis affected all security forces and much of society at large. However, it was often most immediately evident in the armed forces, where it was exacerbated by massive force reductions brought on by the change in geo-strategic, economic and political circumstances. This was attended by a loss of the Communist Party and governmental control mechanisms, which were not replaced by any corresponding mechanisms for democratic control. New democratic governments everywhere lacked military and security expertise and had no adequate mechanisms either to make security policy or to direct the course of affairs in the army, police or intelligence services. Where mechanisms existed they were very crude, for example, establishing an ever-reducing financial ceiling for defence expenditure. In many countries the internal political power struggle also resulted in the armed forces either being split between ministries and agencies (including those which would not normally have expected to control troops) or being re-subordinated, for example, from government to president. In some countries, politicians sought to use the military or the intelligence services directly in their power struggle. This further reduced the degree of real political control.

The second stage in the process saw the armed forces' leaderships in particular rally to protect and preserve their military systems, and strive to keep as much of the old force structure and infrastructure as possible. This was influenced by a combination of motives in which, as was noted above, personal vested interest undoubtedly played a part. However, sincere conviction, based on patriotism and a strong belief in the validity of the former Soviet and Warsaw Pact military system, reinforced by the lack of expertise and competence of new (civilian) governments was the driving factor. This was exacerbated by the militaries' lack of exposure to alternative professional views, and by the naturally cohesive qualities found in all effective military systems.

The effects of this were quickly felt. Trying to maintain a massive, but obsolete military structure at a time of rapid social change and economic decline proved disastrous. As CEE countries moved painfully into a market economy, resources to the military rapidly began to dry up. In most countries, this was not immediately obvious because the military establishment had always drawn on resources in kind rather than in cash, and had its own means of generating income and consumable resources. This was particularly true in countries of the former USSR. Exploiting these assets frequently allowed the core of the military to survive despite the lack of cash from the government.

Furthermore, societies in all CEE countries, having had no internal hard currency financial system, lacked trained accountants and effective accountancy procedures. The culture of financial accountability was completely absent throughout society, let alone the security sector. Neither the police nor judiciary anywhere had the capacity to monitor and control financial irregularities. This lack of control mechanisms was particularly important in the defence and security establishments, where to the general national problem was added the issue of secrecy. Thus the defence and security sectors in CEE were very slow to set up proper budgetary systems. Furthermore, the security forces in some places became a hotbed of corruption. The uncontrollable sale or distribution of military material, officers using their positions and forces under their command for personal business purposes, officers hiring out soldiers, the straightforward theft of money, and other such practices – all highly destructive of military discipline – proliferated. The result was a very rapid decline first in training standards, second in discipline, morale and living standards for both officers and men.

This factor affected police and border forces rather differently because of the nature of their organisations. They did not, for example, have large quantities of material to dispose of. However, in these services the problems of corruption were commensurately worse as personnel used their powers to generate income in the absence of the proper salaries, which the state was unable to provide. For the intelligence services, information was their special product. Those services, which (unlike for example the Czech) were not thoroughly restructured at an early stage, soon began to use information to secure either their income or their influence within the political system.

During the next stage procurement systems broke down. Defence industries, deprived of a tied domestic market, generally tried to avoid restructuring and reorientation, and in many countries took refuge in the fiction that arms sales abroad would save them. Yet in fact, because of corruption and lack of expertise in market economic realities, CEE defence industries missed the window of opportunity they had in the early 1990s to seize a share of the rapidly shrinking world market. With this export opportunity lost, and with domestic demand collapsed, the defence industries looked to governments to save it. Defence factories soaked up massive state subsidies, but used these to keep vast numbers of idle workers on subsistence pay instead of reorganising and converting to civilian products. In the long term, no country can maintain the quality and cost benefits that make for attractive exports without the security of a good home market. The ability to draw on vast reserves of fundamental research and existing military R&D enabled the industries to survive for some time in their obsolete form and avoid painful reform. However, when these reserves ran out defence industries in CEE faced near-total collapse. Reform was far more difficult and painful than if it had been undertaken ten years previously.

The impact of all these problems was, in most CEE countries, a drastic fall in the image of the profession of soldier and policeman, coupled with a drop in conditions of service. The result was most immediately felt in the conscript ranks of the army. They were the first to suffer from the catastrophic drop in training and living standards. During this stage in the reform process the failure of the military establishment to keep pace with the changes in society meant that young people were no longer willing to serve, and the breakdown of the established system meant that they could no longer be compelled. The universal conscription system decayed rapidly, and with it the pre-service patriotic military training in schools and universities that was a particular feature of CEE. Henceforth, only a fraction of the eligible age groups in CEE would serve in the army. Legal exemption, the ineffectiveness of the draft system, and bribery would ensure that the well-off and the well-educated would never have to serve in the ranks.

It was at this point that the old social-based system of a 'working-class-in-arms' failed definitively. It cannot be restored, because the social basis it sprang from and depended upon has gone forever. This did not mean that conscription as such was rendered invalid. Just that it would have to be on a different social basis. Yet in fact this was so difficult to achieve that it pushed many countries to seek what appeared to them as an easy option – a solution by proposing a conversion to fully professional forces.

It is easy now to point to this failure of the conscription system with the wisdom of hindsight, but at the time, in the early-mid 1990s (depending on the country), this was not so obvious to those within the system. The decline in the armed forces became evident much more quickly than in other security forces. The fall in the number and quality of conscripts, the endemic problem of physical abuse of conscripts by senior soldiers and officers, and the catastrophic drop in training (with consequent collapse of the armed forces' prestige) next hit the ranks of young officers. Many simply quit. Standards of entry to officer training colleges dropped and many cadets, having had a good technical education, never went into the army at all but simply left on or just before graduation.

This completed the self-destruction of the old system, particularly in countries of the former Soviet Union. The armed forces of the USSR and Warsaw Pact, working to a common Soviet model, had relied on young officers to conduct in units (rather than in training depots) all the junior command and training tasks which in many Western armies are done in depots or by regular professional long-service non-commissioned officers (NCOs). The lack of young officers meant that the steady downward spiral of the whole training system accelerated. A vicious circle had now established itself – training standards fell – kit broke down and was not replaced – poor treatment of soldiers increased – the gap between the command and the soldier increased – recruitment of young officers became more difficult – morale fell, along with public respect. The result was a steadily increasing incompetence of the forces, accompanied by a steady command and administrative drain as officers fled their posts at all levels and the force structure crumbled away.

As armies shrank, their officer corps structures became grossly 'top heavy' and this itself created the next obstacle to reform. However, attempts to reduce the officer ranks clumsily and drastically were also harmful. The sight of the government casting off unwanted senior officers without thanks, without real pensions or social security, and with no real chance of taking up a new career did two things – it reinforced the decisions of many who were not qualified for other employment to do all in their power to stay in the armed forces (thus maintaining the imbalance); and, it demoralised the younger officers and deterred many a keen young man from engaging in a military career at all.

The deterioration of the armed forces and security forces did not advance everywhere at the same speed, even within a single country. Successive ministers and chiefs of defence attempted to rationalise their shrinking armies and succeeded to differing degrees. In units and formations with exceptional commanders, competence and combat capabilities were retained. By concentrating efforts and resources on a small number of units (regiments, squadrons or ships), some of these were maintained at a reasonable standard of military readiness. Nevertheless, in the main, the decline was not halted and during the 1990s not a single one of the armed forces of countries in the former USSR or of its former Central European allies managed to satisfactorily reconstruct an effective and sustainable military and security system on modern lines. The slow pace of reform in the policing sector and border security regimes created conditions for organised crime to flourish and to establish international links. The failure to reform intelligence services meant that countries were ill-prepared to deal with new threats such as terrorism.

A point was reached in most CEE countries where the situation, that is the failure to reform, became so bad that the armed forces turned desperate. Their plight was obvious, but the solution was not. The only way they could see how to pursue reform was to get more money from the state. Requests from the armed forces for funding to initiate reform were therefore commonplace. It is true that reform does cost, but experience in CEE showed that, whenever money was made available to the defence establishment before reforms had taken place, the money was spent not on reform, but on keeping the old system alive. Small cosmetic improvements were made, but reform was actually put off and the situation became worse. Reform was in fact made more difficult because the money stiffened resistance to reform. Many countries experienced this stage in the process.

The 'NATO factor' played a role in complicating the reform process in many CEE countries. In some countries keen to join NATO, the military command on occasion proposed the procurement of unnecessary (and frequently unaffordable) equipment on the grounds that this would facilitate entry into NATO. When the political leadership and their civilian staffs (and also parliamentarians and journalists) did not know enough about military issues, this argument could sound very persuasive. Frequently Western arms companies would peddle the same line. In other countries, governments sometimes used NATO 'demands' as the excuse for pushing for defence reform because they lacked the self-confidence to tackle this issue on their own authority. Both of these approaches damaged civil-military relationships and eroded public confidence. The aggressive lobbying of Western arms producers provoked suspicions both in the military and in the public, which worked against the interests of reforms, allowing these to be misrepresented as only serving the interests of Western defence industries at a time when local defence industries were dying for lack of orders. Most central European countries have experienced this stage in the reform process.

In Russia the 'NATO factor' was used differently. The maintenance of a perception of a military threat from NATO was used to justify the preservation of much of the old military infrastructure. This in turn distracted attention from, and siphoned off money from, real defence and security sector reform.

The final element in the 'NATO factor' was the readiness of CEE governments and militaries alike to look to the West for models of military organisation and reform without discrimination. All NATO members have very different military systems and CEE countries had widely differing requirements for defence reform or building forces anew. It was exceptionally difficult for CEE countries to evaluate successful models and work out what elements were relevant for their own development, and it was hard for them to find unbiased advice that they could rely on. Governments and armies have gone from one extreme to the other, for example, rushing to embrace 'Western' ideas such as 'professionalisation' without any real understanding of what it involves – or costs.

A widely experienced stage during this process was the failure of reform efforts from below. At one stage, some reliance was placed on active young officers who, it was supposed, would rejuvenate the system and bring in ideas from the bottom-up. This movement had some temporary success, but the energetic young officers were too few and they failed, either because they could not overcome the inertia of the mid-level structures or because they were squashed by their seniors who saw them as a threat.

Another widespread experience was that of officers sent for training and education abroad, most frequently to the US, the UK, Canada, France or Germany. It was expected that these would return and infuse their military systems with new ideas. What this system actually did was to protect itself accordingly. In some Central European countries even as late as summer 2000, every single officer who had been sent abroad on training courses were on return, either dismissed, demoted, or sent to serve in a dead-end job in some military backwater. In other countries, although all the senior general staff officers had received training abroad, their lead was ignored by the mass of colonels beneath them, who obstructed the implementation of the orders. Only too often is 'democratic control of the armed forces' taken to mean that the generals will obey the politicians, but democratic control can also fail if colonels do not obey the generals and will not work hard to implement painful reform programmes.

A further common failing was the initial inability of CEE ministries of defence to implement an effective budgetary and planning system. Some countries have not got past this stage even today. Simply put, this meant converting the thinking of the military collective from approaching the problem with a Cold War mentality. Such a mentality argues that if we push for the capability the resources may follow. It was simply not accepted that the situation in the real world makes excessive defence spending unjustifiable and that social and economic changes made the old system unsustainable. Western armies have long had to approach the issue of defence planning based on available expenditure, purchasing power and priorities given the current assessment of 'the threat', that is an assessment as to what roles will be played by our armies. Experience of the last few years in CEE has shown just how difficult it can be to introduce a proper planning and budgetary system of this sort.

Linked to this common failing was the failure almost everywhere to put in place an honest and open system for evaluating the abilities and qualifications of officers in the armed and security forces and using that evaluation to create a promotion and posting system. Without such a process, no minister or head of service would ever be able to institutionalise change and reform because he would have no capacity to identify those officers with the qualities needed to bring in that change and create a new kind of army, or to put them into positions where they could transform words into action. This is also a stage which some CEE countries have not yet passed.

A frequently neglected aspect of democratic control and security sector reform is the issue of whether the government is actually competent to decide on and implement a security policy and direct the course of military and security sector reform. This is a common failing, with often disastrous results. The fact is that CEE countries have not been able to develop that body of civilian expertise in defence issues which is needed to ensure balance and to provide dispassionate advice. The very rapid turnover rate of CEE governments was a serious factor in maintaining this lack of expertise. When the government is *wholly* reliant on, for example, the uniformed military for advice on defence issues, it is the armed forces, and not the government, which effectively decides policy. The same is true for policing and intelligence issues. This state of affairs still persists in some CEE countries, despite the existence on paper – and in law – of what would otherwise be adequate mechanisms for democratic control.

Conclusion

This chapter, in reviewing experience of the last ten to fifteen years, points specifically to a number of problems and difficulties of conducting security sector reform. To complete our evaluation we can comb this experience to identify those most important features which are essential for success at each stage or level of the process.

The first is knowledge. There can be no successful fundamental reform if the civilian government does not have available an independent basis of knowledge of defence and security sector issues. This essential 'strategic community' of civil servants, journalists, academics, parliamentarians and even businessmen need not be large. However, it must be trusted as well as trustworthy. It can be built, and it can grow of its own accord, but without it reform will be limited to a matter of detail. An expert civilian community is essential to develop that relationship of mutual respect between armed and security forces and government, which is necessary for both a healthy society and effective security forces.

The second feature essential to success is a realistic threat assessment. Without this, how can a country know what sort of armed forces or security forces it needs? This seems so obvious, yet it is surprising how often it is lacking, and how often the real drivers in the reform process are such things as finance, vested interest, power struggles or ideological conviction. Some countries find it difficult to make a real threat assessment for political reasons – fear of offending a neighbour, for example. These countries are in an impossible situation unless they have a national consensus on the threat, which allows that the threat need never be openly voiced.

Political will to respond to the threat is the third *sine qua non*. Without political will it is impossible to drive through the very difficult radical changes that fundamental reform requires. Without political will a population will not be persuaded of the necessity to find the required resources for reform. 'Political will' does not just denote a ruthless politician. It means having an effective political system that permits policy to be turned into action when the will is there, gaining the support of voters that is essential in a democracy. It is a measure of a country's political maturity.

The fourth essential element is closely linked to the third. A country undertaking serious reform needs allies, help and friends. Certainly under some circumstances countries have pursued defence and security sector reform alone, but this is not an option for many countries today, when new security threats have created such new conditions. Only with allies or friends one can trust is it possible for a country to let down its guard – reduce its security capabilities – whilst it reforms its structures. The smaller and poorer a country is, the more this is so. Help – and the ability and preparedness to accept it – will also ensure that a country can learn from the mistakes of others. For many reasons it has proved easier for countries to accept help to reform armed forces than to reform interior forces and police. Yet, it is in this latter area that reform is now arguably more important, given the nature of today's threats.

It is at first glance, then, both surprising and not a little depressing that, after so many years of effort, so much remains to be done in the field of security sector reform in Europe as a whole, as well as in CEE. The central conclusion from the current situation, particularly in the military field where levels of real capability are so low in comparison with the resources invested, is that this is a far more important area of social activity than many governments have appreciated or have been prepared to admit. Under the umbrella of superpower confrontation during the Cold War, most countries in Europe, East or West, could afford to reduce investment in security to historically very low levels of expenditure. Since the end of the Cold War, expenditure has decreased even further, and much expertise has been lost. This leaves many countries in the security doldrums, becalmed as it were, in a state of mind where most political leaders consider it enough to spend less than two per cent of GDP on defence, and where no one considers it scandalous that so little useable military capability is achieved in Europe for the expenditure of what is still a great deal of money. Until this attitude changes, until governments and populations believe that there is a real danger from the new security threats, which they acknowledge, there is little likelihood that the failures of security sector reform will be rectified. European countries need to invest much more intellectual effort in addressing this problem so as to be prepared for unforeseen future events. Other countries need to learn from Europe's failings.

Chapter 4

Security Sector Reform as an Instrument of Sub-Regional Transformation in West Africa

Adedeji Ebo

Introduction

Since 1989, security has been the major concern in the West African sub-region, to the extent that the Economic Community of West African States (ECOWAS) has become better known for its achievements in peace and security (with the ECOWAS Ceasefire Monitoring Group, ECOMOG, as its prominent cornerstone) than for its economic integration credentials. While it may yet be ambitious to configure an integrated West African security sector, it can be argued that there are emerging discernible elements of a West African security architecture, which are crucial for peace and security in West Africa.[1] The experience of ECOWAS in Sierra Leone and Liberia has shown that the transnational and cross-border nature of conflicts in the sub-region means that many conflicts cannot be resolved or transformed exclusively within borders. Sub-regional security mechanisms, therefore, form an important component of security sector reform (SSR) and can be crucial in conditioning the security environment, thus representing both an input and output of security sector reform. A major concern of this paper is to further explore the relationship between the concept of SSR and the emerging sub-regional institutional security frameworks and how such processes can be rendered more responsive to sub-regional security needs in a manner that is accountable and transparent.

The chapter contends that security sector reform cannot be viable in the absence of a sub-regional framework and unless such reforms represent part of a change in the overall governance agenda based on transparency, accountability, and, as much as possible, participation. It is contended that what is required is not mere incremental adjustments (defined as reform) in the security sector, but rather a transformation, which institutionalises transparency and accountability as the basis not only for the security sector, but also for governance as a whole. Such a transformation agenda must recognise and be predicated on the indivisibility of security. Ultimately, security at individual, group, regime, national, regional, and international levels are directly and indirectly interlinked, enhanced by globalisation of the means of production and communication. This chapter leans towards a holistic approach, which recognises the intrinsic link between security, governance and development. In the specific case of West Africa, the unique experiences of the collective security cooperation in Liberia, Sierra Leone, and Guinea Bissau by ECOWAS member-states have provided the basis for the evolution of, at least, a rudimentary sub-regional framework as encapsulated in the ECOWAS Mechanism for Conflict Prevention, Management and Resolution, Peacekeeping and Security (hereafter the ECOWAS Mechanism). The sub-regional context has been defined by a collective search for peace in a conflict-ridden environment populated by some of the poorest countries in the world and where the imperial security umbrella of the Cold War has been removed.

The chapter starts with a discussion of conceptual issues related to the security sector, and attempts to define the character of the security sector in West Africa based on these concepts. It then considers the extent to which the elements of a sub-regional security architecture can be said to exist, and the opportunities and limitations which these present for SSR. It is argued that the ECOWAS Mechanism is at the core of West Africa's emerging sub-regional security architecture. Issues which are considered relevant for a sub-regional transformation agenda for the security sector are identified, putting forward the argument that West Africa is caught between the scissors of *Westphalian* realities of the present global system and the desirability of a transformation agenda.

The Character of the Security Sector in West Africa

The security sector in West African security is not people-oriented, often disarticulated from the larger society and anachronistic in structure. Thus, it is unable to provide security for the populace, often rather functioning as sources of insecurity and tools of oppression, dictatorships and maintenance of power at all cost. Rather than being agents of the law, their flagrant abuse of, and impunity and immunity to the rule of law has been the means through which they have brutalised and terrorised the very population which they are supposed to protect. In addition, imperatives and vagaries of the Cold War permitted, and to a large extent encouraged the characterisation of security as 'regime security' in much of Africa. The essential point of emphasis is that the disarticulated basis of the security sector in much of the West African sub-region emanates from a governance deficit. Nnoli has adequately captured the core of the link between security and governance:

> 'Eventually opposition to the state arises as a result of the reckless abuse of state power in a process in which the accumulation of power and its ruthless projection gradually generates a critical mass of desperate enemies. Government makes decision without consultation and takes action without providing remedies for those adversely affected by these actions. The people react with hostility towards government, which in turn represses them, setting off a spiral that culminates in violence.'[2]

The drought of good governance in contemporary Africa resulted in a rain of violent resistance movements, rebel groups and militias whose commonality has lain in the use of force to effect regime change (Nigeria, Ghana, Sierra Leone, Liberia, Côte d'Ivoire). In virtually all civil wars in West Africa since the end of the Cold war, small arms have featured as the favoured instrument for the capture and illegal exploitation of natural resource-rich areas.[3] The small arms in turn provide the finance for prosecution of internal wars resulting in mass mutilation, displacement, sexual enslavement, gross abuse of human rights, and sheer plunder and murder of West African citizens. Under challenge from militia and insurgent groups, criminal gangs and networks, and structurally weakened by the call of the World Bank and the IMF to 'roll back' the state, much of Africa has lost the monopoly over the means of coercion, making statutory security forces one of *many* security actors rather than *the* security actor. The significance of the weakness of the state and its increasing incapacity to provide security as a public good, is the increasing privatisation of security services at both formal and informal levels, featuring a range of actors beyond the state. This has direct implications for the definition and evolution of the security sector both at state and regional levels.

From a relatively narrow perspective, the *security sector* is defined as those institutions which have been entrusted with the protection of the state and its citizens, based on a monopoly of the use (or threat of use) of coercive force, that is military, paramilitary, intelligence, police and penal forces. It also includes civil authorities mandated to control and oversee these agencies (ministries of defence, finance, interior, national security agencies, judiciary, and parliament).[4] However, a major shortcoming of such a definition is its state-centric focus and the assumption of state monopoly over the means of coercion. Such a definition takes on a superficial value in view of the diffusion of the sources of the means of coercion and the subsequent expansion of the security community, which has taken place in most African states, particularly following the end of the Cold War. The United Nations Development Programme (UNDP) provides a broader definition of the security sector, which includes non-statutory security forces (such as liberation armies, private security companies, guerrilla armies) and civil society groups.[5] In terms of universal validity, however, the suitability of non-statutory security forces such as guerrilla armies or private security and private military companies for inclusion in the security sector remains debatable.[6]

In order for security sector reform to be viable and sustainable either at state or sub-regional levels, it must lead to security institutions which are better able to respond to the threats faced by the populace, and not merely threats to the government. Such a policy environment necessarily extends beyond immediate concerns with *regime* security. The task of the contemporary security sector reform agenda is the articulation and operationalisation of a transformative, people-centred conception of security. In this regard, the necessary point of departure is the identification of the sources of threat, the targets of such threats, and the purpose and goals of SSR.[7] Even though the outcomes of objective threat analysis and strategic defence reviews for West Africa are admittedly unlikely to be uniform, it is evident that the sources of threat are often internal and the targets/victims are not merely states and security forces. In addition, the purpose of security extends beyond protecting the state. West African citizens, communities and states are threatened by criminals of various levels of sophistication, armed insurgents with various levels of callousness and poverty of various levels of misery. For many, the very governments whose statutory responsibility it is to protect, has become the major source of insecurity through corruption, abuse of power, and the lack of state capacity to deal effectively with pressing social problems. Diseases such as HIV/AIDS and malaria routinely threaten human existence in West Africa, and other parts of the continent.[8] Thus, blessings have become curses, and protectors have become predators.

Viable and sustainable post-conflict reconstruction cannot occur without a systematic promotion and infusion of democratic principles into broader socio-political structures and processes. A transformation agenda would also need to recognise the externalities of the security sector in African states:

> '...for peace to be embedded, the objects of reform should not be confined merely to the security sectors of the target countries but should also incorporate the broader global structures and agents that condition them. In other words, a transformative approach places as much emphasis on healing the physicians as well as the patients'.[9]

Furthermore, in the context of underdevelopment, any viable change in the governance of the security sector would need to address issues of poverty alleviation, predicated on a human security agenda. However, the concept of human security, while very appealing at a conceptual and rhetorical level, confronts real difficulties at the level of operationalisation and implementation. Conscious therefore of the dilemma between the desirable (security sector transformation) and the practical (security sector reform), perhaps the ideal framework of analysis is one that pursues the latter with the former constantly in view. Ultimately, this chasm between reform and transformation can only be bridged by democratic governance processes and institutions.[10]

The contradictions related to the crisis of governance (governance gap) in many West African states are responsible for instability and conflict, conditioning the role of security forces in society. As aptly noted,

> '...to the extent that the ordinary people do not see themselves as stakeholders in the nation-building project, the state in West Africa lacked popular legitimacy and remained a shell since independence. Unable or unwilling to lead societal transformations that would have guaranteed the security of the majority, and fearful of societal backlash, the post-independence African leadership yielded to their instincts of self-preservation. The preoccupation with assuring personal power and regime security blocked any moves towards democratic institution building'.[11]

It is important to recognise that non-statutory security organisations (such as liberation armies, guerrilla armies, traditional militias, political party militias, private security companies, civil defence forces, local, regional and global criminal groups) have, particularly since the end of the Cold War, been at the core of West African security concerns. Their role has been either to supplement government provision of security services, or to directly compete with the state for control of the means of coercion, including the use of illicit instruments of force to capture power from the state. Of direct relevance in this regard is the role of militias in the Mano River Union (MRU)[12] conflicts, the role of heavily armed criminal gangs and the evolution of vigilante response mechanisms, which further expand the space for non-statutory actors in the West African security community.

In much of West Africa, the state, both as a result of bad governance and in response to Structural Adjustment Programme (SAP) conditionalities, has been stretched beyond the limits of its capabilities. In Nigeria, for example, vigilante groups such as the *Bakassi Boys,* or the *Oduduwa Peoples Congress*, have often enjoyed the confidence and admiration of the populace, in contrast to a perception of the police as corrupt and ineffective. In Ghana, local manufacturers of small arms have become renowned for their expertise not only nationally, but also with the capacity for export to other parts of the sub-region. In Sierra Leone, traditional hunters and militia were primary actors in a civil war, which witnessed the active participation of European mercenaries.[13] Throughout the entire sub-region, indigenous mercenary elements have emerged, participating in civil wars in Sierra Leone, Liberia, and Côte d'Ivoire for material gains and access to natural resources.

Given the expansive nature of the security community in West Africa, an operational definition of the security sector must include the non-statutory actors whose paradoxical roles have been both to threaten and to provide security (selectively) to elements within and states alike. There is a need to accommodate the complexity and diversity of actors in the African security landscape. Effective and democratic control of the armed and security forces so that they respond more effectively to the needs and priorities of the population remains the objective of SSR. This cannot be achieved without an adequate and inclusive mapping of what constitutes the security sector and an articulation of the conditions which propel a sustained challenge to the monopoly of the state in West Africa over the legitimate means of coercion. The task of reforming the security sector is, therefore, directly related to democracy and good governance. In this regard, security sector reform seeks to ensure that the institutions entrusted with the protection of the people and the state *(les gens d'armes)* are supervised in accordance with the principles of accountability, transparency and participation. Such reforms must seek ways to either accommodate or extinguish those non-state actors who have established themselves as stakeholders in the West African security complex.

In addition, a tragic irony which is becoming increasingly clear, is that the prospects for more thorough and fundamental changes (transformation) in the security sector can be enhanced by the near collapse of state structure. In other words, the nearer a state approaches total collapse, the more the opportunities for the reconstruction of its security sector in a manner that is accountable and transparent. Contrast, for example, the extensive reconstruction of the security sector in Sierra Leone and Liberia with the 'stealth reforms' in various other West African states. SSR in post-conflict societies is denoted in most literature as security sector reconstruction, signifying a more comprehensive approach, which alters relations of power between the *state* and the *citizenry*.[14] It must however be noted that such 'opportunities' also expose the post-conflict society to the vagaries of an externally-driven agenda which may be implemented at the expense of local ownership.

The Challenges of Regional Democratic Governance of the Security Sector

Several factors propel the need for an active sub-regional actor as a vehicle for addressing West Africa's increasingly interconnected security challenges, thus making ECOWAS an indispensable instrument for the collective transformation of the security sector in West Africa. The ever-increasing and widespread loss of monopoly of the instruments of force by the state, the limits of externally-driven security sector reform agendas, and the growing prominence and potency of cross-border security threats (such as illicit small arms proliferation, HIV/AIDS, mass refugee movements and other types of forced displacement, illicit exploitation of natural resources, sometimes to fund wars, the use of child soldiers and mercenaries) are factors which singularly and collectively reflect the need for a shared instrument such as ECOWAS. This could provide a common sub-regional definition and mechanism for the security sector reform agenda.

The history of West Africa since the 1990s has demonstrated clearly that state-based approaches to SSR are crucial and necessary, but not sufficient for achieving and sustaining peace and stability in the reforming state(s).[15] While the specificities of historical and political contexts, institutional background and social conditions of each country cannot be denied, the need for a broader sub-regional path to addressing security sector transformation is becoming increasingly evident in West Africa. Cross-border threats such as the proliferation of illicit small arms and light weapons

(SALW), illegal trade in natural resources, human trafficking, and transnational criminal groupings are all examples of security challenges which fall beyond the reach and capability of any particular state and which can only be viably resolved through a collective regional approach.[16] Moreover, unilateral SSR programmes may be well-meaning, but threatened by developments in the neighbouring states. In addition, geographical proximity facilitates experience sharing, lessons learned processes and coordination among states. Sub-regional approaches therefore strengthen co-operation and facilitate confidence building.[17] With the benefit of hindsight, it can be said that the Liberian civil war ignited this realisation in West Africa in the late 1980s and early 1990s, arising from its ramifications in the immediate neighbouring countries of the Mano River Union (MRU) and the entire sub-region.

While the ECOMOG intervention demonstrated that sub-regional interventions could make a positive difference, its various shortcomings and operational difficulties in its intervention missions in Liberia (and subsequently in Sierra Leone and Guinea Bissau) exposed the limits of ad hoc interventions. The creation of the ECOWAS Mechanism was, to a large extent, an attempt to devise a more systematic framework for addressing conflict and to define security within the broader framework of human security. The ECOWAS Mechanism has emerged as the main framework for conflict management in the sub-region and the nucleus of West Africa's emerging sub-regional security architecture. It is, therefore, worthy of more detailed examination.

Although the ECOWAS Mechanism was signed in December 1999, its evolution began with regional efforts to address the Liberian civil war.[18] The Mechanism supersedes and borrows from the two previous regional security agreements as encapsulated under the 1978 Protocol on Non-Aggression and the 1981 Protocol on Mutual Assistance in Defence (MAD). It can in fact be argued that the ECOWAS Mechanism is the result of incremental progression in the evolution of a sub-regional normative framework for addressing conflicts. While the 1978 Protocol merely called for peaceful settlement of disputes, the 1981 Protocol went further to provide for mutual assistance against external aggression and the formation of standby forces. Even though ECOWAS members failed to establish the standby forces as provided by the MAD, such a provision provided the necessary precedent upon which the ECOMOG intervention could later be based. Moreover, it meant that the notion of joint military operations was, at least in theory, not being entertained for the first time. The Mechanism is, therefore, the end result of incremental gains in regional cooperation in security matters. It has emerged to form the core of a sub-regional security architecture which is not merely a product of regional security cooperation, but which increasingly has implications for the priorities and agenda of security sector reform in respective West African states.

Figure 4.1 shows the organisational structure of the ECOWAS Mechanism, whose implementation is the direct responsibility of the Deputy Executive Secretary for Political Affairs, Defence and Security (DES/PADS), under the direction of the Executive Secretary. The office of the DES/PADS oversees four directorates – political affairs, humanitarian affairs, defence and security, and observation and monitoring. It is significant to note the supranational element in the ECOWAS collective security arrangement 'to give mutual aid and assistance for defence against any armed threat or aggression on a member-state,' as contained in the 1981 Protocol on Mutual Assistance in Defence, and as recalled in the Preamble to the ECOWAS Mechanism. It would therefore seem that there is, at least, a supranational aspiration, which is admittedly so far hampered by the lack of a common foreign and security policy comparable to that of, for example, the European Union.

The creation of a Mediation and Security Council (MSC) introduced an element of transparency, which had hitherto been lacking, residing as it previously did exclusively at the level of Heads of State. The creation of the MSC is significant in view of the fact that it represents practical experience learnt from the collective efforts at addressing the Liberian civil war. It signifies a metamorphosis of the Committee of Nine, which had been the main organ for collective decision-making over the Liberian civil war. The MSC has a wide range of tasks, including *inter* alia, decisions on all matters relating to peace and security; decision and implementation of all policies for conflict prevention, management, resolution, peacekeeping, and security; and authorisation of all forms of intervention and decision particularly on the deployment of political and military missions.[19] The MSC operates at three levels (a) Heads of State, meeting at least twice a year (b) Ministers, meeting once every three months and (c) Ambassadors accredited to Abuja. The Defence and Security Commission and the Council of Elders were established to support the work of the MSC.[20]

Figure 4.1: Organisational Structure of the ECOWAS Mechanism[21]

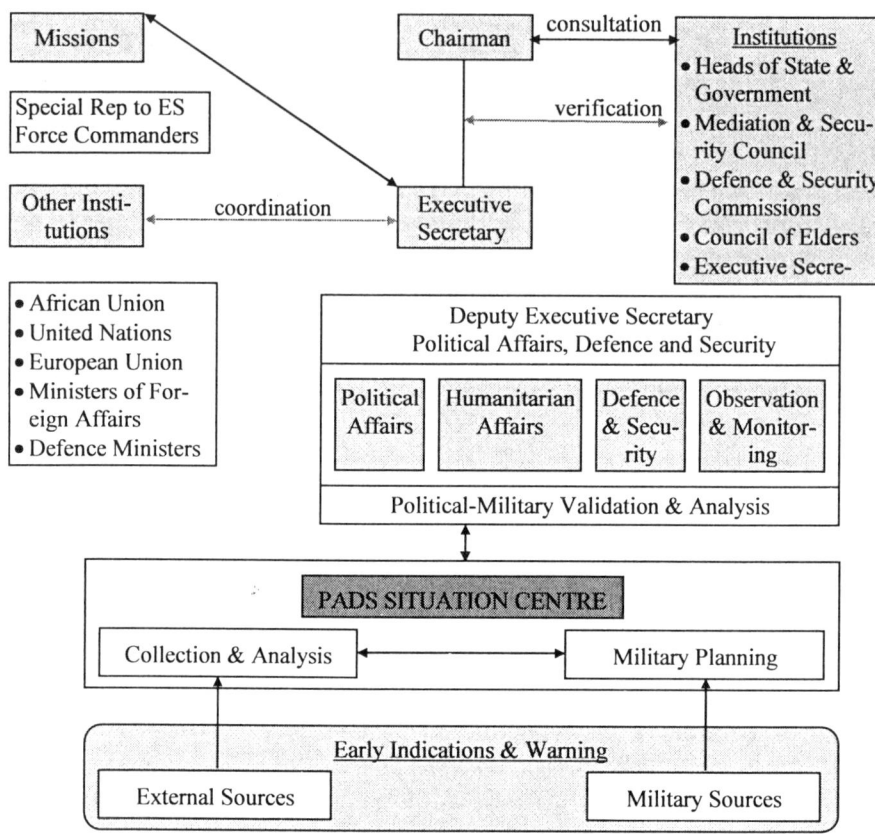

Table 4.1 sets out the basic elements of sub-regional security sector architecture in West Africa. The normative basis for these elements resides essentially in the Protocol on Democracy and Good Governance (2001), which is, in fact, a Supplementary Protocol to the ECOWAS Mechanism. Section 1 of Article 1 of the Supplementary Protocol is titled 'Constitutional Convergence Principles' upon which the ECOWAS Mechanism is predicated and provides for:

    (a)   Separation of powers (the Executive, Legislative and Judiciary); empowerment and strengthening of the parliaments and guarantee of parliamentary immunity; independence of the Judiciary (judges shall be independent in the discharge of their duties).

(b)   Every accession to power must be made through free, fair and transparent elections.

(c)   Zero tolerance for power obtained or maintained by unconstitutional means.

(d)   Popular participation in decision-making, strict adherence to democratic principles and decentralisation of power at all levels of governance.

(e)   The armed forces must be apolitical and must be under the command of a legally constituted political authority; no serving member of the armed forces may seek to run for elective political office.[22]

These principles affirm the constitutional and democratic basis of not only the security sector, but also of the political system in all ECOWAS states. While Article 1(a) provides the statutory basis for the principle of separation of powers, sections 1(b) and 1(c) outlaw military coups d'état, while section 1(e) expressly provides for civilian oversight of the armed forces. This is further reinforced by Article 20(1), which states that 'the armed forces, the police and other security agencies shall be under the authority of legally constituted civilian authorities'.[23] The Supplementary Protocol recognises the role of civilian elites in often instigating military coups when it suits their political interests. Thus while Article 19(1) provides that 'the armed forces and police shall be non-partisan', Article 20(2) makes a corresponding demand that 'civilian authorities shall respect the apolitical nature of the armed forces and police'. The norms of transparency and accountability are contained in Article 34 of the document, which states that 'member states shall ensure accountability, professionalism, transparency and expertise in the public and private sectors'.[24] Popular participation as a norm is statutorily addressed in Article 1(j), which provides that 'the freedom of association and the right to meet and organise peaceful demonstrations shall also be guaranteed'. Furthermore, Article 22(1) provides that 'the use of arms to disperse non-violent meetings or demonstrations shall be forbidden. Whenever a demonstration becomes violent, only the use of minimal and/or proportionate force shall be authorised'. Overall therefore, the Protocol on Democracy and Good Governance addresses the essential norms and principles of accountability, transparency and participation, which are the essential elements for the democratic governance of the security sector.

Table 4.1: Instruments of Sub-Regional Security Sector Governance in West Africa

	Instrument	Features	Source(s)
Conflict prevention	Early Warning System	4 observation and monitoring zones in Banjul, Monrovia, Ouagadougou, and Cotonou Central Observatory at ECOWAS HQ, Abuja	Chapter IV of Mechanism
Conflict resolution	Mediation and Security Council	9 members, including present and immediate past Chair of ECOWAS. 2 year tenure. Operates at 3 levels: Heads of State, Ministerial, Ambassadorial	Articles 7 & 8 of mechanism.
Peace support operations	ECOMOG	stand-by units in member states	Articles 21,22 & 28 of mechanism
Trans-Border Crime	Close coopera-tion among the security services of member states Assistance and proper coordina-tion for the apprehension of criminals	Establishment of spe-cialised departments in ministries of Justice, Defence and Security Harmonisation of domestic laws Crime Prevention and Criminal justice Centre (ECPCJS) Small Arms Control and Prevention Meas-ures	Article 46 Articles 50 & 51

However, the application of these instruments and the accompanying normative principles face various challenges, which demonstrate a degree of reluctance by ECOWAS states to adopt a sub-regional approach to security sector governance. These challenges include:

i) Political will: Perhaps due to its binding nature, both the ECOWAS Mechanism and its (Supplementary) Protocol on Democracy and Good Governance have witnessed a disappointing level of assent. To date, the Mechanism has been ratified by only four states (Burkina Faso, Mali, Sierra Leone and Togo), while Ghana is the only country to have ratified the (Supplementary) Protocol on Democracy and Good Governance.[25] Even though the historical anglo-francophone divide which has plagued the organisation has been on the decline particularly since the end of the Cold War, political cohesion remains far from ideal.[26]

ii) Funding: ECOWAS is a collection of states whose economies are basically fragile and where human development remains among the lowest in the world. The financial difficulties faced by ECOWAS are characteristic of the material conditions of its member states. Most member states remain in arrears in terms of their annual contributions to ECOWAS. With particular regard to the ECOWAS Mechanism, peace support operations in most of the conflicts have depended on external funding, including current efforts in Côte d'Ivoire and Liberia. Current efforts by ECOWAS to set up a Peace Fund would go some way in addressing the issue of funding.

iii) Institutional capacity: The operationalisation of the ECOWAS Mechanism has also been plagued by the limited human and institutional resources of the Secretariat, which is also directly related to funding constraints. Although the office of the DES/PADS was created in 2000, it has been slow in recruiting the necessary human resources. For much of the period since its establishment the DES/PADS has operated with a skeleton staff, often overstretching available staff and leaving crucial programme areas uncovered. The situation witnessed some improvement with the appointment of all four Directors under the DES/PADS in 2003, but many middle level positions remain unfilled. The ECPCJS in the Department of Legal Affairs (see Table 4.1) is yet to be established.

iv). Lack of standard operating procedure and doctrines: ECOWAS is a collection of states with different and varying levels of military training, doctrines, colonial background, and therefore, operating procedures. Language and communication present major problems since anglophone and francophone military operate different systems of staff training for officers. In order to address this gap, ECOWAS is devising a peacekeeping doctrine the concept and structure of which were approved by the Defence and Security Commission in June 2004. The Defence and Security Commission also agreed to form a 5,000 strong brigade by 2010, with initial and immediate focus on the creation of a Task force of 1,500.[27]

v) Political expediency versus practical imperatives: Implementation of the ECOWAS Mechanism has also been hampered by the conflict between the demands of state diplomacy and the practical demands of implementation. Criticism has been made, for example, of the decision to locate two of the Observation Bureaux in Ouagadougou (Burkina Faso) and Monrovia (Liberia).[28] Another example relates to the decision to locate the offices of the Programme for Coordination and Assistance for Security and Development (PCASED) in Bamako, Mali. While this decision was probably intended as a reward for Mali's pace-setting role in micro-disarmament in West Africa, it created operational difficulties due to the fact that the ECOWAS Secretariat is located in Abuja. Eventually, it was decided to deploy a PCASED Liaison Officer at the ECOWAS Secretariat in Abuja in 2003, by which time institutional and operational gaps had already been created. The decision to create a Small Arms Unit within ECOWAS can partly be explained by the perception within ECOWAS that PCASED could not respond adequately to its needs.

The ECOWAS Mechanism provides the basis for a regional security framework, based on a normative framework provided by the Protocol on Democracy and Good Governance. However, various factors (including lack of political will, inadequate financial resources, lack of standard operating procedures and a clearly articulated peacekeeping doctrine, and short term imperatives of political interests) retard the scope and pace of the implementation of the Mechanism and its corresponding norms and principles. These obstacles inform and define the key issues for the democratic transformation of the security sector within a regional framework.

Key Issues for Security Sector Transformation of the West African Security Complex

The harmonisation of security arrangements as encapsulated in the ECOWAS Mechanism is central to security sector reform on a sub-regional basis. In this regard the West African sub-region manifests specific issues, which are likely to affect the prospects for security sector reform within and between states in the sub-region. The extent to which developments in the security sector could transform the West African sub-region depends on addressing a number of key issues identified below.

A Critical Mass of Reforming States

The relationship between security sector reform in individual states and the sub-region is a dynamic and mutually reinforcing one. SSR within member states affects collective security arrangements while the latter also affect the pace and direction of reforms within the constituent states. In the particular case of West Africa, therefore, the ECOWAS Mechanism is, to a large extent, the product of reforms and developments in the ECOWAS member states (civil conflicts in Liberia, Sierra Leone and Guinea Bissau attempts to address the proliferation of SALW, trans-border crime, corruption etc). Concurrently the Mechanism also affects the pace and direction of reforms in the armed and security forces of ECOWAS member states. Thus, the available space for security sector reform at the sub-regional level would depend to a large extent on the existence of a coalition of willing reforming states, the collective effect of which would be to create and sustain the political will for SSR (and hopefully, transformation) at the sub-regional level. The ability of each state to influence the SSR debate at the sub-regional level is necessarily a function of its power and strategic position relative to other member states, thus making the role of hegemonic states crucial in the transformation of the regional security arrangements. It has been aptly noted that

> 'the extent to which they (regional powers) themselves have achieved a reform of their security sector will determine the extent to which reform can be useful at the sub-regional level. Nigeria, for example, has consistently contributed about seventy per cent of the ECOMOG force. The extent to which that country succeeds in reforming its security sector will ultimately impact positively or negatively on the overall conduct of the force...Successful transition and reform processes in Nigeria will only enhance any progress realised at the sub-regional levels. However, developments in ECOWAS could also assist the process of transformation of the Nigerian security establishment'. [29]

It would seem, however, that this critical mass of reforming states in the security sector remains lacking, as evidenced by a recent study looking specifically at state security sector governance in the West African sub-region. Nigeria is yet to attempt any far reaching reform of its security sector while, with a few exceptions, regime security, as opposed to people security re-

mains the primary objective and concern of most West African governments.[30]

The Role of Armed and Security Forces in Emerging Democracies and Post-conflict Societies

Against the context of contemporary fundamental changes in the nature of
war, the role of the state, and the increase in internecine conflicts worldwide,
there is a multiplicity of demands on armed and security forces in Africa.
Despite developments in the global and domestic environment, armed and
security forces in West Africa have maintained the characteristics inherited
from the colonial period. As Rocky Williams aptly noted, they are 'uncan-
ningly Eurocentric in origin'.[31] While some have embarked on various levels
of institutional reform, doctrines, operating procedures and orders of battle
(ORBAT) they have essentially been modelled after the armies of developed
countries. The essential question of 'security sector reform for what?' has
remained essentially outside the purview of most SSR programmes in West
Africa. The armed forces are largely unable (and unlikely?) to perform the
'primary function' of protecting the territorial integrity of the state, while the
police are not only unable to provide public security, they often represent
sources of insecurity. Corruption and excessive use of force, within a context
of lack of accountability, promote a culture of impunity which is self-
perpetuating. In the words of Claude Ake, 'in the absence of a credible external threat the African military is redundant. Against a credible external
threat it is expensively useless'.[32] Therefore, African armed and security
forces are essentially unable to respond effectively to the contemporary
threats facing their populations. This is particularly due to the fact that armed
and security forces in Africa, as with many African institutions, have failed
to evolve beyond their colonial origins. [33]

The threats that confront African populations are less territorial and
more people-centred, rendering the traditional focus on territorial defence
rather superfluous. There is, therefore, a palpable need to reposition the African military towards a more developmental role.

Inverted Civil-Security Relations and Civilian Control of the Military

Given the protracted history of military rule in much of West Africa, the
armed forces have traditionally operated without, and often against the fundamental democratic principle of civilian oversight. The end-result has been

inverted civil-security relations, characterised by a *superiority complex* on the part of the military and a debilitating *incapacity complex* on the part of civilian oversight institutions. Hence while most SSR programmes identify the need to encourage and empower civilian (particularly parliamentary) oversight of the armed and security forces, little attention has been given to the need to orient the military towards appreciating and accepting the need for civilian oversight. It is argued here that there is a need to sensitise and educate the military to objectively appreciate and be favourably disposed to the principle of democratic civilian oversight, with the objective of submitting to supervision by civilian institutions.

Local Ownership

Much of the literature on SSR recognises the need for local ownership of reform, while conceding that the SSR agenda is often externally and donor-driven.[34] The rationale is that SSR, no matter how well intended, can neither be successful nor sustainable without the support of the consumers of such programmes. A recent overview of security sector reform in Africa has specifically noted that

> '...a major problem in the area of security sector reform and transformation in Africa has been precisely the lack of African input to and ownership of the emerging reform agenda. Donors of both security assistance and development assistance aimed at supporting changes in the security sector have tended to dominate the process of defining the reform agenda'.[35]

The dilemma, however, is that security sector reform is a particularly sensitive area, which many states perceive as being at the core of their 'sovereignty'. Moreover, armed and security forces are often part of the security problem, they often enjoy the support of incumbent regimes, and they often serve as agents of regime security. While donor states and agencies may pursue the alternative track of securing a 'local partnership' with opposition elements, the media, academia, civil society and some parliamentarians, this can ultimately only be for the purpose of pressurising the government. Donor enthusiasm cannot replace local ownership, and perhaps the most practical path is for the former to support and encourage the necessary conditions for the latter, rather than seeking to supplant it.

The Role of Civil Society

Civil society organisations (CSO) have been identified as watchdogs, agents of change and sources of technical input in the SSR process.[36] The reasons for CSO involvement in SSR as well as their contributions to the promotion of local ownership have been clearly discussed.[37] A central shortcoming, however, is that SSR remains a rather specialised subject in much of Africa, on which there is both limited expertise and interest, sustained by the traditional secrecy with which security-related issues have been cloaked.

> 'African CSOs have been reluctant, as well as unequipped, to influence security policy and oversight...The problem is magnified by the relative rarity of African research institutes specialising in security issues; certainly the theme of SSR is striking in its absence from the work of mainstream political scientists and university departments in Africa'[38]

The end result is a limited circle of experts and non-governmental research organisations in this area of interest. In this regard, the SSR debate in West Africa has benefited from 'the vision and efforts of a very small number of concerned individuals with a high level of experience on or knowledge of security matters'.[39] There is a need to broaden the limited circle of experts and expertise, expand the space for SSR debate and democratise popular participation and interrogation of the concepts, norms and practices of SSR in West Africa. There is also a need to avoid complacency in assuming that CSO are, by their mere existence, structurally superior to state structures and inherently better equipped to contribute positively to the SSR debate.[40] As already cautioned, civil society may not always be 'civil' and 'may be similarly unrepresentative and unaccountable to society'.[41] The democratisation and expansion of the space for SSR research would also be further enhanced by scholarship and exchange programmes with West African universities and institutions of higher learning for the security studies.

Rule of Law

Lack of transparency and accountability characterises not only the security sector, but also the entire web of social relations. No sector is spared the ramifications and effects of corruption and impunity. Corrupt judges, porous legal systems, impunity leading to lack of faith in the legal system, corrupt police services, all threaten the prospects for democratic governance generally, and of the security sector in particular.

The rule of law requires that government must itself respect and uphold the law. The situation in which governments disregard judicial injunctions and tamper with the judicial process ultimately deprives the government of the legitimacy which flows from the rule of law as the fundamental principle of collective coexistence based on democratic principles. In this regard, it must be emphasized that the spirit of constitutionalism is an indispensable condition for the rule of law to operate. Strong consensus is essential for the self-binding procedures of governance which is at the basis of constitutionalism.

Parliamentary Oversight

Civilian, especially parliamentary oversight raises particular challenges for West Africa while presenting unique opportunities for the transformation of the sub-region. Firstly, decades of military rule have impacted negatively on parliamentary oversight capacity. Secondly, parliamentarians often lack the specialised knowledge necessary for oversight of the security sector. Such shortcomings are carried over from national assemblies to the ECOWAS Parliament, which is not elected directly, but seconded from national legislatures. Thirdly and significantly, West African parliaments are, to a large extent, a mirror of the societies which they serve and from which they emanate. In this regard, it is worth mentioning that in order for the legislature to be in a position to transform the sub-region, the fundamental principles of democracy such as rule of law, transparency and accountability would need to apply to the parliamentarians as they apply to other members of society. The same principles of professionalism demanded of the armed and security forces would also need to apply to the legislators. Experience from some of the major parliaments in West Africa indicate that there is a danger that the principle of 'separation of powers', which is a *sine qua non* for effective parliamentary oversight, is in danger of operating as a 'collusion of powers'. While an objective study of the state of affairs with regard to the integrity of the legislature is yet to be conducted, *public perceptions* are no less significant, particularly in terms of democratic oversight. An assessment of the Nigerian legislature of the fourth republic by the Nigerian press is indicative:

> 'In legislative and oversight functions, the National Assembly seems to have found it difficult living above the mire and the mud. Allegations are rife that many Assemblymen have been breathing down the spines of the ministries and parastatals under the so-called oversight functions all in the name of graft. This is believed to be the usual means by which ministries and parasta-

tals lobby members of the various committees of the National assembly during budget defences. Those Chief Executives who do not hope to be in trouble are quick to do the bidding of such powerful assembly committee chairmen. This is believed to be why a sizeable volume or portion of contracts at the ministries are normally reserved for members of the "oversighting committees" of the National Assembly'.[42]

It must be emphasised that this assessment is by no means either scientific or representative of the Nigerian legislature. It certainly is not characteristic of parliaments in West Africa. What this assessment affirms is that the legislature is only a product and a reflection of the society which its serves. Corruption is the very antithesis of oversight. The prospects for democratic oversight simply melt away in the face of a corrupt legislature.

International Cooperation

ECOWAS has since 2001 been involved in a P-3 Agreement with the US, France and the UK to build ECOMOG capacity for peace support operations. Under this arrangement an officer from each of these donor countries is seconded to the ECOWAS Secretariat, the first of which (American) reported for duty in 2002.[43] Known initially as the African Crisis Response Initiative (ACRI), the American programme has been renamed the African Contingency Operations Training Assistance (ACOTA). The French programme, known as RECAMP involves practical training to strengthen cohesion and effectiveness of African capacity for peace support operations.[44] RECAMP held its ECOWAS Strategic Conference from 7-11 June 2004.[45] British assistance is carried out under the auspices of the African Peacekeeping Training Support Programme.

Within the context of sub-regional security cooperation, a major challenge facing West African states is the need to maintain a delicate balance between external assistance and the need for local ownership of security arrangements and reforms. At both sub-regional and bilateral levels, lessons have been learnt in the realisation that African armed and security forces cannot be mere clones of their donor counterparts, and superior resources do not automatically translate into superior capability. The example of the ACRI is indicative:

'It (ACRI) was established in order to reduce the demand for UN peacekeeping assistance in Africa. The training provided under ACRI by UN troops has tended to focus on conventional peacekeeping doctrine and techniques rather than on doctrines and techniques relevant to the difficult conflict environment in which African armed forces now find themselves, including operations against guerrilla forces in difficult terrain'.[46]

Implementing the Moratorium on SALW

The widespread proliferation of small arms and light weapons (SALW) has necessitated the institution of a small arms moratorium regime in West Africa.[47] While there is no reliable data on the exact number of illicit small arms in circulation in West Africa, estimates have ranged between seven and ten million. Whatever the exact figure, the devastating conflicts in the sub-region, particularly in the Mano River axis, confirm that SALW are West Africa's Weapons of Mass Destruction (WMD). Independent assessments indicate that the Moratorium has had a marginal effect on the security situation in West Africa.[48]

Despite the shortcomings in implementing the ECOWAS Moratorium, there can be little doubt that it could be a viable regional instrument for transforming the security sector. Regional provisions necessitating application for exemptions to the Moratorium promote the building of sub-regional norms, while the joint training required as part of the Moratorium regime could entrench elements of transparency, professionalism, and facilitate the evolution of standard operating procedures among the armed and security forces. Implementation of the Moratorium regime offers a unique opportunity to transform the West African sub-region, and represents a barometer for sub-regional cooperation in the security sector. With on-going discussions to transform the Moratorium into a Convention, it is evident that the prospects are bright for the evolution of a normative framework for sub-regional practical disarmament in West Africa.[49]

In essence, the prospects for transforming the security sector would depend on key considerations including the presence of a critical mass of reforming states to propel the reform agenda; the extent to which the armed and security forces can evolve beyond their colonial origins to respond more effectively to contemporary threats; the prospects for local ownership of the reform agenda and the related role of civil society in this process; the ability of the legislature to perform oversight functions over the armed and security forces; the quality of international cooperation and assistance; and the pace and quality of practical disarmament in the sub-region.

Recommendations and Conclusion

The key issues discussed above would arguably define the prospects for security sector transformation. The following specific recommendations would, in our view, provide paths to addressing these keys issues in order to enhance the prospects for the transformation (as opposed to mere reform) of the security sector. Firstly, SSR reform programmes need to move beyond the usual gravitation towards reform of the armed and security forces and to extend, in operational and programmatic terms, to justice and police reform. The political will and courage for addressing corruption is a necessary condition for bringing an end to the culture of impunity, which is endemic in the sub-region, and which tends to position the citizens as victims rather than benefactors of the security services.

Secondly, the parliament is the engine of democracy and the foremost institution for civilian oversight of the security sector, along with relevant ministries, political authorities, civil society and the media. In view of the several identified shortcomings of the security sector, there is a need for capacity building for parliament generally and the committees on defence and security, justice and police affairs in particular.[50] In order to lend credence to, and to empower regional approaches to parliamentary oversight, particular emphasis should be laid on enhancing the capacity of the ECOWAS Parliament through training of both ECOWAS Parliamentarians and staff.

Thirdly, steps should be taken to promote professionalism and conditions accepting civilian oversight within the armed and security forces. The objective is to create an enabling environment for the forces to accept the benefits and constitutionality of civilian oversight. The specific methodology may include integrating democratic and civilian oversight principles and practices in the training curricula of West African security forces. These should focus on military academies, command and staff colleges, war colleges, and peacekeeping courses. Such intervention would expose security personnel to the principles, benefits, and challenges of civilian oversight. There should also be democratic and civilian oversight lectures, roundtables and colloquiums, organised in participation with civilian oversight bodies, to create a feedback channel. In addition, there should be development of civilian oversight training modules for use in security and military training institutions.

Fourthly, there is a need to reposition African armed and security forces to respond more effectively to contemporary threats not merely to

West African states, but to West African populations. Such efforts should focus on post-conflict reconstruction, including Demobilization, Demilitarization, and Reintegration (DDR), military humanitarianism, that is deploying military expertise and skills for development especially in civil engineering, agriculture, medicine (including the scourge of HIV/AIDS), regional peace support operations, internal security challenges, including search-and-rescue operations.

Fifthly, there is a need to expand the knowledge pool and debate on SSR within the sub-region. The limited circle of expertise should be expanded to accommodate new actors, which should extend to West African tertiary institutions. One specific avenue is to sponsor scholarships in the study of SSR and to make literature available *gratis* to institutions of higher learning. There should be closer collaboration between African universities and think tanks in the sub-region in the study of the security sector.

There is also a clear need for closer collaboration among donors and other technical partners, with regard to their cooperation with institutions and governments in West Africa. Networks, technical assistance programmes, and other external interventions should be coordinated and informed by a common set of criteria and benchmarks. It would be useful to activate a sub-regional security sector network among donors.

There is a continuing need for the enhancement of the capacity of ECOWAS to inform and contribute to SSR in member states. This translates into an enhanced capacity for the implementation of the ECOWAS Mechanism. It is recommended that specific timelines on specific aspects of the Mechanism should be developed by the ECOWAS Secretariat under the coordination of the Mediation and Security Council which could be reviewed periodically.

This chapter has attempted to define the essential character of the security sector in West Africa and argued that the ECOWAS Mechanism has emerged as the core of a sub-regional security architecture. Essentially, it is argued that unilateral and sub-regional approaches to security sector reform exist in a dynamic and mutually reinforcing relationship. In this regard, there is a need for a critical mass of reforming states, which could collectively propel the agenda and pace for security sector reform in the West African sub-region. Although the role of civil society is crucial, there is a need to expand the space for such civil society participation so as to democratise and intensify a popular interrogation of the security sector reform in West Africa. Civilian, particularly parliamentary oversight of the security sector is essential, but grossly inadequate. The legislature manifests various shortcomings, which are indicative of the larger crisis of governance within the sub-region and which hamper its effectiveness to function as a veritable vehicle for security sector transformation within and between states in West Africa.

Notes

[1] See Chapter 2 in this book for a similar argument on the emergence of a Euro-Atlantic security sector.

[2] Nnoli, O., 'Security of Africa in the Emerging Global Environment: What Role for the Military', Graduation Lecture Series No. 8 (National War College: Abuja, Nigeria, 29 July, 2003), p. 25.

[3] For a detailed overview of the effects of illicit small arms proliferation in West Africa, see Ebo, A., 'Small Arms Control in West Africa', *Security and Peacebuilding Programme (MISAC)*, (International Alert, London, October, 2003).

[4] For a fuller elaboration of the narrower definition of security sector, see *A Conceptual Framework for Enhancing Policy Coherence* (OECD, Paris, 2000).

[5] See *Human Development Report* (UNDP, 2002).

[6] Greene, O., 'Security Sector Reform, Conflict Prevention and Regional Perspectives'. *Journal of Security Sector Management*, Vol 1 No 1, (March 2003).

[7] Williams, I., 'Why Africa Needs Security Sector Reform', in A. Lala and A. Fitz-Gerald, eds, *Providing Security for People: Security Sector Reform in Africa,* GFN-SSR, (Shrivenham, 2003).

[8] Malaria is particularly dangerous to Africa. The disease is responsible for 900,000 deaths in Africa. Every thirty seconds, an African child dies of Malaria. Every day, at least 3,000 Africans die of Malaria. At least twenty per cent of all under-five child deaths in Africa is attributable to Malaria. Available at: <http://allafrica.com/stories/200405270802.html>. AIDS is widely acknowledged as the number one cause of death in Africa. Disaggregated data for West Africa are not available but some thirty million Africans (seventy per cent of global infections) are in Africa. Available at: <http://www.data.org/whyafrica/checkthefacts/>.

[9] Cooper, N. & Pugh, M., 'Security Sector Transformation in Post-Conflict Societies', *The Conflict, Security and Development group*, Working Paper Number 5 (London, 2002), p. 6.

[10] Security Sector *Reform* often denotes incremental changes which often fail to address structural and institutional deficiencies in the security sector. Security Sector *Transformation*, on the other hand, requires fundamental changes in the governance process so as to permit for transparency and accountability and often involves radical changes in power relations, particularly between the security forces and the civilian population.

[11] Musah, A.-F., 'Small Arms-A Time Bomb Under West Africa's Democratization Process, *The Brown Journal of World Affairs*, Spring Vol IX Issue 1 (2002), p. 241.

[12] The Mano River Union (MRU) came into being on 3 October 1973 when President Siaka Stevens of Sierra Leone and President William Tolbert of Liberia signed an economic cooperation pact at Malema, a small town on the Mano River in Sierra Leone. Both Presi-

dents were conservative and had little admiration for radical and military regimes. The MRU Declaration made provision for other West African countries to join the Union and, subsequently, Guinea became a member on 25 October 1980.

[13] Aning, K. E. 'Africa's Security in the New Millennium: State or Mercenary Induced Stability?' *Global Society: Journal of Interdisciplinary International relations,* Vol 15 No.3 (May 2001).

[14] On the details of security sector transformation in Liberia and Sierra Leone, see chapter 8 this book.

[15] For a detailed discussion of the country-specific nature of Security Sector Reform, see Hutchful, E., 'Reforming the Security Sector in Africa: An Overview', lecture delivered at the DCAF-UNOG Seminar, Geneva, 26 January 2004.

[16] For details of cross border security threats in West Africa, see Report of the (UN) Secretary-General on Ways to Combat Sub-regional and Cross-border problems in West Africa', (S/2004/2000). It is worth noting that even though the Presidential Security Council Statement of 25 July 2003 (S/PRST/2003/11) had requested a focus specifically on the issues of mercenaries, child soldiers and small arms, the reported noted that 'This is not an exhaustive list of such problems. The culture of impunity, the spread of HIV/AIDS, the continued weakening of the security sector, the proliferation of roadblocks, youth unemployment, environmental degradation, social exclusion, remnants of war, mass refugee movements and other forced displacement, inequitable and illicit exploitation of natural resources, weak national institutions, and civil society structures, and violations of human rights, including the rights of women, are some of the other serious cross-border problems afflicting many parts of the sub-region' (page 1). The report further notes that 'the need for security sector reform lies at the heart of most cross-border regional problems...' (page 7).

[17] For a more detailed analysis of the appeal of regional approaches to SSR, see Greene, O., 'Security sector reform, Conflict Prevention and Regional Perspectives', *JSSM,* Vol 1 No 1 (March, 2003), p. 7; Ball, N. et al., *Security Sector Transformation Handbook,* forthcoming.

[18] For a historical analysis of the evolution of the ECOWAS Mechanism, see Kwesi Aning, 'The new ECOWAS: Democracy and Security Sector Governance in West Africa', paper for the *Research Network on Security Sector Reform and Democratization in Africa: Comparative Perspectives,* (Accra, 24-28 Feb, 2002). See also Summary report of the Conference on Collective Regional Security in West Africa, Akosombo, Ghana, 21-24 July, 1999, organised by Centre for Democracy and Development (Lagos) and Centre for Conflict Resolution, Accra. Available at: <http://www.cddnig.org>.

[19] See Article 10 of ECOWAS Mechanism. Even though the MSC is statutorily composed of seven members and the immediate past and current chair, the Council is currently composed of all ECOWAS member-states except Guinea Bissau. This is an anomaly, which is due to an 'administrative glitch' and will be corrected in 2005 (Email communication with a Director at the ECOWAS Secretariat, 4 June, 2004).

[20] The Defence and Security Commission comprises the Chiefs of Defence Staff, officers responsible for internal affairs and security, and officers from the Ministry of Foreign Affairs.

[21] Source: Ball, N., et al, *Security Sector Transformation Handbook* (forthcoming).

[22] Protocol A/SP1/12/01 On Democracy and Good Governance (Supplementary to the Pro-
      tocol Relating to the Mechanism for Conflict Prevention, Management, Resolution,
      Peacekeeping and Security. Executive Secretary, December 2001.
[23] Ibid., Article 20.
[24] Ibid., Article 34.
[25] Interview with General Cheick Diarra, DES/PADS, Lome, Togo, 24 April, 2004. General
      Diarra commented that it is ironic that the only country to have ratified the Supplementary
      Protocol (Ghana) is yet to ratify the main Protocol (the Mechanism). He further noted
      that its inconsistency and lack of political will places the ECOWAS Secretariat in an em-
      barrassing situation in its discussions with donors and international agencies.
[26] Some of the factors which have facilitated the blurring of the anglophone-francophone
      divide in West Africa include the demands of the politics of European integration on
      France (such as the devaluation of the CFA Franc), the decision by France and United
      Kingdom to adopt a common African policy, closer collaboration and mutual confidence
      gained through ECOMOG operations, closer socio-economic interaction enabled by the
      Protocol on Free Movement, and the winding down of the French-sponsored *Accord de
      Non-Aggression en Matière de Défense* (ANAD).
[27] Telephone interview with Colonel Dickson Dikio, Principal Programme Officer for
      Peacekeeping, ECOWAS Secretariat, 29 June 2004.
[28] It has been noted, for example, that 'both Burkina Faso and Liberia are rogue states that
      fan the flames of insurgency in West Africa. Due to the nature of governments in place in
      these two states and their complicity in and support for rebel groups in West Africa, it is
      highly probable that it twill be nearly impossible for these offices to work to gather in-
      formation upon which ECOWAS can make informed decisions'. See Kwesi Aning, *op cit*,
      p.10. The author was writing during the rule of Charles Taylor.
[29] Ball N., et al, *Security Sector Transformation Handbook* (forthcoming).
[30] Bryden, A., N'Diaye B., & Olonisakin, F. (eds), *The Challenges of Security Sector Gov-
      ernance in West Africa* (forthcoming).
[31] Williams, R. 'Africa and the Challenges of Security Sector Reform', *ISS monograph* No.
      46, (February, 2000), p. 7.
      See also <http://www.iss.co.za/pubs/monographs/No46/Africa.html>.
[32] Ake, C., 'The Causes of Conflict in Africa: A Research Proposal', *CASS* (Port Harcourt,
      1995)
[33] Interview with General Ishola Williams (rtd), Lome, Togo, 25 April, 2004.
[34] See Brzoska, M., 'Development Donors and the Concept of Security Sector Reform',
      DCAF Occasional Paper No. 4, (2003); Lily D., et al, 'A Goal Oriented Approach to
      Governance and Security Sector Reform', (International Alert, London, 2002); Ball, N:,
      'Enhancing Security Sector Governance: A Conceptual Framework for UNDP', (New
      York, 2002); Ball, N., 'Transforming Security Sectors: the IMF and World Bank Ap-
      proaches', *Conflict, Security and Development*, Vol 1, No. 1 (2001).
[35] Ball, N., Fayemi, J. K., *et al*, 'Governance of the Security Sector', in N. Van de Valle &
      N. Ball (eds), *Beyond Structural Adjustment : The Institutional Context of Development*'
      (Palgrave Macmillan, 2003).
[36] Ball, N., Fayemi, J. K., *et al.*, *op. cit.*

[37] Hutchful,E., 'A Civil Society Perspective', in Anicia Lala & Ann Fitz-Gerald (eds), *Providing Security for People: Security Sector Reform in Africa*, GFN-SSR, Shrivenham, 2003.

[38] See Hutchful, E., 'A Civil society Perspective', *op cit.*, p. 38.

[39] Ball, N., Fayemi, J. K., *et al.*, op cit, p. 278. Some of the pioneer CSOs in the SSR field include African Security Dialogue and Research (Ghana), Centre for Democracy and Development (Nigeria), African Strategic and Peace Research Group (Nigeria), Groupe d'Etude et de Recherche sur la Democratie et le Développement Economique et Social en Afrique (Benin), and African Leadership Forum (Nigeria).

[40] The establishment in November 2003 of the African Network of Networks on Security Matters (under the aegis of the SSR-GFN) should address these challenges to a considerable extent.

[41] Lilly D., *et al.*, *op. cit.*, p. 7.

[42] *THISDAY* (Newspaper), 27 January 2002, p. 17.

[43] Interview with Colonel Dickson Dikkio, ECOWAS Principal Programme Officer in charge of Peacekeeping, 7 May 2004.

[44] RECAMP holds cycles of practical training in peace-keeping for sub-regional armed forces. The cycle lasts two years and comprises three phases. Phase 1 is a political-military seminar which studies a crisis situation and how to deal with it, phase 2 is a staff exercise stimulating the details at theatre command level of military decisions to put a peacekeeping operation in to effect, and phase 3 is a field exercise with troops to test on a real scale methods of action developed in the preceding phase. See <http://www.un.int/france/frame_anglais>.

[45] Interview with Colonel Dikkio, ECOWAS, 7 May 2004.

[46] Ball, N., Fayemi, J. K., *et al.*, *op. cit.*, p. 280. Others have similarly argued that the peace-keeping record of American troops in Africa, particularly in Somalia, does not make for a model which ECOWAS states should emulate. See Ebo, A.& Mondeh, K., 'The African Crisis Response Initiative and Conflict Management in a 'New' World Order', *Defence Studies Journal*, Vol 8, July 1988, pp. 23-32.

[47] West Africa's moratorium regime is composed of three main related instruments. (1) Moratorum Delaration, signed on 31 October 1998, renewable every three years; (2) Plan of Action for the Implementation of the Programme of Coordination and Assistance for Security and Development (PCASED), March 1999, and (3) Code of Conduct, 10 December 1999.

[48] Report of the Panel of Experts Appointed Pursuant to Security Council Resolution 1306 in Relation to Sierra Leone (2000) S/2000/1195, New York, 15 December 2000; Cortright D & Lopez G, 'Sanctions *Sans* Commitment: An Assessment of UN Arms Embargoes', Project Ploughshare *Working Paper*, 2002; Sola Ogunbanwo & Chick Faye, 'The ECOWAS Moratorium on the Importation, Exportation, and Manufacture of Small Arms and Light Weapons: Evaluation Study', October 2002.

[49] Cattaneo S. & Ebo, A., 'Report of the ECOWAS-DNI/UK Conference on Combating Illicit Small Arms Brokering and Trafficking' (ECOWAS Secretariat , Abuja, Nigeria, 22-24 March 2004).

[50] This rationale informs DCAF's commitment to, and focus on a programmatic agenda for parliamentary oversight capacity building in West Africa, based on a clear articulation of trends, priorities and needs. In this regard, DCAF is engaged with partnership training

programmes with the ECOWAS Parliament and has collaborated with the United Nations Centre for Peace and Disarmament.

Chapter 5

Security Sector Reform in the Arab Middle East: A Nascent Debate

Arnold Luethold

Introduction

With the publication of the first two *Arab Human Development Reports* in 2002 and 2003[1], Arab intellectuals have brought the short-comings in the Arab world to the forefront and underscored the need for urgent economic, political and social reform. Since then, the debate on reform in the Arab world has proliferated. Its central themes evolve around three priorities: promoting democracy and good governance, building a knowledge society, and expanding economic opportunities.

One would expect that the recent popularity of the security sector reform concept in modern development discourse would have had an impact in shaping the discussion on political reform in the Arab world and the wider Middle East. Yet, with the exception of Iraq and Afghanistan, where security is key in the reconstruction process and rebuilding of the security sector part of it, security sector reform has to date not played any significant role in the reform debate in the Middle East, and even less so in practice. This may surprise, if one considers that the outbreak of numerous conflicts and a series of grave human rights violations in the region have been attributed to an unchecked and inflated security sector; that military aid budgets and military expenditure are amongst the world's highest; and that respect for political liberties and civil rights is commonly rated amongst the world's lowest.[2]

This chapter seeks to make a modest contribution to the discussion of security sector reform in the Arab Middle East,[3] a still much under-researched area. The material provided here is preliminary and meant to give insight into work in progress and to invite comments, rather than to present final conclusions. This chapter examines in the first part the rationale for change from within the security forces. The second part tries to argue the case for reform from the perspective of civil management and oversight of the security apparatus. The third part looks at changes in the strategic environment and discusses their impact alongside internal and external pressures on the prospects of security sector reform. All three parts lead to the conclusion that despite ongoing transformations in their security apparatus, countries in the Arab Middle East have not yet engaged in an encompassing security sector reform, which would imply a move towards transparent, accountable and participatory governance, in short *good governance* of the security sector. In contrast to Latin America and Africa, for example, where development agencies have played a critical role in promoting good governance of the security sector, practitioners and intellectuals in Middle Eastern countries have so far had little exposure, if any, to the security sector reform discourse. The Middle East, it appears, has still not absorbed, less assimilated, the security sector reform concept. However, one of the conclusions of this chapter is that this may change. The need for wider political and economic reforms, as a result of various domestic and international pressures, could create conditions from which a SSR discourse could soon emerge in the region.

The Need for Reform from within the Security Apparatus

The security apparatus in most countries of the Arab Middle East represents a blend of regular armed forces, paramilitary forces, such as national guards or royal guards, border guards, coast guards, a number of often competing intelligence and internal security services, police forces, judicial and correctional systems, militias and a rapidly growing number of private military and private security companies. Troops positioned in the Middle East on the basis of bilateral agreements, by the US and other foreign powers, have to be considered integral part of the security sector of the host country.

Several factors interact to exert pressure for change from within the security apparatus. These are:

- The shift from external to internal security challenges;
- The search for interoperability with US forces and regional cooperation;
- The need to reduce military expenditures;
- The need for force reduction, demobilisation strategies and modernisation;
- The privatisation of security.

Shift from External to Internal Security Challenges

Arab countries were, until recently, posed to deal mainly with external challenges to their national security and threats to regime stability from military coups. Growing exposure to terrorist threats has made evident that the real challenge to their security is internal. For some Arab governments this has highlighted the failures of their past policies. In the 1990s, Saudi Arabia, Kuwait, Yemen, the United Arab Emirates, were among the countries that had hoped to be able to export and control the Islamist threat by tolerating and facilitating official recruitment and enrolment of their nationals in military training in Afghanistan. Several years later, the returnees from Afghanistan[4] openly challenge their own governments and constitute a threat at home and abroad.

To cope with the new type of security challenge, Arab countries are under domestic and international pressure[5] to develop a wide range of new skills and capabilities. These include establishing and training anti-terrorist units and rapid intervention troops, extended surveillance, improving communication and liaison both between various segments of the security sector and with foreign intelligence services, enhancing coordination between different internal intelligence services, control of money flows and monitoring of activities undertaken by charity organisations.

Traditional reliance on existing structures within the Ministries of Interior and intelligence services will in itself not be a sufficient answer to the new threat. In countries like Saudi Arabia, where opposition strategies aim at 'winning over powerful factions in the military and subsequently convince them to move against the regime'[6] ruling elites are faced with the question to which extent they will be able to count on the loyalty of their security forces in case of need. One may assume that such and similar fears have paved the way to a series of internal force transformations and the setting up of further systems of checks and balances, which would require thorough research in order to be properly understood.

The shift in threat perception may act as the most important single driver for transformation within the security apparatus for years to come. Yet, it bears the potential risk of increased repression in countries which by international indices have ranged already low in terms of political freedom and civil liberties, and make violence a more appealing option to an ever growing number of people. However, if it were successfully managed, for example, in a politically inclusive and accountable manner, it could strengthen the citizens' trust in the state's capability and become a vehicle for greater cohesion.

Interoperability with US, Allies and Regional Cooperation

US interests and threat perceptions have been and still are a decisive factor in shaping national security structures in many of the Arab states. Furthermore, the US military remains the dominant force in the Middle East and has thus to be considered an integral part of the security sector in the region.

Since the 1980s, and more so since the Gulf War in 1991, the regional military balance of power has shifted and is now in favour of the US. Arab states in the Persian Gulf remain heavily dependent on US forces for their defence.[7] Interoperability with forces from both the US and regional allies is therefore an important factor in the restructuring and training of armed forces in all member-states of the Gulf Cooperation Council (GCC).[8]

Reliance on foreign forces for the provision of security or training has also made governments in the Gulf more vulnerable to mounting domestic pressure, particularly in Saudi Arabia, where foreign military presence has been a contentious issue since the deployment of American troops in August 1990. To appease internal opposition, Saudi Arabia's crown prince Abdullah found himself compelled to decree in February 2003 a military disengagement from the United States. It would, however, be illusionary to believe that the withdrawal of US troops from Saudi Arabia constitutes a fundamental departure from Saudi Arabia's defence policy. As other states in the region, Saudi Arabia has, in the short-term at least, no viable alternative, but to continue to rely on US security cooperation for maintenance, repair, replacement and often operating of its advanced equipment, as well as for training purposes. In the shorter-term, the announced disengagement, and the tactical shift of US military operations to Qatar, is thus more a matter of reducing US visibility in Saudi Arabia. In the longer-term, and contingent on regional developments, both Saudi Arabia and the US may seek to reduce their mutual reliance by following a strategy of diversification.

Despite shared threat perceptions and common defence partners, Gulf States only reluctantly engage in regional cooperation inside the GCC. The main reason for this is that the smaller Gulf States have always resented Saudi hegemony. Some unresolved border-disputes have further added to these reservations. As a result, the GCC, as a sub-regional organisation, has never been able to play an important role in defence.

The need for enhanced US interoperability also exists in Arab states beyond the GCC, in Yemen, Jordan, Egypt, and more recently in Iraq and Arab states in North Africa. *Bright Star,* the world's largest multinational training exercise, mobilised in 2001/2002 in Egypt some 18,000 US troops and over 52,000 troops from ten coalition countries, including Egypt, Jordan, Kuwait and the UAE.[9] Co-hosted by the US and Egypt, this biennial exercise may have contributed to shape President Clinton's perception of Egypt as 'the most prominent player in the Arab world and a key US ally in the Middle East,' that provides substantial 'political and security benefits that no single other Arab state can provide'.[10] Jordan, the Arab world's second largest recipient of US military aid after Egypt,[11] has also conducted large-scale joint military exercises with US troops.

Aside from training, multilateral defence cooperation has remained underdeveloped and also fallen short of US expectations. There have been in the past numerous calls for wider Arab military alliances, but concrete attempts remained short-lived. The *Damascus Declaration*,[12] a loose military alliance between GCC-states and their Arab coalition partners, Syria and Egypt, existed more on paper than in practice. It had been created in March 1991, mostly as a reaction to Islamist criticism of Arab governments' reliance on foreign military forces. Due to inner Arab divisions, however, the member states failed to develop any meaningful security cooperation and their official communications remained limited to echo the wider Arab concerns as expressed in the resolutions of the Arab League. A collective Arab defence pact,[13] signed as early as 1950, remained ink on paper. Yet, the treaty's explicit links between security and development on one side, and between national and regional security aspects on the other, as well as the broad scope of the proposed cooperation conceal a potential for reform, which still waits to be exploited. The single example for practical engagement by Arab states in a form of alliance is thus the October 1973 War.

Dominant security thinking in the region still remains heavily influenced by the traditional balance-of-power approach with the disadvantage that security is conceived in a very narrow sense and hence does not address major imbalances at both national and regional level. Regional asymmetries in population and income remain a source of protracted instability. Ideas of a wider regional security system in the Gulf that would include the GCC, Iraq and Iran have circulated since the mid-1990s, but failed to translate into concrete steps, as the political conditions for cooperation were not met.

Reduction of Military Expenditure

Arab military expenditure has pursued a long-term rising trend. SIPRI calculated an almost ten per cent increase in real terms for the year 2003 for the Middle East, Iran and Israel included.[14] This amounts in absolute terms to approximately US$ forty-three billion for the Arab Middle East alone, without taking into account Iraq, Qatar and Yemen, countries for which figures have not been made available. However, Omitoogun assumes that military spending would have been even higher, if most Arab leaders had adopted a less ambiguous stance towards the war in Iraq.[15] By comparison, military spending increased by thirty-four per cent in 1991. Many Arab countries are notorious for purchasing expensive and often minimally used equipment, which is spurred by a taste for state-of-art technology and, in some cases, lucrative commissions. Measured by the share of military expenditure in GDP, Oman, Kuwait, Saudi Arabia, Jordan, Yemen and Syria are among the world's top military spenders (see Table 5.1).

Widespread public opposition to these levels of military spending in most Arab countries have compelled states to make efforts to increase social spending at the expense of military spending. Such concerns are shared by a wider development community and reflected in the normative position taken by the Bretton Woods institutions, which demand tighter control over military spending. Leverage by the international community has remained limited, partly due to major arms-producing countries with a vested interest in the status quo have sent out mixed signals.

Yet, it would be consequent to expect that the emphasis on internal threat perceptions has been accompanied by a shift in the resource allocation from defence budgets to internal security budgets. Saudi Arabia's Security Budget, which is estimated to have been around US$ 5.5 billion in 2003, less than one third of the defence budget, reportedly increased by fifty per cent in 2004.[16] However, as the details of internal security budgets in most countries, not only in the Middle East, are classified, it is difficult to assess the effective expenditure. For full transparency, it would further be necessary to understand how the costs and expenditure for various private sector companies are accounted for, which in many Middle Eastern countries have taken over multiple police and military support functions.

This illustrates that military expenditure alone may be a less useful indicator of the real costs at which a country purchases its security. Because of the vested interests of donor countries, Arab governments have hitherto been subject to little pressure, domestically and internationally, to account for defence and security-related expenditure. This, however, could change in the future, if the development community were to adopt a more coherent approach and insist on greater transparency with regard to defence and security budgets.

Table 5.1: Military expenditure in the Middle East (in US $m)[17]

Country	2002	2003	% change from 2002
Bahrain	330	456	+ 38
Egypt	2,766	...	...
Iran	15,369	19,189	+ 25
Iraq	...	...	...
Jordan	750	798	+ 6
Kuwait	3,547	4,834	+ 36
Lebanon	800	798	0
Oman	2,536	2,723	+ 7
Qatar	...	...	...
Saudi Arabia	18,704	19,102	+ 2
Syria	5,366	5,930	+ 11
UAE	2,466	2,549	+ 3
Yemen	600	...	...

Need for Force Reduction, Demobilisation and Modernisation

The war in Iraq has brought about the most dramatic force reduction in the Middle East. Following the downfall of the regime, there was general agreement on the need to disband the Republican and Special Republican Guards and to downsize and restructure a heavily oversized regular army. However, the Coalition Provisional Authority's (CPA) decision to dissolve all the forces, including the police forces, without prior consultation with Iraqis, has met considerable criticism in Iraq and abroad, for it was perceived to undermine Iraq's stability. Meanwhile the CPA has reversed several of its former decisions and allowed some members of the police and regular army to return to duty. Initially, it was planned to draft by mid-2004 some 150,000 Iraqis into various police, military and intelligence forces.[18] Various observers, however, estimate that CPA has largely missed this target and that only a fraction of this force will be available on 1 July 2004, when CPA will hand over authority to Iraq's transitional government. Compared to pre-war levels, where the armed forces alone totalled 430,000 and close to one million at the height of the war with Iran,[19] the projected force strength of 35,000 to 40,000 for the *New Iraqi Armed Forces* constitutes a reduction of more than ninety per cent of Iraq's armed forces. While in the long-term such cuts are designed to reduce the risks and costs associated with an inflated security sector, they can present considerable downsides in the short-term, especially if the process of downsizing is poorly managed, if there are no proper demobilisation and reintegration strategies in place. Downsizing or rightsizing requires also a redefinition of the mission focus and the construction of a new identity. The new Iraqi army reportedly suffers from an unclear mission focus and a low acceptance within the Iraqi population.[20]

With the exception of Oman, all Gulf States face severe manpower shortages in their armed forces and, despite growing unemployment rates, have to recruit third-country nationals.[21] For most GCC-nationals, military service, as any other job involving physical labour, lacks prestige. Young people consider it a personal right to get an undemanding high-paid job from their government.

Some Arab states find it increasingly difficult to translate burgeoning populations into a source of effective military power, as modern effectiveness is associated more with technological advantages and the quality of human resources (education, training, motivation etc.), than with the numerical strength of forces. Furthermore, the open desert terrain in large parts of the Middle East favours technology-intensive forces over traditional conventional forces.[22] The logical trend would be towards much smaller, lighter, more flexible and better-trained forces.

Consequently, large Arab forces like those maintained by Egypt (430,000) and Syria (380,000)[23] are a heavy liability for the state. Egypt has attempted to alleviate the fiscal burden by moving its armed forces towards self-sustainability by allowing them to take over large parts of the economy. However, because of the adverse consequences on the national economy, this policy has in the view of most economists only added to the burden and further delayed a solution to a problem that grows bigger by the day. The Saudi National Guard, with an estimated strength of some 100,000, provides a good example of a parallel force to the regular army. Originally set up as a counterweight to the Saudi regular armed forces, it was meant to provide protection for the crown prince. Over time it has developed into an internal security force, similar in size to the regular armed forces. Cordesman takes the viewpoint that Saudi Arabia can no longer afford to maintain two parallel ground forces with roughly the same manpower and an unclear separation of mission, especially when interoperability is not guaranteed and suggests that both should be brought under the same command structure.[24]

GCC member states have built their national defence systems mainly on air-superiority, naval capabilities, and air defence in response to perceived threats from Iraq and Iran. In comparison to Iran, the Gulf States are seen to be at least a generation ahead, if not more, in terms of the quality of their equipment.[25] However, there remain fundamental doubts about the military capabilities that have resulted from large investments in military technology in all the Gulf States. Rathmell et al. argue that, despite its investments, Saudi Arabia will not be able to acquire even modest operational military capabilities without broader transformation of its dysfunctional defence establishment.[26] Success of modernisation of the armed forces will not only be determined by investment in hardware, but by the countries ability do develop the human skills required for operating it and the political culture that gives it social acceptance.

Privatisation of Security

Given the high expectations in professional security services and in several cases, because of limited trust in both the capabilities and the loyalty of their own citizens, some Arab governments have increased their reliance on private military companies (PMCs) and private security companies (PSCs).[27]

In the oil-rich Gulf States, where demand for PSC services has been spurred by the perceived terrorist threats to oil production and transportation facilities and the risks from instability in Iraq, the roles of the police and the private sector have become intertwined in such a way that it is often difficult to distinguish between the two. Driven by American security policy in Iraq, the booming demand led many companies to establish offices in the region, mostly in Baghdad or Kuwait.[28] The potential for current and future transformation of the security sector from privatisation is evidenced by the scale and scope of activities undertaken by private companies. In Saudi Arabia, 30,000 men reportedly guard the oil facilities. In the last two years $750 million was added to the kingdom's $5.5 billion security budget.[29]

Enrys International recruits, trains, equips and manages an Iraqi Oil Security Force of 14,000 Iraqi security guards. *Global Risk International (GRI)* maintains a counter-terrorist division and offers protection to Middle

Eastern Royal families. Other companies specialise in surveillance and counter-surveillance, combat support services, maritime protection and propose their services for operations on land, in the air and in the water.[30]

While growing privatisation of security may appeal to pressured governments as a cost-effective alternative, it could alienate various segments within Arab societies. The extension or expansion of contested Western presence would likely fuel further criticism by Islamists and support their perception of the private sector as a covert agent for governmental interests. For a large number of unemployed Arab youth the missed job opportunities could result in further grievance and increased frustrations, and differential treatment of foreign security personnel may disconcert local security staff and weaken their commitment and loyalty. Under the current circumstances, the drawbacks of privatisation risk outweighing the associated benefits. It remains, however, uncertain to what extent governments in the Middle East maintain effective control over the privatisation of their security. Given their strong reliance on the US, privatisation may reflect more the current trend within the US than a real political choice.

In all countries of the Arab Middle East, the various components of the security apparatus are under pressure to adapt to changed threat perceptions and to reduce overall defence and security related expenditure in order to cope with limited resources and to stimulate economic growth. Close cooperation with and reliance on foreign powers, particularly the US, drives and constrains change in most countries. This promotes professionalism, modernisation and regional cooperation but also encourages external dependence and high levels of spending, the utility of which remains questionable.

The Need for Reform of Civil Management and Oversight

Increasingly, as important tradeoffs have to be made, defence and security decisions in the Arab Middle East will also have to be analysed and weighed in relation to their impact on development and social cohesion. This calls for subjecting the armed and security forces to a system of checks and balances at state level that helps prevent abuse. In functioning democracies, armed and security forces are accountable to all three branches of the state (executive, legislative and judiciary).

Civil Management

It is manifest that the concept of civil management and even more so that of oversight of the armed forces, as developed and understood in the West, have so far had no practical application in a region where 'a combination of outdated paternalism, exaggerated and pointless secrecy, and treating defence (…) as a fiefdom of the ruling elite is the rule (…) and not the exception'.[31] Many Arab countries thus have either no established Ministry of Defence, as for example Jordan, or have a Ministry of Defence, which is run by the military (Egypt, Syria, Yemen and Saudi Arabia). As a result, the armed forces manage themselves with the support of the ruling elites. In Jordan the king personally heads the Army, the Navy and the Air Force, in Oman the sultan is also the Minister of Defence.

From a legal point of view, civilian management and control over the armed forces is poised to be strengthened in Iraq. Chapter 1, Article 5 of the 'Law of Administration for the State of Iraq for the Transitional Period' of 8 March 2004, explicitly subjects the Iraqi Armed Forces to the civilian control of the Iraqi Transitional Government.[32] Nevertheless, the effectiveness of this law still remains to be tested in practice.

Political Control of Armed Forces and Military Effectiveness

Ruling elites, for securing their stability and survival, traditionally ensure political control of their armed forces by a mix of the following strategies:

- Extending corporate and private benefits to the officers corps in exchange for loyalty;
- Aligning army interests with those of the regime through appointments based on kinship or belonging to certain minority groups;
- Managing the military through purges, frequent rotations and tight monitoring from competing internal security-agencies;
- Limiting military influence on politics through a policy of diversification that seeks to build up regime support in various social, economic and religious groups.[33]

As a result of these strategies, military effectiveness has been seriously undermined in all Arab countries.

In several countries, military professionalism has also been hampered by the armed forces' involvement in commercial activities. According to official sources, which have to be received with caution, total proceeds from the military production sector have reached ten billion Egyptian pounds (US$ 1.6 billion) during the past four years, an unprecedented figure since the sector had emerged.[34] The availability of cheap labour through general conscription has provided the armed forces with a competitive edge over the private sector that favoured its expansion into the production of a wide range of civilian goods and services, which include agricultural products, hospitals, tourist facilities, sophisticated electronic devices, joint ventures with private sector developers etc. and secured it control over the bulk of Egypt's economy. As Springborg observes, 'the military has its own sources of revenue for which it is not accountable and is under no observable political pressure either better to utilise its capital or to divest itself of enterprises, as is the case with regard to the civilian public sector'.[35] Syria's armed forces have allegedly used their bases in Lebanon for black-market and smuggling activities. Military involvement in commercial enterprises potentially undermines training, readiness, discipline and internal cohesion due to economic rivalry, especially when associated with corruption and opportunities for private gain.[36] At the level of national economy, because of unfair competition, it leads to market distortions, which in turn reduce the attractiveness for foreign investment.

Military involvement in the commercial sector thus represents a trade-off between the potential gains in terms of political control for regime-stability and the negative impacts on military effectiveness and national economy.

Poor and Expensive Management

Cordesman's description of weaknesses in the management and organisation of the Saudi forces is characteristic for every military force in the Middle East to some degree, including Israel.[37] He points at poor leadership and the absence of proper management systems for effective planning, programming and budgeting as major causes of waste and corruption. Important challenges for a new management lie in developing a much needed focus on force effectiveness rather than on force build-up and in introducing tight top-down budget and programme management, a condition for effective fiscal controls over procurement, manpower and operating and maintenance systems. Some of these problems are exacerbated by measures of political control, particularly when personal relationships and family ties determine key promotion and staffing decisions. The problem is more acute where members of the royal family serve in the military.[38]

Absence of Effective Legislative Oversight

Many of these weaknesses could be addressed if Arab countries would take measures to subject their security organisations to effective oversight from parliaments, if budgets, procurement decisions, appointments and dismissals had to be approved, if not by parliament as a whole, at least by a committee that is assigned responsibility for it. However, for practically all Arab parliaments, defence and security matters are considered taboo. National assemblies may have to approve, as is the case for Jordan, defence expenditure as part of the government's annual budget, but this is regarded a pure formality. In Jordan, a country which otherwise has made significant progress in freedom of expression, the parliament's limited role in security affairs is evidenced by the fact that none of the twenty permanent parliamentary committees has been assigned responsibility for defence or security.[39]

Baaklini et al. have illustrated that legislatures in Egypt, Lebanon, Kuwait, Morocco and Yemen are constitutionally authorised to study and approve the budget, but in practice play a minimal role.[40] Although in theory, the legislature can reject the budget, only rarely does it exercise that power, since doing so could lead to the parliament's dissolution. They argue that legislatures in the Arab world still lack professional staffs with capacities to provide fiscal analysis and to develop budgetary information systems that would allow legislators to play a more significant role in the budgetary process. Effective legislative oversight is thus limited by both political and technical constraints.

Effective oversight would also require proper legal frameworks, which provide for a division of authority and a clear distribution of roles. In most countries of the Arab Middle East, these are either missing or dysfunctional. While Egypt and Syria have long-standing states of emergency in place, Jordan's government used the temporary suspension of the parliament from June 2001 to September 2002 to enact a number of laws that restricted various freedoms, including the freedom of the press and the freedom of assembly.

As an instrument for regime stability, armed and security forces in the Arab Middle East are subject to tight political control of the ruling elites. Civil management and oversight of these forces, as required for the transparent and accountable management of the security sector, thus remain largely underdeveloped in practice. This has encouraged nepotism, waste and corruption, which in turn have proved detrimental to the professionalism of the forces and the national economies. In order to enhance the professionalism of their security organisations, and introduce cost-effective budget and programme management in defence and security, countries of the Arab Middle East will have to strengthen civil management and oversight. Arab countries thus face the challenges of developing the required civil capabilities, re-defining the role of political actors, and engaging in a meaningful political reform process that that sets the stage for broader participation in political decision-making, including in areas such as defence and security.

Changes in the Strategic Environment and Pressure for Wider Reform

Hitherto, the Arab Middle East has shown considerable resistance towards political reform. The political discourse of the ruling elites however has recently been modified to reflect an acknowledgment that reform is overdue. Several changes in the external environment may have favoured this change in attitude and are likely to influence both the depth and pace of reform in the future.

Strategic Changes

As a result of the war in Iraq that in April 2003 brought the downfall of Saddam Hussein and his regime, many countries in the Middle East find themselves in a dramatically changed strategic environment. Iraq, once feared for its military might and its suspected arsenal of non-conventional weapons, has ceased to constitute a military threat. As this is unlikely to change in the next few years, it provides an opportunity for states in the region, which had essentially built their defence on the perceived military threat from Iraq, to revisit their defence expenditure.

In the perception of the smaller Gulf States, Iran has become less threatening in recent years. This has been driven by a combination of an uncomfortable presence of US troops in its immediate neighbourhood, in Afghanistan, Iraq, and Central Asia and the joint determination with which the US and Western European governments, notably Germany, France and the United Kingdom, has convinced Iran of the need to make concessions and to suspend some of its nuclear activities. By signing the Additional Protocol, Iran has accepted a more far-reaching verification regime by the International Atomic Energy Agency (IAEA), in order to reassure the international community that it is not developing nuclear weapons. Ambiguities over Iran's long-term intentions nonetheless persist, but are perceived to constitute a lesser threat than in the past.

Syria's security concept has been sharply weakened since it lost superpower support with the disintegration of the Soviet Union. Over the last two decades, the fading out of Arab unity, Egypt's and Jordan's peace treaties, the fall of the Iraqi regime and most recently the economic sanctions imposed by the US have all contributed to Syria's marginalisation. Even in the Arab community, where Syria had claimed uniqueness as a front-line state engaged in the struggle against Israel, Syria's rhetoric begins to be perceived as outdated and disconnected from regional change.

Libya's leader, Mohammad Qadafi, has made it plain that Israel has ceased to be considered a threat for his country's security. In the new strategic environment, the risk of a major Arab-Israeli confrontation outside the occupied territories has practically disappeared. Israel thus enjoys broad security margins that even in the views of Israeli analysts open a window of opportunity for a withdrawal from the occupied territories.[41] There are also indications that in the longer-term, regional concerns over Israel's nuclear capabilities may no longer simply be disregarded and double standards addressed. The announced visit to Israel by the Head of the International Atomic Energy Agency (IAEA), Mohammad Baradei, this summer, may mark the beginning of long-term change in the way the international community deals with Israel.

As a result of these changes, the role of the Arab military has diminished further. This could accelerate their progressive retreat from direct politics, a trend that has been observed over the last two decades.[42]

Demographic and Economic Pressure

All countries of the Arab Middle East have fertility rates above 3.0 children per woman. Robust population growth and growing urbanisation have increased pressure on governments in the region to adjust the infrastructure and to stimulate economic growth in order to reduce unemployment and create new jobs for the ever increasing number of young Arabs who seek integration into the labour market.

The World Bank estimates that 100 millions jobs will have to be created by 2020 in the Middle East and North Africa to absorb the growth in labour forces from 104 million in 2000 to 185 million in 2020 and to cope with current unemployment rates of about fifteen per cent.[43] Meeting this challenge will require the transformation of the region's societies and economic structures. Any reinvigoration of the private sector will be closely linked to public sector reform. In Arab republics, as for example Egypt, economic neo-liberalism, labelled as the Washington Consensus, will inevitably clash with the dominant military economy. Springborg sees the primary threat to Egypt, as to most Arab republics, in economic decay and resultant political instability, rather than military confrontation. In the struggle to develop the economy the military is a liability.[44] He argues that regional and global contexts are not conducive to the continued expansion of the military's role and will, over time, expose the military public sector as anomalous and gradually bring about pressure for its privatisation.

With burgeoning populations, countries practicing general conscription face the challenge of absorbing a fast growing number of military manpower reaching military age. Egypt absorbed in 2003 an estimated total of over 743,000 new recruits.[45] Information on how these recruits were distributed amongst the 430,000 strong armed forces, the military production facilities and the Ministry of Interior, is not easily obtained, as all statistics in connection with military production facilities are surrounded with opacity.

As Nichiporuk[46] observes, sources of conflict also tend to shift, partly as a result of demographic trends. One important security challenge from demographic pressure is acute shortage of drinking water, which affects disproportionately poorer countries, unable to afford costly desalination plants and pumping stations.

Pressure from Parliaments

In an overview of six countries (Egypt, Jordan, Kuwait, Lebanon, Morocco and Yemen), Baklini et al. concluded that Arab legislatures, particularly those of Jordan, Kuwait and Morocco have generally become more important in recent years, because governments have made them a primary vehicle of their reform efforts, and because opposition forces are struggling to enhance their influence within and through them.[47] Egypt, by contrast, was the only country studied where parliament was playing a less important role than it did in the 1980s or 1970s.

Arab regimes have had an interest in strengthening parliaments in order to broaden their popular base and increase their domestic and international legitimacy. As platforms of political contestation, parliaments responded to demands for wider political participation and lessened political tension. In some contexts, they provided public support for their occasionally unpopular policies (austerity measures, repression of Islamists) and enhanced their liberal image to the outside world, which in turn influenced their ability to gain access to loans and credits.

Baklini et al. take the view that Arab transition to democracy share features that distinguish them from democratisation experiments elsewhere. Building on the political vocabulary used in the Arab press, they use a four-step model to explain the democratic evolution in Arab countries.[48] In stage one, *Al-Mithaq (the Pact)*, the regime accepts that different political interests and views exist and need to be reconciled and declares unilaterally a number of concessions, such as relaxing controls over the press, allowing greater freedom of expression and participation in professional organisations, which previously were under strict governmental control. In stage two, *Al-Hiwar (Dialogue)*, ruling elites, usually out of necessity to broaden political support or to avoid a breakdown of the political order, engage in a trade-off with the counter-elites or opposition. Stage three, the *assertion of the legislature's authority*, is characterised by a gradual redistribution of power away from the executive, normally reflected in constitutional changes. The last stage, *sustainable democracy*, would be reached with the widespread agreement among all key participants on the rules governing access to state institutions and on their respective prerogatives, as well as on the mechanisms that protect the democratic institutions against infringements by executive elites.

While none of the Arab states has yet reached the level of sustainable democracy and while it is unlikely that any Arab state will reach it for many years,[49] Lebanon may be seen as having entered stage three. Its constitution accounts for an atmosphere of political freedom and a modern participatory system, where groups, parties and sects can compete for power and limit the power of others,[50] despite Syria's influence which continues to constrain parliamentary activities there.[51] Kuwait, Jordan and Morocco are not far behind.

If Arab parliaments still exert no effective control over the armed forces, it must not be overlooked that they have gradually moved in the realm of legislative concern issues, which previously had been taboo including human rights and political prisoners; the normalisation of relations with Israel (for example, Jordan); the demand for separating the office of the prime minister from that of the crown prince and the accountability of the ruling family in managing the country's overseas investments (for example, Kuwait).[52] Kuwait's opposition also demanded to take over control of 'sensitive ministries', such as Interior or Defence, and critically questioned in televised debates the government on defence arrangements with foreign countries and procurement issues.

Pressure from Islamist Groups

Throughout modern history, much evidence supports the idea that the West has 'stood in the way of democracy'[53] in the Middle East. The Western track record in the Arab Middle East, marked by financial, military and political sponsoring of Arab authoritarianism, has fuelled suspicion and distrust of Western policies and alienated democratically minded forces amongst Islamists and secularists.

Islamist discourses differ widely on a variety of dimensions, but generally concur that the West has a case to answer for poor governance in the Middle East,[54] and yet favour, in their majority, a dialogue with the US and Europe. Even in discourses located at the extremist side of the continuum, certain elements have often been too superficially and too hastily dismissed as psychopathic. Without conferring legitimacy to terrorist methods, a less biased and less passionate analysis of these discourses could help gain better insight in underlying grievances and the reasons for much of their public appeal, as well as the high approval rates of their exponents. [55]

Several of Bin Ladin's statements capture popular discontent with security sector governance across the Arab Middle East. He for instance criticises 'the police states in the Arab world' for their excessive spending on the military sector and other security organisations for regime protection, 'at the expense of the rights of the people and their security'.[56] He also blames the Saudi government for the country's economic downslide by having aligned Saudi foreign policy to US security interests and entered into civil and military contracts, which overstretch the country's financial capabilities.[57] A reiterating point of grievance in the popular discourse is 'the state of the ill-trained and ill-prepared army and the impotence of its commander in chief despite the incredible amount of money that has been spent on the army'.[58] Related thereto is the call to free the Arabian Peninsula from all foreign military presence.[59] Ayman Al-Zawahiri, a close ally of Bin Laden, not only elaborates on the strategic objectives underlying US military deployment in the Arabian Peninsula, but also claims that the US set up a US intelligence bureau inside the headquarters of the Egyptian State Security Investigation Department and military bases west of Cairo, in Wadi Qina, and in the Ra's Binas Naval Base. He further explicitly criticises the joint military exercises *Bright Star* that the US conducts with Arab armies in Egypt as preventing the fundamentalist movement from seizing power. [60] Aware of the limitations resulting from an asymmetric relationship of power, Bin Laden advocates to abstain from conventional fighting and to engage instead in 'guerrilla warfare, (…) using fast moving light forces that work under complete secrecy'.[61] The recent series of attacks on oil-installations in Saudi Arabia, for which Al-Qaeda has claimed responsibility, suggest either a departure from the earlier strategy not to target oil facilities[62] or a fragmentation within the movement.

Security sector governance in the Arab Middle East occurs in a contested space and the outcome is shaped by many actors with varying degree of legitimacy. As evidenced in 2003 by the pullout of most US troops from Saudi Arabia and the transfer of the US air operations centre for the Middle East from Saudi Arabia to Al-Udeid Air Base in Qatar, Islamist militant forces have to be considered as an actor which can impact on security sector governance in the region. Security sector governance and the rise and spread of armed opposition groups in the Middle East may be interrelated and thus would have to be analysed and understood in their mutual interdependence.

International Pressure

The Arab World reacted with a mix of open consternation and hidden delight to the programmatic speech in November 2003 at the National Endowment for Democracy, where the US President outlined his new policy, a forward strategy of freedom in the Middle East that would support political change throughout the Middle East. [63] The Middle East Partnership Initiative (MEPI), structured in four reform areas (economic, political, education, women), was presented as the administration's primary diplomatic and developmental tool to support this new policy. Although in the Arab public perception scepticism over the seriousness of US intent to encourage democratic transformation generally prevailed, the announcement triggered some discomfort amongst Arab governments who resented the change in discourse.

The leaking of a preliminary working paper on a US 'Greater Middle East Initiative'[64] in February 2004, which the administration was preparing for the G-8 summit at Sea Island (Georgia) in June 2004, added further momentum to the reform debate and divided opinions over the external role in reform assistance. Building on President Bush's call for democratic transformation of the Middle East, the paper spelled out a series of measures that could be taken by G-8 members to assist the countries of the Middle East in their political and economical reform. Arab governments, led by Saudi Arabia and Egypt, rejected these proposals for two reasons. First, they regarded with scepticism any initiative targeted at the 'Greater Middle East' that would include not only the Arab world, but also Afghanistan, Iran, Pakistan and Israel. Second, they presented the initiative as an attempt of political interference that seeks to impose Western values and views on the Arab world. Reform in the Arab world cannot be imposed from outside, but must come from inside.

European countries too have in recent time sought to project an image of more active engagement of the Middle East. First the events of September 11, then the adoption in December 2003 of a *European Security Strategy*[65] and preparations for the Istanbul NATO summit have accelerated the proliferation of initiatives directed at the Middle East.

As these projects show, there is now recognition across the region, and around the world, of the need for reform in the Arab world to meet the daunting challenges it faces.[66] At a closer look, however, many of the programmes overstate the economic objectives and appear driven more by interests of the donors than the beneficiaries. Efficiency and effectiveness of many of these initiatives risk being reduced by a lack of coordination in the design, planning and implementation stages. Furthermore, the various national initiatives appear only loosely aligned, if at all, with international development policy and, at a national level, they demonstrate limited horizontal integration with action by other agencies or ministries. The ten-point action plan proposed by Youngs could help overcome several of these weaknesses by injecting greater clarity, dynamism and coherence into democracy promotion programs in the Middle East.[67] Nevertheless, one of the greatest weaknesses of all Western initiatives, perhaps, remains the uncertainty over the extent to which governments and societies in the US and Europe are prepared to accept the outcome of a political transformation process in the Middle East that could ultimately bring into power groups who are less lenient to their interests. As long as this uncertainty prevails, Arab societies will receive with suspicion all democracy initiatives directed at them and international pressure will remain weak.

Changes in Development Policy

Within the development community, security sector reform is seen as a key component of the broader *Human Security* agenda, developed by the United Nations Development Programme (UNDP) and extends, therefore, well beyond the narrower focus of transforming the traditional security organisations and the authorities in charge for civil management and oversight. The Organisation for Economic Co-operation and Development (OECD) governments and their development agencies are beginning to translate the conceptual links that have been established between peace, security, and development into more concrete policies.[68] This implies that the traditional concept of security in the Middle East, hitherto centred almost exclusively on protection of states from military threats and regime protection, is broadened to include the well-being of the populations and the guaranteeing of their rights. The security apparatus is seen as only one security policy instrument, aside other instruments, be they economic, social, or legal. This paves the way to public and international evaluation of the performance of all these instruments in delivering security to the people.

From this perspective, a future security sector reform agenda for the Middle East will have to address a wide range of issues that include beyond the traditional security concerns, job security, water and energy security, housing, the lowering of corruption,[69] the timely development of strategies to contain an increase in the HIV/AIDS prevalence level,[70] drug traffic control, population control etc. Up to now, conservative societal values have prevented the region from addressing many of these issues openly. Progress in the wider security agenda in the region will depend to a large extent on the states' ability to deliver better education to a larger number of people. With a greater international emphasis on a system approach to security, developing countries, not only in Africa, but also in the Middle East, might find in the future increased difficulties in getting access to international economic assistance without opening up the whole range of security policy instruments to greater domestic and international scrutiny, provided that donor countries are serious about reform and prepared to use the leverage available to them.

Conclusion

Up until today, there have been no serious efforts in any of the countries of the Arab Middle East towards good governance of the security sector, as implied by the concept of security sector reform. A World Bank study revealed that governance is typically weaker in Middle East and North Africa (MENA) than in the rest of the world, qualitatively and in measures of good governance, and within the region weaker in countries with lower income.[71] MENA governments remain the most centralised of all developing countries.[72] Nowhere may these weaknesses be more apparent than in governance of the security sector in the Arab Middle East.

Accountability of the security sector, both internal and external, has remained weak, because of limited access to information on its management and the denial of the possibility for contestability. Good governance would imply greater transparency – a right to know about the functioning of the various institutions – and an open discussion about their performance and possible alternatives. It would also imply greater inclusiveness by all those who have a stake in security sector governance, the civilian administration, the parliament, political parties, men and women, whose security is directly affected, and a proper grievance procedure to redress occurred violations.

While this is not about to change very soon, it is unlikely that governments will be able to continue to ignore calls for greater transparency and a more participatory approach to governance for much longer. Against the background of a changed regional environment and a shift from external to internal threat perceptions, changes in the security configuration are already under way. Internal and international stakeholder groups bring combined pressure to bear on governments for greater internal and external accountability and inclusiveness. External powers, whose manipulative involvement in regional politics has often been criticised for having delayed political reforms, may, as a result of a critical review of their past performance, be more prepared to consider refocusing their intervention on longer-term interests in the Arab Middle East.

In the context of the Arab Middle East, there are opportunities for security sector reform to assist conflict prevention by addressing underlying grievances and concerns. Popular aspirations for enhancement of distributive justice and respect for civil and political rights, for elimination of waste and corruption, for establishing rule of law and order, for improved accountability of government and a wider-faceted and more balanced approach to security will only be met, if the role of the security sector is opened up to questioning and its institutions included in the reform process.

Despite important differences, countries in the Arab Middle East face many similar challenges. Improved regional cooperation would not only assist the internal reform process, but would also enable countries to stand a better chance in facing up to the challenges of many externally driven processes. Knowledge gained from national reform processes could, if better documented and shared throughout the region, assist governments in developing new and adapted solutions 'from inside', if they cannot be brought to the region from outside.

The regional strategic environment, external conditions und internal pressures combine to create conditions, which, over all, can be seen as rather favourable to the emergence of a security sector debate in the Middle East.

Notes

[1] United Nationals Development Programme, *Arab Human Development Report 2003: Building a Knowledge Society and Arab Human Development*; and Report 2002, entitled: *Creating Opportunities for Future Generations*. Both reports are available at <http://www.undp.org > .

[2] With the exception of Kuwait and Jordan all countries of the Middle East are listed as 'not free' in the Freedom House Index.
<http://www.freedomhouse.org/pdf_docs/research/freeworld/2003/map2003.pdf>.

[3] In this chapter 'Arab Middle East' refers to Bahrain, Egypt, Iraq, Jordan, Kuwait, Lebanon, Oman, Palestinian Territories, Qatar, Saudi Arabia, Syria, the United Arab Emirates and Yemen.

[4] There are no reliable figures that would tell how many have undergone training in Afghanistan. For Saudi Arabia, estimated figures range between 8,000 and 15,000.

[5] See for example the UN Security Council Resolution 1373, which established the UN Counter Terrorism Committee and requires member states to report in regular intervals on the follow-up measures taken. (See also UNSCR 1267).

[6] See Abedin, M., 'A Saudi oppositionist's view: An interview with Dr. Muhammad Al-Massari', in *Terrorism Monitor*, vol. 1, issue 7 (4 December 2003).

[7] None of the Gulf States is seen capable of securing its own defence. Kuwait has integrated these limitations into its doctrine and formulates the objective for its forces the capability to delay a ground attack for forty-eight hours, the time needed for the coalition to respond.

[8] The Gulf Cooperation Council was founded in 1981. Member states include Bahrain, Kuwait, Oman, Qatar, the United Arab Emirates and Saudi Arabia.

[9] See <http://www.globalsecurity.org/military/ops/bright-star.htm>. According to the Pentagon's News Release No. 584-03, of August 9, 2003, Bright Star 2003/2004 had to be cancelled due to 'continued operations in the Global War on Terrorism in Iraq, Afghanistan and elsewhere'.

[10] *Human Rights Watch World Report 1999.*

[11] Military aid to Egypt amounted to US $ 1.3 billion for the fiscal year 2003. Jordan received US $ 450 millions. See also: <http://www.cdi.org>.

[12] The amended constitutive text of the Damascus Declaration is available at <http://meij.or.jp/text/Gulf%20War/damascus.htm>.

[13] The English translation of the 'Joint Defence and Economic Cooperation Treaty between the States of the Arab League' is available at <http://www.middleeastnews.com/arabLeagueDefenseTreaty.html>.

[14] See *SIPRI Yearbook 2004*, Chapter 10, Appendix 10E.

[15] See Omitoogun, W, *'Military expenditure in the Middle East'*, in: *SIPRI Yearbook 2004*, Chapter 10, Appendix 10E (Oxford University Press: Oxford, 2004), p. 2.

[16] See Obaid, N., 'Attack highlights threat to Saudi infrastructure', *Jane's Intelligence Review* (20 May 2004).

[17] Source: *SIPRI Yearbook 2004*.

[18] Cordesman, A., 'The Current Military Situation in Iraq' (CSIS, 4 December 2003). See also Chapter 10 in this book.

[19] See Baram, A. 'The Iraqi armed forces and security apparatus', *Journal of Conflict, Security and Development*, Issue 1:2 (2001), pp. 113-123.

[20] See *ICG Middle East Report* No 20, 'Iraq: Building a new security structure' (23 December 2003), p. 16.

[21] Recruits come from Jordan, Palestine, Pakistan, Sudan and Yemen. Kuwait's armed forces include also persons considered stateless, so called Bidoons (without papers).

[22] See also Nichiporuk, B., 'Security implications of Demographic Factors in the Middle East', in: Murawiec, L. and Adamson, D., *Demography and Security*, Proceedings of a Workshop, Paris, (Rand, Santa Monica, 2000:12f.),available at <http://www.rand.org>.

[23] IISS, The Middle East Military Balance. Egypt also has over 400,000 paramilitary forces and over 250,000 reserves. Syria's paramilitary forces include the Gendarmerie (8,000) and the Workers' Militia (400,000).

[24] Cordesman, A., "Saudi Arabia Enters the 21st Century", Vol. 2: *The Military and Internal Security Issues*, V, (2002), p. 14. <http://www.csis.org/burke/saudi21/>.

[25] Byman, D. and Wise, J., *The Persian Gulf in the Coming Decade: Trends, Threats and Opportunities*, (Rand, Santa Monica, 2002, p.33), available at <http://www.rand.org>.

[26] Rathmell, A. et al, *A New Persian Gulf Security System* (Rand, Santa Monica 2003), p. 8, available at <http://www.rand.org >.

[27] Makki, S. et al. "Private Military Companies and Proliferation of Small Arms: Regulating the actors", International Alert Paper (2001). Distinguish between corporate entities that provide 'offensive services' and are designed to have a military impact – the PMCs – and those that provide defensive services to protect individuals and property – the PSCs.

[28] Companies with offices in the Arab Middle East include AD Consultancy, Blackwater Security Consulting, CACI, Combat Support Associates (CSA), Control Risks Group (CRG), Custer Battles, Diligence LLC, Erinys International, Genric UK, Global Risk International (GRI), Halliburton, Hill and Associates Ltd, ICP Group Ltd, ISI Group, Overseas Security and Strategic Information, and several more. For more detailed information see the websites of these companies.

[29] See Obaid (2004), 'Attack highlights threat'.

[30] See for example Jane's Foreign Report, 'Bush's secret army – The USA hires contract soldiers to fight in Iraq', 9 June 2004, or consult the websites of the Private Military Companies listed above.

[31] Cordesman (2002) II, 'Saudi Arabia Enters the 21st Century', p. 6.

32 The more detailed guidelines for the Iraqi Armed Forces are spelled out in Chapter 3, Article 27 of this law.

33 For a detailed discussion of political control over the military in Arab states, See Brooks, R., *Political–Military Relations and the Stability of Arab Regimes*, Adelphi papers 324 (IISS:London 1998), pp. 19-44.

34 See Arabic News, 16 March 2004. Official figures on the military economy have in the past not proved reliable.

35 Springborg, R., 'Military Elites and the Polity in Arab States', Development Associates Occasional Paper No 2, (Arlington, 1998), p.6.

36 See Brooks, R , *Political–Military Relations*, p. 50.

37 See Cordesman, 'Saudi Arabia Enters the 21st Century'.

38 See Byman et al., *The Persian Gulf in the Coming Decade,* p. 39.

39 For a complete list of the existing committees within Jordan's Lower and Upper House see http://www.jordan-parliament.org/comm/.

40 Baaklini et al. *Legislative Politics in the Arab World: The Resurgence of Democratic Institutions*, (Lynne Rienner, London 1999), p. 53.

41 See Feldman, S., 'A National Moment of Truth?', *Strategic Assessment*, Vol.6, No.4, 8 (February. 2004), p. 5-7 , avaibale at: <http://www.tau.ac.il/jcss/sa/v6n4p1Fel.html>.

42 For a detailed description of the evolution of civil-military relations since the late 1970s, see Springborg, 'Military Elites and the Polity'.

43 World Bank, *Unlocking the Employment Potential in the Middle East and North Africa: Toward a new Social Contract.* (Washington, April 2004).

44 Springborg, 'Military Elites and the Polity', p. 12.

45 IISS, Military Balance 2003. The duration of military duty varies in function of the educational level, between one and three years.

46 Nichiporuk , 'Security implications of Demographic Factors', p. 12.

47 Baklini et al, *Legislative Politics*, pp. 2-4.

48 Ibid., pp. 33-44.

49 See also Schnabel A., 'A rough journey: Nascent democratisation in the Middle East', in: Saikal, A. and Schnabel, A. (2003), *Democratisation in the Middle East: Experiences, Struggles, Challenges*, (The United Nations University, New York, 2003), p. 19.

50 See Abu Jaber, K., in A.Saikal and A. Schnabel, *Democratization in the Middle East*: *Experiences, Struggles, and Challenges*, (United Nations University Press, 2003), p. 136

51 See Baaklini et.al., *Legislative Politics*, p. 42.

52 Ibid., p. 5 and pp. 191-194.

53 Glenn E. Perry (1990), 'Democracy and Human Rights in the Shadow of the West', quoted in Sadiki, L., *The Search for Arab Democracy: Discourses and Counter-Discourses*, (C. Hurst London., 2004), p. 345.

54 Sadiki, *The Search for Arab Democracy,* pp. 358-373. Presents a collection of quotes from his interviews with Islamist leaders that offer an interesting insight in Islamist perceptions of how Western governments have shaped polity in the Middle East.

55 A government-commissioned poll of 15,452 Saudis found that forty-eight-point-seven per cent think favourably of Bin Laden's sermons, but only four-point-seven per cent would want him as their president. See Donna Abu-Nasr, "Islamic doctrine that enthroned Saudi royals is proving hard to control", *The Associated Press*, 19 April 2004. According another poll by the Pew Research Centre, Osama bin Laden is viewed favourably in Paki-

stan (sixty-five per cent), Jordan (fifty-five per cent) and Morocco (forty-five per cent). See 'A Year After Iraq War. Mistrust of America in Europe Ever Higher, Muslim Anger Persists', *The Pew Research Centre*, 16 March 2004.

[56] Interview with 'Nida'ul Islam', 15th issue, October-November 1996, p.,2.

[57] Ibid, p. 4.

[58] Usamah Bin Muhammad Bin Laden, *Fatwa 23 August 1996*, p. 5.

[59] Ibid, p. 10.

[60] Ayman Zawahiri, leader of the Egyptian Al-Jihad Organisation and closest ally of Bin Ladin, published 'Knights under the Prophet's banner', made available in serialised excerpts by *Al-Sharq Al-Awsat* in Arabic as of 2 December 2001.

[61] Bin Laden, *Fatwa 23 August 1996*, p. 11.

[62] Ibid, p. 8.

[63] Speech of 6 November, 2003, available at <http://mepi.state.gov/mepi>.

[64] See U.S. Working Paper for G-8 Sherpas published in Al-Hayat, 13 February 2004.

[65] Solana, J. (2003), "A Secure Europe in a Better World", Brussels 12 December. available at <http://ue.eu.int/solana/list.asp?BID=111>. (The European Security Strategy endorsed last December makes the Middle East a priority).

[66] Security Sector Reform does usually not figure explicitly in these proposals, but is implicit in the promotion of 'good governance'. Youngs (see Youngs, R., *European Policies for Middle East Reform: A Ten-Point Action Plan*, available at <http://www.civility.org.uk> (2004). Page 7 mentions 'Security Sector Reform' in relation with a contribution that the EU could make to post-conflict reconstruction in Iraq.

[67] Youngs, *European Policies for Middle East Reform*.

[68] See OECD, *Security System Reform and Governance: Policy and Good Practice. A DAC Reference Document* (OECD, Paris 2004).

[69] See Leenders, R. and Sfakianakis , *Moyen Orient et Afrique de Nord*, in Rapport mondial sur la corruption (Transparency International 2003), pp. 273-286.

[70] The World Bank Report on 'HIV/AIDS in the Middle East and North Africa' estimates that continued inaction could give rise to accumulated costs for the period 2000-2015 that are equivalent to one-point-five per cent of today's GDP for each year of delay. Under conservative assumptions, expected costs over the next twenty-five years could be on the order of thirty-five per cent. See World Bank, *HIV/AIDS in the Middle East and North Africa. The Costs of Inaction* (Washington 2003), p. xix.

[71] World Bank, *Governance for the Middle East and North Africa: Enhancing Inclusiveness and Accountability* (Washington, September 2003), p. 5.

[72] Ibid., p. 5.

PART III

SECURITY SECTOR RECONSTRUCTION

Chapter 6

Security Sector Reform and Post-Conflict Reconstruction under International Auspices

Michael Brzoska and Andreas Heinemann-Grüder

Introduction

In the aftermath of violent conflict and military interventions, international organisations or coalitions of countries increasingly engage in post-conflict reconstruction. One part of the international post-conflict agenda is the 're-construction' or 'reform' of the security sector (SSR). In post-conflict situations, the security sector is often characterised by politicisation, ethnicisa-tion, and corruption of the security services, excessive military spending, lack of professionalism, poor oversight and inefficient allocation of re-sources. The term 'reconstruction' of the security sector pertains to the ne-cessity of rebuilding domestic public security institutions, and particularly to re-establish a legitimate monopoly of violence. Such reconstruction is neces-sary where security forces cannot provide for order and protection of citi-zens, either because they were *de facto* dissolved, too small, or suffered from a loss of credibility. In peace support operations,[1] where local security for-mations were among the targets of international military intervention, such as in Haiti in 1994 or in Afghanistan in 2001, the need for reconstruction will go even further. The term 'reform' highlights necessary or desired changes to governing principles and procedures of existing, but not properly functioning domestic security institutions, particularly with respect to 'soft' issues, such as democratic civilian oversight and observance of human rights. Both aspects are part of post-conflict transition, which primarily fo-cuses on the prevention of renewed conflict, the introduction of rule of law, the democratisation agenda, and the promotion of conditions for sustainable development.

Situations where the international community plays a prominent role, through a peace support operation or has a major political influence in post-conflict situations are becoming increasingly frequent. The most prominent post-conflict cases of externally sponsored policy measures in the security sector include Afghanistan, Azerbaijan, Bosnia and Herzegovina, Georgia, Haiti, Iraq, Kosovo, Liberia, Macedonia, Mozambique, Tajikistan and East Timor. It seems safe to predict that the international community will be faced with more cases where national order breaks down, or where internal warfare destroys the social and political fabric of societies, increasing the need for instruments and policies that can support state-building. Yet, views held in the international community about state-building are often competing, highly normative and not well tested. For instance, as regards economic development, international financial institutions such as the World Bank have developed sets of policies and measures whose success rate, when applied, is not very impressive.[2]

Security sector institutions provide another example of a policy area where the need for action is not concomitant to the stock of sound advice. While much has lately been produced in terms of suggestions for instruments and policies of security sector reconstruction and reform, there is still very little knowledge about the effects of priorities and sequencing in particular constellations. In this regard, situations with significant international involvement are particularly prone to yield useful insights for the accumulation of knowledge about the application of instruments and policies of security sector reconstruction and reform, as the international community is in a strong position to apply recently designed recipes.

This chapter explores a number of issues which seem particularly relevant for empirical analysis of the priorities in security sector reconstruction and reform. It offers some tentative ideas about dominant themes and respective priorities for external actors. Security sector reconstruction and reform is subject to, and generates, a number of policy dilemmas, some of which are identified in this chapter. The chapter concludes with a hypothesis about priorities for post-war security sector reconstruction and reform, which need to be put to further empirical scrutiny.[3]

Cues in the Security Sector Reform Debate

Security sector reconstruction and reform needs to begin with an appropriate identification of the security related problems to be solved in the short and midterm perspective. In all past, and likely future, cases of prominent international commitment to post-war reconstruction, the provision of physical security is the key near-term task on which international and national actors need to focus their efforts. The near-term priority issues for the provision of physical security include curbing warlordism, disarmament, demobilisation and reintegration (DDR), the formation of a national army and police reform, as well as transitional justice. To make the newly created, or reconstructed, institutions sustainable after the initial phase of security consolidation, their compatibility with available resources needs to be achieved. While disarmament, demobilisation and reintegration of military forces make sense for a number of reasons early on, later 'rightsizing' of forces, which entails a downsizing of military forces, is often crucial, particularly for long-term financial viability. In addition, security forces need to have clearly identified mandates, be accountable to civilian oversight bodies and be regulated by law.

Security sector reform is a relatively new concept, originally introduced by development donors.[4] In the late 1990s a comprehensive approach to the security sector began to be propagated by some development donors, international organisations and consultants working for them.[5] SSR is supposed to deliver on three fronts:

- Provision of security. This pertains to political violence by state or non-state actors, criminality, militant opposition group activity etc., and it is a major problem in most post-conflict situations, particularly those with international presence. Linked to this provision of physical security, which primarily involves the police and the military, is the proper functioning of the courts and the prison system, as well as, small arms control.
- Governance and Rule of Law. One of the roots of security sector reform is to bring security institutions within the realm of rule of law. Issues which affect the conditions of governance, include the professionalisation of the armed forces in the sense of Huntington's 'objective control' as well as the ethnic composition of security forces.
- Effectiveness and efficiency. In many post-war cases there is a need to de-militarise, for example, to reduce the number and size of armed forces and to bring military expenditures in line with economic means as well as to overcome clientelism and corruption.

According to the standard SSR argument, these three objectives need to be pursued in parallel. The propagation of such parallelism between performance, governance and efficiency is proclaimed in most reform efforts by development donor organisations as a consequence of criticism of earlier policies, which only focused on performance or efficiency. While sound in theory, such a comprehensive approach presents problems in practice. Often in concrete situations, decisions on priorities and sequencing of steps need to be made. For instance, external actors may be pressed to provide security even though this is detrimental to improving domestic control over security forces. There is no general agreement in the SSR literature which of these clusters should become a priority under what circumstances. Moreover, there is no agreement on how important it is to deal with all three simultaneously or in some order. In the case of East Timor, for example, there were voices among development donors who questioned the necessity of having a military force at all. Yet, as a rule external actors come with at least the semblance of a general idea, which is largely shaped by perceptions of their own security sectors, as well as larger objectives, such as democratisation and economic development.

Elements of what is generally now seen as falling under the security sector reform agenda soon also became an issue for peace support operations.[6] The objectives of massive international interventions in conflict and post-conflict situations have expanded over time, both in number and depth. Interventions have become broader in scope and longer in duration. Earlier interventions, authorised to back-up cease-fires, such as in Somalia, or to support political settlements, such as in Mozambique and Cambodia, were primarily aimed at restoring order and facilitating elections. Demobilisation and disarmament of combatants were an early harbinger of wider efforts towards security sector reconstruction and reform within peace support operations.[7] In parallel, but generally with little coordination, development agencies began to operate in areas relevant to public and human security.

More recent interventions have become very ambitious, attempting to lay the groundwork for sustainable political, economic and security structures. Elements of this expanded interventionism include stabilisation, post-war reconstruction, economic rehabilitation, and democratisation. Next to the concept of 'human security' security sector reform thus turned into one of the most ambitious or holistic approaches.[8]

External contributions to security sector reform have been made under a range of circumstances, including where international agreements adopted following the cessation of armed conflict provided a corresponding mandate (Bosnia and Herzegovina, Macedonia), where the United Nations Security Council provided a mandate for international interim administrations (Afghanistan, Kosovo, Sierra Leone), and where a cease-fire, mediated and/or backed by international actors, which included security sector reform policies, put an end to collectively organised and/or large-scale armed conflict, (for example, in Tajikistan, Nagorno-Karabakh and Northern Ireland). Security sector reform has also been attempted outside such situations, for instance through the support of local initiatives by donor countries, with the focus on administrative reforms. This so far limited experience has been incorporated into the wider security sector reform agenda.[9]

With few exceptions, prescriptions and accounts of SSR are 'holistic', fusing ends and means, prerequisites and results, actors and policies. There are advantages and disadvantages to such an approach. One advantage is that the attempt is made to see societies, where reform is to occur, in their interconnected totalities. However, this advantage only plays out on a rather abstract level of analysis, or when it is filled with empirical detail relevant to a particular society. Otherwise it does not provide much guidance for policy. The major disadvantage of the holistic approach is that it is not very helpful for making decisions about priorities for or sequencing of policies.

Accumulation of knowledge about security sector reform in particular settings has only begun fairly recently. For the time being, the security sector reform debate is marked by a mismatch between long list of general recommendations of what could and should be done and concrete suggestions based on a thorough analysis of the problems in a particular post-conflict situation. This might be one reason why country-specific accounts often show little progress in security sector reconstruction and reform on the ground.[10] Security sector reform needs to be made concrete with respect to priorities and sequences, partial objectives and instruments, to have relevance in particular settings.

Objectives and Assumptions

Recommendations for security sector reconstruction and reform come from a variety of sources, including actors ranging from peacekeepers to development donors and analysts, all of various convictions. The result is a mixed bag of policy prescriptions and an ever-longer list of suggested instruments.

However, what unites all these recommendations is the idea to provide security for the 'people', that is the ordinary citizens living in a given state. This is generally seen as having two interlinked sides. First, the provision of physical security and second, the control of those institutions providing security so that they actually provide security to the citizens, and not to selected groups, or in ways infringing on the rights of citizens.[11] Deficits in the public provision of physical security are usually perceived as one of the core problems in post-conflict situations. Typical manifestations of insecurity include organised crime and illegal paramilitary organisations, trafficking in drugs and weapons, the unregulated possession of firearms, terrorism and violent extremism and the abuse of power by state security apparatuses.

At the same time, post-conflict situations are regularly marked by deficits in governance structures, including democratically legitimised institutions. The creation and reform of such institutions is another key task in post-conflict situations.

Solving the security problem is generally perceived as a prerequisite for development and democratisation. In peace support operations the burden of providing security initially will fall on the international community. Reconstruction and reform of domestic security sector institutions will then have to enable these to successively take on this task.

However, there is also a corresponding link between democratisation and security sector reform in the opposite direction. Without the functioning of democratic institutions, governance of the security sector will be prone to hostage-taking by particular interest groups. It will also be difficult to ensure that security institutions behave lawfully, as long as the rule of law is not broadly established in a post-war situation. Security sector reform is unlikely to be ahead of broader political and institutional reforms, in fact, security sector governance generally lags behind other reform efforts.[12]

The linkage between democratisation and security sector reform is complex and difficult to generalise. In a way, security sector reform and democratisation provide an example of a chicken-and-egg problem. Traditionally democratisation has been prioritised in peace support operations, however, in a number of recent cases, such as Bosnia and in Central Asia, security sector reform has been pushed despite visible deficits of democratisation. This dilemma will be picked up again in this chapter on a more theoretical basis.

In addition to these two core facets of security sector reform, there is, in the view of the authors, a third facet, whose importance is often underestimated in discussions and theoretical prescriptions of security sector reform, but which is of great practical relevance, particular in post-conflict situations under international auspices. This is the economic sustainability of domestic security sectors constructed and/or reformed by international actors. International actors will often find it difficult to sustain funding to build-up national security sector institutions over long periods of time, while domestic funding is often hard to come by. Therefore, security sector reform, which aims at sustainable structures of security provision, will often occur under severe financial constraint, at least after an initial period.

In summary, the authors are guided by the assumption that security sector reform in post-conflict situations is about three clusters of objectives: (i) the build-up of new security sector institutions, where none exist or are acceptable for reform by the international community, or the retrenchment of overwhelmingly controlling, present, repressive and threatening state security institutions from intervention into politics, economy, and society, where such institutions continue to exist; (ii) the disarmament, demobilisation, reintegration, transformation, and prosecution of illegitimate armed non-state actors in order to re-establish a state monopoly of legitimate violence; (iii) the long-term goals of building-up accountable, efficient and effective security forces.

To achieve these objectives, actors can use a wide spectrum of instruments, ranging from (a) strengthening civilian and democratic participation and control through (b) reallocating military (material, economic and human) resources for civilian ends ('conversion', 'demilitarisation' and control of military spending) to (c) reforming military and police institutions to perform specific tasks ('professionalisation', 'capacity building'), (d) developing an independent judiciary and a humane penal system ('rule of law') and (e) undertaking security analysis and creating policy models.

As a rule external actors generally come with broad ideas about which instruments are best suited to the particular situation, often shaped by images of their own domestic arrangements. Since these ideas differ among major international actors, lack of policy coherence is a problem, further complicating the issue of priority setting. In addition, externally sponsored SSR often has to react in an ad hoc fashion to urgent security requirements.

While the security sector reform debate has clearly widened the agenda for reconstruction and reform beyond the military, which earlier was often seen as the only relevant institution, there is no unanimous view of how far this label should be stretched. A narrow definition of the security sector focuses on the provision of *public* security — it encompasses all actors and agencies authorised to threaten or to use violence in order to protect the state, its citizens or its external environment. The extensive use of the term SSR pertains to all potential actors, institutions, policies and contextual factors impacting on security.[13] Notions of physical security, rule of law, civil-military relations, democratic governance, post-conflict disarmament, demobilisation and reintegration and 'human security' intermingle respectively. In its extended version SSR exemplifies a thrust for good governance, for example, transparent, accessible, accountable, efficient, equitable, checked and democratic input, output and process. Accordingly, the concept covers all institutions and actors that in one way or another determine, implement or control the provision of public security or are able to undermine it. Corresponding to this spectrum of understanding of the security sector, international actors have also adopted somewhat different perspectives for reform policies. In some cases, such as Afghanistan, police reform has so far been prioritised over all other possible approaches, while in Bosnia and Herzegovina a very broad understanding was adopted.[14]

Post-conflict security sector reform sponsored by the international community is generally both defensive and offensive. In its defensive mode it is geared towards meeting contingencies that are often brought about by fears of disorder, anarchy, resurgence of violence, gross human rights violations, disloyalty, and mutiny. Compelling recent examples include Afghanistan, Bosnia and Herzegovina, Kosovo, Iraq and Macedonia. In such critical cases security sector reform should concentrate on the domestic security threats, particularly those emanating from an unreformed 'security sector', and potential ways of reducing these threats. In post-conflict situations 'security sector reform' needs initially to focus on activities aimed at reducing public insecurity and to restore the state monopoly on the legitimate use of violence. Early post-conflict security sector reform therefore often requires specific priorities, in contrast to SSR as part of democratic consolidation. These include containing the spread of violence, emergency stabilisation, quelling the remnants of violence (mostly in the form of disarmament and other measures to contain the spread of small arms and light weapons, as well as demobilisation and reintegration of combatants), preventing relapses into violence and the formation of basic security agencies.

Security sector reform is time-sensitive and dependent on the conflict cycle. Given historical experience for the introduction of the rule of law and recent empirical evidence about the attention span of the international community, security sector reconstruction and reform does not often go much beyond initial stabilisation of the security situation, despite the broader issues raised in the security sector reform agenda. Under such circumstances, it makes sense to concentrate on the international actors' time frame rather than on normative ideas about an extended democratisation agenda. Security sector reconstruction and reform programmes should therefore avoid simply enumerating prerequisites or normative goals that can only result from a multi-year, evolutionary change. Externally promoted security sector reform can contribute to capacity building, changing forms of legitimisation, and they add a veto point to the political process. However, security sector reform cannot change the type of domestic political regime.

Democratic consolidation may require a comprehensive, mutually reinforcing combination of human rights, rule of law, development and polyarchy. Regardless of differences among students of democratisation, democratic consolidation usually includes constitutionalism (formal democratic principles), institutional consolidation (formation of democratic institutions), representative consolidation (formation and empowerment of democratic non-state actors), and normative or behavioural consolidation (internalisation of democratic norms and values).[15] Disputes exist with respect to the necessary prerequisites – a pre-existing demos, pre-existing statehood, rule of law, a Weberian bureaucracy, secularism, literacy, urbanism, and a certain distribution of income between social strata. SSR in post-conflict situations is not yet about the agenda of democratic consolidation.

Framing Conditions

Post-conflict situations usually share some legacies or framing conditions with a bearing on public security, few of which can be changed in months or even years.

In many of the cases relevant here, a recent history of war or large-scale violence led to the breakdown of the state monopoly on the legitimate use of violence. Interest groups are often armed. Accordingly, civilian norms of conflict management do not function as internalised guiding principles of public and private behaviour. Institutions of public security and law enforcement are either paralysed or factionalised. Furthermore, most of the post-conflict situations share with typical underdeveloped countries a lack of traditions of rational, efficient and effective state bureaucracies. Instead they are characterised by patrimonialism, clientelism, and informal networks rather than formal institutions.

Most political regimes prior to the conflict, but, given the societal base, also after the conflict, are authoritarian or semi-authoritarian,[16] and they belong at best to the group of 'partially free' or 'delegative democracies' with elected presidential systems, strong majority features, executive power concentrations, and a strong reliance on security forces as instruments to stay in power. Political parties, which are the prerequisite of strong parliaments and provide the crucial state-society nexus, are mostly organised around ethnic affiliations or clientele networks. Clientele and charismatic leader parties dominate over democratic programme parties. Civil societies are usually weak, at least in the sense that evaluative institutions autonomous of the government or the power elite are missing. Additionally, most of these post-conflict situations are on the lower end of the Human Development Index while they rank high on indices measuring rent-seeking and market distortions, such as Transparency International's corruption index.[17]

Even in those post-conflict situations where international actors are limiting the external and internal sovereignty of states through military intervention forces, or administration of territories, they still need to reckon with domestic characteristics of societies and polities. There are no clean slates anywhere. Any kind of reform programme, whether in the security or any other sector, runs its course influenced by reactive, strategic behaviour of domestic actors. International actors will seldom be able to determine outcomes. One important example is the provision of physical security in programmes for security sector reconstruction and reform.

Dilemmas of Externally-Driven Security Sector Reform

In terms of the seriousness of the challenges, post-conflict situations seem to provide fertile ground for security sector reform, but they are characterised by at least six dilemmas.

Firstly, post-conflict situations are marked by a lack of security and the need to quickly build up institutions which can provide security for the people as well as state institutions. Yet, there are often structures and institutions of war present which need to be disbanded. While the need for security is obvious, it is often questionable whether post-conflict situations provide adequate opportunities for security sector reform. Sometimes both actors and analysts assume that there is a clean slate when in fact, as mentioned above, this never is the case. Political and societal legacies may have been thoroughly changed by a war and foreign military intervention, but they remain relevant, mixing with new interests groups. A *tabula rasa* approach with respect to past deeds, for example, blanket amnesty, absence of lustration policy, the transformation instead of dissolution of repressive organs as well as paramilitary forces, is often the prerequisite for buying the acquiescence of former perpetrators. Contrary to the assumed need of an ideational and jurisdictional break with the past, reform often has to begin with the fiction of a zero point in order to limit political opposition and resource needs. Imperatives of transition and legacies evidently clash. The question in many concrete situations therefore is, to what extent well-meaning reform policies can in fact contribute to overcome those legacies? General transition research suggests that after an initial shock, entrenched actors and traditional structures overwhelm one-fit-for-all programmes.[18] Path dependency of societal and political development is difficult to overcome, even in situations where major shake-ups have occurred in the form of wars and subsequent international interventions.

Secondly, in peace support operations, foreign troops and/or police, which initially take over the role of security providers, are faced with the classical 'white man's burden' problem of setting incentives for reactive, seemingly passive behaviour of domestic actors, strategically aimed at exploiting the international actors.[19] However, security sector reform – like all policy which is to be sustainable after the end of international tutelage – needs to be implemented and enforced by domestic actors with particular interests. It is, therefore, generally difficult to find the proper place of external actors in security sector reconstruction and reform. As a rule, internationals have a strong interest that their input is transitioned, as soon as possible, to national institutions. The interest in early transfer is self-evident – high costs, vanishing consensus and support in donor countries, security risks for internationals and disincentives for national stakeholders to take over responsibility. Yet, domestic actors' thrust for a quick transition undermines the very basis of external influence. External input clashes with the need for local ownership. The practical question therefore is what principles should guide transfer strategies.

A third, related dilemma pertains to the fundamental democracy deficit of external interventionism. The power of international actors to bring about security sector reconstruction and reform depends not just on financial or human resources, but on the ability to shape, direct, and control policies and outcomes. International actors may reduce security problems and contribute to capacity building, but they are not subject to principles of popular sovereignty, constitutionalism, elections, and accountability in the territories where they act. The capacity to implement programmes depends on a violation of just those democratic principles to be promoted. The fundamental question is whether basic, non-arbitrary criteria can define readiness for self-determination, self-governance and rule of law in security sector reform agendas.

The fourth dilemma concerns the interdependency of policies. At least in post-conflict situations externally sponsored SSR is *de facto* premised on the assumption that public security and the state monopoly on legitimate violence are prerequisites for long-term democratic, developmental or over-arching 'human security' agendas. Afghanistan, Bosnia and Herzegovina, Iraq and Kosovo are cases in point. They are either politico-military protec-torates or semi-sovereign states. Security sector reform has been prioritised by international actors in these cases compared to democratic consolidation. However, some authors hold that democratisation has to be prioritised, and that with proper democratisation respective governance of security institu-tions will emerge over time. Another view holds that capacity building for 'good governance', particularly professional training, has to be the priority. The question is whether public and physical security issues have to take precedence over the democratisation agenda or whether conditioned capacity assistance with a stabilisation and conflict containment agenda is the ade-quate option.

A fifth dilemma pertains to the self-interests of national actors. As the introduction of rule of law and law obedience in general demonstrate, it is naïve not to take into account the immediate self-interests, in terms of finan-cial and power games, of all relevant actors in security sector reform pro-grammes.[20] Particularly for those key national actors which are powerful prior to reform, security sector reform is often not in their short-term self-interest as it threatens to undermine their power bases. This suggests that security sector reform has to overcome an initial unstable phase where a wide range of actors are faced with short-term increases in insecurity about the new arrangements as well as unknown pay-offs. The benefits of stability through more predictable behaviour of disenchanted segments of society, helping to channel distress, and increasing social cohesion, generally only come in the longer term. Yet, the expected long-term benefit of rule of law may transgress the time frame of national actors primarily interested in power preservation. The question is, therefore, whether and how the incen-tive structure of national actors can be changed in favour of post-conflict security sector reconstruction and reform.

A sixth dilemma concerns the contradicting interests, divergent re-source endowments, and varying levels of expertise among international actors. Due to its resource endowment and organisational capacity, the military often takes the lead in security-related issues in post-conflict situations, including issues of security sector reconstruction and reform. As security sector reform entails instruments not generally in the military's toolbox, this constitutes a stretch of the capabilities and capacities of military organisations, in addition to claiming ground traditionally covered by development agencies. However, development agencies generally have little experience, and often limited willingness, to deal with security institutions or to develop programmes for security sector reform such as police reform or the design of laws for security sector institutions. Discussions about norms, rules and institutions of civil-military interaction in post-conflict situations are just emerging and are highly informed by national cultures and interests. An open question therefore concerns the appropriate qualifications and forms of interaction among international actors.

Priorities to Improve Security

Judging on the basis of a preliminary analysis of a number of post-conflict situations, the initial focus of international efforts in post-conflict situations should be on curbing warlordism and stabilising the security environment, on disarmament, demobilisation and reintegration of former combatants, rebuilding military and police forces and on transitional justice.

Curbing warlordism must involve efforts to undermine the economic foundations of the warlords' power and facilitate a transition to a civilian economy. Rampant violence and disorder in post-conflict areas and the international community's unwillingness to commit sufficient peace enforcement forces is often a major obstacle to security sector reform efforts. Lasting causes of insecurity usually involve warlordism, trade in narcotics, illegal arms and precious resources, the interference of regional states, so-called 'spoilers'[21] and rampant crime. Warlords, or similar actors who can self-finance organised militant groups, in many cases, pose the most potent threat to the post-conflict political order. The lack of law enforcement and unclear legal provisions often allows warlords to create economic and political niches in the transition phase from a manifest violent conflict to stabilisation. Warlords aggressively carve out provincial fiefdoms, use ethnicity for support, and generate resources through drug or arms trade, controlling external aid, imposing taxation and various forms of criminal activity.

If the central government lacks the means to curb the influence of the warlords, it can try to accommodate, co-opt or integrate them. Political dispensation is in the interest of warlords as it provides them with the veneer of legitimacy without curbing their activities. However, 'buying in' warlords may pose a threat to SSR – most are war criminals, guilty of grave human rights violations and unpopular among the general population. Due to the involvement of many of them in the economies of war, the nascent government may become hostage of war oligarchs. To undermine the power of warlords and spoilers security sector reform will have to include concerted efforts to choke off their sources of revenue. The warlords power is often primarily predicated on a financial rather than on a military basis. Accordingly, an effective means to confront warlordism is to equip the nascent government with economic tools to disrupt and dissolve their economic networks, for example through controlling transit trade and bringing customs under central command, and stopping military interference in economic and political affairs.

Disarmament, demobilisation and reintegration of former combatants is an indispensable component of post-war rehabilitation and reconstruction. Its primary purpose should be to demilitarise society by disbanding armed groups and eliminating military structures outside state control. In addition, successfully reintegrating former combatants into civilian society reduces the likelihood that 'violence experts' pick up arms again in order to secure their livelihood. Severing the dependence between militiamen and the warlords often necessitates the offer of alternative employment opportunities. Incentives for former combatants could include appointments in the government, military or police, retraining, assistance in establishing private enterprises and economic inducements. Disincentives refer to the use of force, recourse to legal measures, and banishment. The main problem is political and can result from a number of factors, including popular distrust of the nascent army and police, the existence of armed rival factions, possibly even a security vacuum where no national or international actor is in control and the failure of the international community to deploy robust forces. Small arms and light weapons control programmes can contribute to ridding post-conflict areas of surplus weapons.[22] However, expectations that more than symbolic numbers of weapons can be collected are generally unrealistic. Laws controlling the possession and use of weapons are often comparatively easier to enact and enforce.

The formation of truly national security institutions, whether army or police, is viewed in many post-conflict situations as a litmus test for the entire state-building endeavour (Bosnia and Herzegovina, Macedonia, Afghanistan, Iraq, partially Kosovo). Key problems for the creation of ethnically and politically representative security forces include the resistance of private militias to reform, as well as, political factionalisation, limited capacities of existing forces to absorb additional personnel from formerly excluded groups, lack of equipment and the absence of an overarching ideology. Externally assisted police reform was, all in all, more successful than military reform (Kosovo, Bosnia and Herzegovina, Afghanistan), although lack of sufficient training, basic equipment, miserable payment, and the enrolment of ex-combatants with a militiaman mentality have inhibited effective policing in a number of cases. However, the most serious obstacle to successful police reform is often the lack of lasting international support.

Countless atrocities have been committed in the course of 'civil' wars, including systemic executions, mass killings, mass rape, ethnic cleansing, torture, indiscriminate shelling, armed robbery, extortion, abduction, assaults on civilians, violence against journalists, feminists or political activists. Transitional justice has often treated these atrocities as taboo. While there is much recent experience with various forms of dealing with the past, including international tribunals, the international community and national governments often feel insecure and reluctant about how to address the problem. This issue is intimately linked to the dilemma, identified above, of building post-war power coalitions with limited resources. However, in our preliminary analysis of relevant cases, silence on accountability for human rights violations has more disadvantages than advantages. It emboldens ex-combatants and warlords to consolidate their power. Amnesty might be a necessary compromise in order to successfully demilitarise and reintegrate ex-combatants, but amnesty has to be more specifically defined. In view of the lack of amnesty legislation, the expectation of a blanket amnesty is very likely to stimulate insurgents to relapse into violent or criminal pursuit of interests. The promise of amnesty may even make the international community appear to be aiding and abetting opponents to successful reform the security sector. Blanket amnesties cast a lasting doubt on the democratic credentials of paramilitaries transformed into security agencies, but also inhibit their future control. Evaluation of personnel for post-war security agencies has, therefore, to cover all potential candidates, including commanders. Flagrant violations of humanitarian law, including genocide, war crimes, torture, terrorism, rape, and hostage-taking, should be exempted from any amnesty. Given the wide array of acts of violence, the reintegration and re-assimilation of combatants warrants a proactive reconciliation policy. Insufficient amount of attention has been dedicated to issues of human rights and gender, which have tremendous implications for security. If mechanisms to protect the rights of women and prevent human rights abuses are not erected in the security sector, the SSR process will serve to perpetuate gender-based discrimination and egregious human rights violations.

Suggested Conditions for Success and Failure

The following tentative conclusions and recommendations are derived from a preliminary analysis of post-conflict situations with strong international influence. They constitute hypotheses, which need to be further tested in empirical analysis. Specifically, they include (1) capacities of international actors, (2) local ownership, (3) enabling factors, (4) sequencing of models and (5) cost-benefit and project evaluation.

Capacities of international actors. If international actors intend to play a substantial part in security sector reform, they must be willing to invest substantial political and financial capital. Security sector management will require a multidisciplinary approach involving legal and constitutional experts, military and police professionals, experts in human resources management, persons and agencies with experience in demobilisation, re-trainers and labour market experts. Effective security sector reform is best conducted cooperatively among a wide range of actors. These include, in addition to those involved in peacekeeping and international administration in post-war situations, development as well as national and international donor agencies such as the World Bank and relevant non-governmental organisations. However, while positive in principle, the multiplicity of international actors with similar mandates operating in the same areas constantly creates 'turf wars' sometimes even among competing actors from one donor country. Duplication, parallel chains of command, and fights over allocation of funds have a noticeable toll on efficiency and effectiveness. International resources are often spread over too many independent actors with divergent mandates and limited willingness to coordinate. Overall responsibility for the various aspects of security sector reform is often unclear, or deliberately vague. Security sector achievements have been limited, for example in Afghanistan, because implementation of the division of labour for elements of the overall reform process agreed among national donors has been flawed. In some cases, such schemes have served to disjoint the process, fostering uneven progress in a strategy contingent on simultaneous movement among its constituent elements. Competing national agendas, unclear division of labour, budgetary problems, and bureaucratic sluggishness result mainly from political negligence. A solution could either exist in nominating a 'lead nation' for coordination or in establishing an international working body – not just a supervisory organ – for coordination.

Local Ownership. SSR will only last if it is based on a growing sense of local ownership. Imposition of security sector reform might seem possible in protectorates such as Kosovo and Bosnia and Herzegovina, but even there external leverage has proven to be limited and external dictates counterproductive in the long run. It is vital that reform is seen as an expression of national will and not something imposed by outsiders.

Enabling factors. Within a general framework, external support should be as demand-driven as possible and take the local socio-economic environment into account. Projects are too often generated externally and then 'sold' to the recipient country without needs assessments by independent experts or the recipient government. Needs assessments are rarely performed before measures are decided on. Chances of successful security sector reconstruction and reform increase if they form an integral part of post-conflict agreements, since they tend to reduce the likelihood of a relapse into violence. Keeping security sector reform off the initial agenda for post-conflict reconstruction is likely to increase the long-term costs in political instability and the danger of reigniting conflict. Security sector reform is also aided if the message sent by the international community is unambiguous. Post-war security policy must be geared towards removing the remnants of war, not to rectifying military imbalances or rewarding warlords. Capacity building of security sector forces is the core of successful external security sector reform assistance. In cases where emergency measures for stabilisation of the security situation are necessary, the initial focus must be the provision of physical security. Longer-term issues of security sector governance will need to take second place. Assisting capacity building should clearly be connected with de-militarisation, de-politicisation and strengthening the rule of law. Security sector reform should not result in furthering repressive regimes or authoritarian politics. Raising expectations not backed by capacities only leads to frustration and shifting responsibilities to external actors.

Sequencing. The post-conflict SSR policy sequence should start with deliberations about future tasks of national security, defence and intelligence, cascading down to changes in organisations and personnel. Discrete security sector reconstruction and reform projects should form – as much as possible – part of larger efforts for post-war reconstruction and democratisation and be aimed at sustainability. It is preferable for the long-term success of such programmes that security sector reconstruction and reform flows from a restatement of national security policy and that the development of defence and intelligence policy is a part of that process. In an ideal situation, which can serve as guidance for the overall approach, a restatement of the overall defence policy should form the basis for constitutional and legal reform, democratic control, the roles and functions of each security-related organisation, material and equipment, manning, and force management. Concrete reform elements should be elaborated in detailed plans, including budgets, for the various new security sector institutions. A management structure should be created which is capable of leading and inspiring the respective security organisation, as well as managing its resources efficiently and effectively within the democratic requirements of transparency and parliamentary accountability. Each of these plans will require implementation timelines, as well as the appointment of change managers to oversee the process. Administrative and technical reforms are unlikely to succeed unless they are underpinned by progress on the wider post-war reconstruction agenda. The overarching goal of international assistance must be to facilitate the creation of sustainable national structures, including legal frameworks. Goals and time frames of security sector reform should be clearly stated, otherwise donor fatigue coupled with the slow pace of aid delivery may deprive the process of vital funds.

Cost-benefit and project evaluation. As each layer of the plan is implemented, it is important that the solidity of the foundation is regularly confirmed. The aim of any review should be to conduct a quantitative, qualitative and effective audit of each step in the SSR process. The review phase should assess, among other issues, the quality of internal communications and the distribution of information concerning implementation of the plan, the quality and relevance of legal advice and other external expertise, the soundness of financial management, the effectiveness of the identification of skills and of commercial opportunities for laid-off personnel, and the overall cost of the implementation in terms of 'value for money'.

Conclusion

Post-conflict situations, where the international community is strongly committed, provide particularly pressing needs for security sector reconstruction and reform. If existing at all, domestic security institutions are generally faced with major security challenges, from remaining contenders to power and/or criminality, in some cases also from neighbouring countries. At the same time, security forces are often inadequately empowered or lack legitimacy.

External actors who involve themselves in peace support operations need to combine priority setting with facilitating the long-term build-up of professional, legitimate and efficient domestic security institutions. Unfortunately, little good advice on such priority setting is currently available. This is partly due to the relative novelty of international peace support operations including security sector reconstruction and reform, and partly to deficiencies in the debates on security sector reform, particularly a lack of empirical studies.

On the basis of preliminary analysis, taking into account the specific nature of each post-conflict situation, a number of hypotheses are developed for further empirical testing. One cluster of hypotheses pertains to the priorities for international actors in the reconstruction and reform of domestic security sectors. Near-term priority issues generally include curbing warlordism, disarmament, demobilisation and reintegration, the formation of a national army and police reform as well as transitional justice. Related to this are the long term goals of building-up accountable, efficient and effective security forces. Moreover, conditions for the advancement of security sector reconstruction and reform are often difficult, because of the existence of semi-authoritarian or authoritarian power structures. However, in these situations, security sector reform cannot be a substitute for political reform and democratisation.

Another cluster of hypotheses developed in the chapter address the enabling conditions for security sector reconstruction and reform. The success of security sector reconstruction and reform will likely depend on a number of factors, including the capacities of international actors, the degree of local ownership, the successful sequencing of models and, finally, the proper application of cost-benefit analysis and project evaluation.

These hypotheses need to be further tested in field studies. The goal of such work should be to assess whether security sector reform and reconstruction has helped to provide more security to people, to avoid politicisation, ethnicisation, and corruption of the security forces, to reduce excessive military spending and inefficient allocation of resources, and to improve transparency and accountability. A number of major external contributions to security sector reconstruction and reform have by now been made, or are under way, providing a growing body of evidence which needs to be systematically scrutinised.

Notes

[1]   The term is used here loosely, for international interventions with the primary objective to restore peace and establish sustainable structures for conflict management. See also Fitzgerald, A., 'Security Sector Reform – Streamlining National Military Forces to Respond to the Wider Security Needs', *Journal of Security Sector Management*, Vol. 1, No. 1, (2003).

[2]   See World Bank, *The Role of the World Bank in Conflict and Reconstruction. An Evolving Agenda*, (Washington, D.C., 2001), available at <http://lnweb18.worldbank.org/ESSD-/sdvext.nsf> (2001) for an official policy statement and Batchelor, P., Kingma, K., and Lamb, G., (eds.) *Demilitarisation & Peace-Building in Southern Africa: The Role of the Military in State Formation & Nation-Building,* (Ashgate, London, 2004), for a critical account for the Southern African region.

[3]   An edited volume, the result of a joint DCAF-BICC research project, with case studies on post-conflict security sector reconstruction and reform, for which this chapter provides a framework, is planned to be published in early 2005.

[4]   See DFID (UK Department for International Development) , *Poverty and the Security Sector. Policy Statement*, (London, 2000); Welch, C., and Mendelson Forman, J., *Civil-Military Relations: USAID's Role*. Centre for Democracy and Governance, (US Agency for International Development, Washington, D.C. 1998); World Bank, *Security, Poverty Reduction and Sustainable Development: Challenges for the New Millennium*, (Washington, D.C., September 1999); GTZ (Gesellschaft für Technische Zusammenarbeit), *Security-Sector Reform in Developing Countries: An Analysis of the International Debate*, (Eschborn. 2000); OECD/DAC, 'Security Issues and Development Co-operation: A Conceptual Framework for Enhancing Policy Coherence', *The DAC Journal: International Development*, Vol. 2, No. 3, (2001).

[5]   See Chalmers, M., *Security Sector Reform in Developing Countries: An EU Perspective*, Saferworld, London, January 2000; Williams, R., 'Africa and the Challenges of Security-Sector Reform', in: J. Cilliers, A. Hilding-Norberg (eds.), *Building Stability in Africa: Challenges for the New Millennium*, ISS Monograph Series No. 46, Pretoria 2000; Hendrickson, D., *Understanding and Supporting Security Sector Reform*, DFID, London.2002; Cooper, N., and Pugh, M., *Security Sector Transformation in Post-conflict Societies*, The Conflict, Security & Development Group, Working Papers, King's College, London, February 2002; Ball, N., *Enhancing Security Sector Governance: A Conceptual Framework for UNDP*, October 9, 2002.; UNOG and DCAF (eds.), *Security Sector Re-*

form: Its Relevance for Conflict Prevention, Peace Building, and Development. Compilation of Presentations Made at the First Joint Seminar of the UNOG and DCAF, Geneva 21.1.2003, Geneva, 2003; Commission on Human Security, *Human Security Now*, New York, 2003.

6   See United Nations, *Report of the Panel on United Nations Peace Operations*, Chaired by Lakhdar Brahimi, (New York, 2000) , available at <http://www.un.org/peace/reports/peace_operations/>.

7   See United Nations Department for Peacekeeping Operations, *Disarmament, Demobilization and Reintegration of Ex-Combatants in a Peacekeeping Environment*, New York: United Nations 2000.

8   Some authors see SSR as a carrier for 'democratisation of the state', 'establishment of good governance', a basis for 'economic development', 'international and regional conflict prevention', 'post-conflict recovery', and 'professionalisation', see, for example Karkoszka, A., 'The Concept of Security Sector Reform', in: UNOG and DCAF, eds., *Security Sector Reform*, Geneva , 2003. In this paper, none of such claimed links are further investigated.

9   See Saferworld/International Alert/Netherlands Institute of International Relations 'Clingendael', *Towards a Better Practice Framework in Security Sector Reform. Broadening the Debate*, Occasional SSR Paper no. 1 (The Hague.2002).

10 See Buwitt, D., *Internationale Polizeieinsätze bei UNO-Friedensmissionen. Erfahrungen und Lehren aus Bosnien-Herzegowina und im Kosovo*, BITS Research Report 01.1, Berlin, December 2001; King, J., Dorn, W.and Hodes, M., *An Unprecedented Experiment: Security Sector Reform in Bosnia and Hercegovina*, Saferworld and BICC, (London, September 2002); Yusufi, I., *Security Sector Reform in South East Europe*, Center for Policy Studies, (Gostivar, 18 February.2003); Sedra, M., *Confronting Afghanistan's Security Dilemma. Reforming the Security Sector.* Brief 28 (BICC: Bonn, 2003).

11 See Ball, N. and. Brzoska, M, (with Kees Kingma and Herbert Wulf), *Voice and Accountability in the Security Sector*, BICC Paper 21 (BICC: Bonn, 2002).

17 OECD/DAC, *Security System Reform and Governance. Policy and Good Practice*, (2004). Available at: www.oecd.org/dataoecd/26/44/31870339.pdf .

13 See Hänggi, H, 'Making Sense of Security Sector Governance', in: Hänggi, H., Winkler, T. (eds.), *Challenges of Security Sector Governance* (LIT: Münster, 2003), pp. 3-18.

14 See King et al, *An Unprecedented Experiment,* and Sedra,*Confronting.*

15 See Collier, D. and Levitsky, D., 'Democracy with Adjectives: Conceptual Innovation in Comparative Research', *World Politics*, Vol. 49, No. 3, (1997), pp. 430-451, Beichelt, T., *Demokratische Konsolidierung im post-sozialistischen Europa. Die Rolle der politischen Institutionen*, (Leske und Budrich, Opladen 2001); Diamond, L., 'Thinking about Hybrid Regimes', *Journal of Democracy*, Vol. 13, No. 2, 2002, pp. 21-35,; Merkel, W., Puhle, H.-J., Croissant A., Eicher, C., and Thiery, P., *Defekte Demokratie*, Bd. 1, (Leske und Budrich, Opladen, 2003).

16 Measured e.g. by the Freedom House Index, see <www.freedomhouse.org>.

17 See <www.transparency.org.>.

10 See Linz, J. J., and Stepan, A. *Problems of Democratic Transition and Consolidation: Southern Europe, South America, and Post-Communist Europe*, Johns Hopkins University Press, (Baltimore 1996) and Lauth, H. J., Pickel, G. and Welzel, C. (eds.), *Demok-*

ratiemessung. Konzepte und Befunde im internationalen Vergleich, (Westdeutscher Verlag, Opladen, 2000).

[19] See Chandler, D., *Bosnia: Faking Democracy After Dayton,* (Pluto Press, London 1999)

[20] See Maravall, J. M.and Przeworski, A. 'Introduction', in: J. M. Maravall and A. Przeworski, (eds.), *Democracy and the Rule of Law,* (Cambridge University Press, Cambridge. 2003); Weingast, B. R., 'A Postscript to "Political Foundations of Democracy and the Rule of Law"', in: J. M. Maraval and A. Przeworski, (eds.), *Democracy and the Rule of Law,* (Cambridge University Press, Cambridge, 2003), pp. 109-113.

[21] See Stedman, S. J., 'Spoiler Problems in Peace Processes', *International Security,* Vol. 22, No. 2, (1997), pp. 5-53.

[22] See Faltas S. and diChiaro J.III, (eds.), *Managing the Remnants of War,* (Nomos, Baden-Baden, 2001).

Chapter 7

Security Sector Reform and Post-Conflict Stabilisation: The Case of the Western Balkans[*]

Marina Caparini

Introduction

The states of the Western Balkans region[1] differ from other transitional democracies in Central Europe in important ways, which affect the conditions and challenges for security sector reform (SSR).[2] In their transition from state socialism and authoritarian rule, the Western Balkan societies also bear the lingering material and psychological effects of recent armed conflict and ethnic cleansing. Their security sectors tend to be fragmented, underdeveloped (although some sectors, typically the armed forces, are overdeveloped for peacetime conditions), over-politicised and structured along ethnic or religious lines. Non-state armed formations, including paramilitary organisations formed along party or ethnic lines, private military companies, criminal groups and guerrilla movements may exist alongside state security structures weakened by corruption. The problems of refugee return, resettlement and reintegration of displaced persons, and return of property remain unresolved in key areas. Individuals and communities continue to be scarred by the psychological traumas inflicted by war and extreme nationalism. Nationalistic (ethnic and religious) divisions persist, and the resurgence of nationalist parties in recent elections throughout the region, followed by the open violence in Kosovo in March 2004, provides daunting evidence of the fragility of both democracy and peace in these societies.

In the Western Balkans, the task of SSR must be approached concurrently with post-conflict stabilisation. The continued presence of interna-

---

[*] This chapter was first published in the SIPRI Yearbook 2004. It has been updated and slightly revised for this publication.

tional peacekeeping forces in most parts of the region including international police forces in Bosnia and Herzegovina (BiH) and in the Former Yugoslav Republic of Macedonia (FYROM) and the international administrations with wide-ranging internal powers in Bosnia and Herzegovina and in Kosovo has interrupted the local authorities' monopoly of security responsibilities for years. The goals of SSR, as normally conceived, can only be reached by completing the localisation of security functions as part of the general transfer of authority from international actors to national and regional governments. Plans for this normalisation could be interrupted at any time by a resurgence of security problems anywhere in the region. The goals of reform and normalisation, and external efforts to promote them must, therefore, be conceived more in regional terms than has been the case elsewhere in post-cold war Europe. A special complication is the dispute and uncertainty over the ultimate status of Kosovo, which aspires to independence, but has been ruled as a United Nations (UN) protectorate since 1999.

This chapter examines some of the main efforts to reorganise and modernise those institutions representing the state's legitimate monopoly of the use of force in the five Western Balkan states and in Kosovo. The first section considers the impact of two key external actors and other factors on SSR in the region through the development of relationships between the Western Balkan states and the European Union (EU) and the North Atlantic Treaty Organisation (NATO). The second section surveys common challenges in the component areas of security sector reform – armed forces, police, intelligence and border management. The third section addresses recent SSR developments in individual Western Balkan countries, and the final section offers some brief conclusions and remarks on the way ahead.

External Factors

One of the main pressures, which the Western community has been able to wield for reform and for post-conflict normalisation in the Western Balkans, has been the conditional offer of integration into the key Western institutions – the EU and NATO. Under the EU's Stabilisation and Association Process (SAP), the Western Balkan states may negotiate Stabilisation and Association Agreements (SAAs), giving them trade access and other ties to the EU on condition of meeting further specific political and economic conditions. The road towards membership of the EU is generally considered to start with the conclusion of an SAA. The EU thus invokes the prospect of an eventual invitation to join the Union as leverage for insisting on a series of reforms to bring the candidate states' political and economic systems in line with European standards.[3]

SAAs were signed with FYROM and Croatia in April and October 2001, respectively,[4] and another has been under negotiation with Albania since January 2003. A November 2003 feasibility study for Bosnia and Herzegovina concluded that the country was not yet ready to start negotiating an SAA, but the EU will conduct a re-evaluation by mid-2004. The feasibility study for Serbia and Montenegro was initiated in the autumn of 2003 but was postponed after the parliamentary elections in Serbia in December 2003, in which the ultra-nationalist Serbian Radical Party, led by Vojislav Seselj, won the largest proportion of votes.[5] The EU supports transition processes financially through the Community Assistance for Reconstruction, Development and Stabilisation (CARDS) programme,[6] worth about €4.65 billion for the region in 2002-2006 and politically *inter alia* through the EU-Western Balkans Forum, launched at the Thessaloniki European Council on 21 June 2003. The forum met for the first time on 28 November 2003, and focused strongly on internal security.[7]

The Stabilisation and Association Process deals with those aspects of security sector reform proper to EU competence, through the monitoring of discrete elements such as the rule of law, independence of the judiciary, democratic control of the armed forces and anti-corruption measures by way of annual country reports. Detailed Stabilisation and Association reports assess each state in the area of justice and home affairs (JHA) and include recommendations for reforming legal and institutional arrangements. The reports uphold European (EU and Council of Europe) norms and standards, such as those embodied in the 1950 Convention for the Protection of Human Rights and Fundamental Freedoms.[8] In the field of policing, the SAP monitors national adoption of the 2001 Code of Police Ethics, the establishment of the police as a public service, and the existence of clear internal and external measures for the control and accountability of police.[9] The SAP also focuses attention on effective border control, management of migration flows, and visa and asylum regimes. The emphasis of the 2004 annual SAP report was on internal security through building up individual state capacities and regional cooperation to deal effectively with organised crime, illegal immigration and border security.[10] In addition to meeting the 'Copenhagen criteria' for membership,[11] the Western Balkan states must fulfil the SAP criteria, which are primarily focused on the development of adequate institutional capacity.

The possibility of joining NATO drew particular interest from the Western Balkan nations in 2002-2003, partly because it is considered easier than meeting the EU's far more elaborate demands (*vide* the entry of Bulgaria and Romania into NATO before the EU) and partly because of the symbolism for local countries turning from being 'consumers' to 'producers' of security. Albania, Croatia and FYROM have filed formal applications for membership, and Serbia and Montenegro is currently concentrating on entry into the NATO Partnership for Peace (PFP) programme – in all cases with political support from the US. Meeting NATO's criteria and defence capability standards can be a force for both democratic reform and military modernisation, but it also requires subordinating nations' defence culture to NATO's (fast-changing) collective needs, which are not always well-attuned to the post-communist SSR environment.[12] In addition, entering the world of NATO politics is not always a simple or pleasant experience, as shown by the story of US pressure on states to sign Bilateral Immunity Agreements exempting US personnel from the jurisdiction of the International Criminal Court (ICC). All the Western Balkan states were pressured by the US on this issue, although it concurrently urged them to collaborate fully with the ICTY. Albania, Bosnia and Herzegovina, and FYROM complied, but Croatia and Serbia and Montenegro refused and thereby lost quantities of US military aid.[13] The leverage inherent in the enlargement processes of the EU, the PFP and NATO for aspiring countries may be even further enhanced with the agreement in 2003 between the EU and NATO to develop close consultation through enhanced dialogue leading to a concerted approach to security and stability in the Western Balkans.[14] Their 'joint strategic approach' identifies a common vision for the region based on self-sustaining stability, democratic and effective government, a viable free market economy and closer integration with the Euro-Atlantic structures. The agreement implicitly recognises a certain division of labour in the field of security-relevant reform, with the EU taking the lead in police reform and governance issues and NATO in defence reform. Aside from agreeing to meet regularly and exchange information on security matters in the Western Balkans, the agreement leaves the way open for further joint EU-NATO initiatives.

Common Challenges in Security Sector Reforms

New defence and security approaches, such as that of regional security cooperation and those based on the goal of PFP and NATO membership, require doctrinal shifts and structural reform of the region's armed forces. The reform and downsizing of bloated armed forces and paramilitary forces are common challenges throughout the region and hinge on effective policies for the disarmament, demobilisation and reintegration of former soldiers. The requirements for modernisation and structural reform account for the continued relatively high levels of military expenditure in the region.[15] The introduction of norms concerning the democratic control of armed forces, transparency and accountability requires the adaptation of legislative frameworks, national security policies, and the mindsets of both civilian and military actors. While the focus on the military is understandable in a region emerging from armed conflict, the experience of the Western Balkans has provided one of the clearest illustrations that military capabilities are but one component of security and that other security institutions are even more vital for the security of individuals and society during peacetime.

Police reform in the Western Balkan countries confronts the dual legacy of state socialism and recent involvement in armed conflict. The legacy of the Titoist state of Yugoslavia is broadly similar to that of other state socialist regimes in Central Europe. The regular police functioned as a key instrument of state security and control of the population, becoming a centralised and militarised force which, through its close links with state security police, directly served the interests of and protected the ruling regime. With the break-up of Yugoslavia in 1991, police across the region became directly involved in violent conflict and ethnic cleansing, aided by massive increases in their strength, heavy arms and equipment.[16] They were often highly politicised and paramilitarised and were sometimes built up as an institutional counter to the armed forces. Inter-ethnic conflict affected their composition. They were ethnically diverse in large urban centres and largely homogeneous in ethnic sub-regions. The rapid increase in the numbers of police resulted in a loss of professionalism, as recruitment standards were lowered and normal education and training requirements were waived.

International actors during and after conflict have identified police reform as a priority component of lasting conflict resolution in the Western Balkans, but the results are still not satisfactory. Major problems remain with criminal networks, which use these states as transit corridors for smuggling humans, drugs and other contraband. Frequent scandals suggest the widespread collusion of state and political authorities, including police, border guards and customs officials, in organised crime. In addition to weaknesses in national laws, enforcement and institutional infrastructure, the countries of the Western Balkans region are also limited in their cooperation with each other by a lack of structures and networks for joint action of a transnational nature, for example, through cooperative border management and police and judicial cooperation.

One of the major issues in security sector reform throughout the Western Balkans region is the management of international borders, 5,000 kilometres of which were created by the break-up of Yugoslavia and the emergence of five new states. Many of these borders have yet to be delineated, and border control agencies are often inefficient, under-equipped and subject to corruption. Apart from smuggling, the region is both a source of and a transit corridor for illegal immigrants into the EU. One estimate holds that over 100,000 illegal immigrants per year have come from the Balkans to the EU, of which fifteen per cent originated from the region itself.[17] The border regions also tend to have minority populations, which when under-privileged – as they often are – may become a focus of unrest and source of secessionist pressures.

The EU has placed strong emphasis on improving border control to address smuggling and as a means to stabilise state-to-state and inter-community relations. Integrated border management among national agencies and regional strategies against transnational threats are specifically encouraged and supported through the EU's CARDS Programme. At the May 2003 Ohrid Regional Conference on Border Security and Management, the EU, NATO, the Organisation for Security and Co-operation in Europe (OSCE) and the Stability Pact for South Eastern Europe adopted a Common Platform for the Western Balkans aimed at creating 'open but controlled and secure borders in the entire region in accordance with European standards and initiatives'.[18] The inter-institutional group's ultimate goal is to put border control throughout the region in the hands of civilian (police) services, with overall control exercised by civilian authorities.

Developments in Security Sector Reform in Individual States

Albania

Albania has not been involved in an overt interstate conflict or frontier change during the past decade, but carries heavy legacies in the backwardness and isolation resulting from its Cold War orientation followed by more than a decade of highly polarised politics. A spell of internal disorder in 1997 required a brief international military intervention (the multinational protection force Operation Alba).[19] Since then, there has been international support for security improvements, and there is widespread public and political support in Albania for closer integration with NATO and the EU. However, progress in institutional reform, strengthening central and local government, and combating organised crime and corruption has been slow.

Albania has faced a difficult task of transforming its armed forces, requiring both significant de-politicisation and modernisation. Under the preceding totalitarian, isolationist and highly militarised communist regime, the Albanian Army was under the strong control of the party, whose purges and other measures severely eroded the sense of military corporate identity and professionalism. In the post-communist period, defence issues have remained associated in the public mind with isolationism, hardship and underdevelopment. The drastic reductions in military personnel since the change in regime further undermined the attractions of a military career for young people.[20]

Albania adopted a Military Strategy on Defence in July 2002, outlining the objectives of developing a professional army, reducing the number of conscripts, and increasing the defence budget by 0.1 per cent of gross domestic product (GDP) per year until 2010. However, Albania has far to go to reach NATO standards in terms of equipment and training. During the civil disorder of March 1997 following the collapse of government-supported financial pyramid schemes, the army disintegrated while the country was flooded with looted weapons, creating a legacy of illegal arms trafficking and hoarding. The left-wing coalition government that subsequently came to power purged the armed forces of 1,500 officers, 400 of whom had received Western education or training in 1992–96, and brought back some old regime loyalists.[21]

Legislative oversight of the armed forces, including the defence budget, is weak and perfunctory.[22] Lack of money and staff with sufficient expertise hinders the functioning of oversight by parliamentary committees.[23] Parliamentarians acknowledge the problem and are attempting to find ways to overcome it. On a more positive note, despite the events in Kosovo and the unrest and political conflicts in Albania over the past decade, the army has not attempted to intervene in politics or demonstrated any praetorian tendencies.[24]

More vigorous efforts by Albania to control illegal immigration to the EU and the conclusion of re-admission agreements with EU members and other countries have slowed considerably the flow of economic migrants across the Adriatic Sea to Italy. Albania still experiences major problems, however, as regards trafficking in human beings and in hard drugs, including heroin and cocaine; organised crime; money laundering; and widespread systemic corruption of key state institutions, including the judiciary, police and customs. Trafficking in women and children from Albania for prostitution or slavery has been a major problem fed by high unemployment, deep rural poverty and the traditionally low status of women in society. Albania has also served as a major transit route for traffic in third-country nationals. Only relatively recently, and under international pressure, has the government acknowledged the problem and adopted more aggressive anti-trafficking measures.[25] The problem remains serious. A legislative and functional framework for witness protection has been lacking, traffickers often receive lenient sentences when convicted,[26] and police commonly collude in trafficking with impunity.[27] In June 2003 the Albanian Government finally established the Task Force on Witness Protection, including international experts, to aid witnesses materially and to help the government prepare and implement witness protection legislation.[28] A draft law is now before parliament for approval.[29]

The EU has drawn special attention to Albania's need to address reforms in the JHA sector.[30] The judicial system is weak, with corruption and inadequately trained individuals at all levels of the system. Court rulings are not always enforced and judicial proceedings for serious crimes, including organised crime, trafficking and corruption, frequently fail. The Albanian public consequently lacks trust in the system.

Policing is being reformed, albeit slowly, according to the Reform Strategy of the State Police. Despite the international police training missions,[31] significant problems remain, particularly concerning the corruption and lack of professionalism of police, most of whom have been described as 'untrained, ill paid and often unreliable'.[32] Physical mistreatment and torture of detainees by the Albanian police are widespread and largely go unpunished, although this may now be less common.[33] The judicial police who carry out investigations for the prosecution service are not adequately trained or equipped. Cooperation is poor among the various law enforcement bodies, management remains ineffective, and political influence on selection procedures is frequent.[34]

A major obstacle to tackling corruption and holding government and state officials accountable is the tendency of the Albanian government to respond to perceived critical reporting by interfering with the media through physical intimidation, the threat of defamation trials and financial or regulatory pressure, such as the application of aggressive financial audits or inspections. State advertising is also used as an instrument of pressure and is channelled only through supportive media outlets.[35] Such problems underscore that progress in democratisation and SSR cannot rely on institutional reform alone, but also depends critically on civic society's ability to debate and challenge government policy without fear.

Bosnia and Herzegovina

Reform of armed forces has been one of the most sensitive issues in Bosnia and Herzegovina since the signing of the Dayton Peace Agreement. The agreement created two autonomous entities in the country - the (Bosniac-Croat) Federation of Bosnia and Herzegovina (FBiH) and the (Bosniac-Serb) Republika Srpska. Each entity is responsible for its own defence and has its own armed forces. In practice, however, the country has three armed forces. Although the FBiH Army was designed as a single force, it is divided into the Army of the (Bosniac–Muslim) Federation of Bosnia and Herzegovina (AFBiH) and the (Croat) Hrvatsko Vijece Obrane (HVO).

The Dayton Peace Agreement conceived military reform in terms of a division and balance of power between the two (now almost ethnically homogeneous) entities.[36] The development of a 'train and equip' programme was agreed between Bosnia and Herzegovina and the US specifically to build up the military capabilities of the FBiH Army so that it would be as strong and professional as its opponent during the war, the Army of the Republika Srpska.[37] The programme was implemented by the US Military Professional Resources Incorporated (MPRI) private military company,[38] officially from 1996 until 30 October 2002. This strengthened the FBiH Army, but at the cost of fuelling mistrust among Bosnian Serbs and undermining attempts to integrate the armed forces of Bosnia and Herzegovina.[39] Since then, a key challenge of SSR in the country has been to restore a modicum of authority and control in the realm of security to the weak central authorities, something that matters for democratic accountability and transparency as well as efficiency and equality of standards.

Defence reform lagged after the implementation of the initial downsizing of the BiH armed forces in 2001–2002.[40] The existence of ethnically based, parallel security institutions has been a huge drain on BiH public resources, and the country has spent more than five per cent of GDP on defence every year since the conclusion of the 1995 Dayton Peace Agreement.[41] This has been criticised by NATO as excessive, while the Office of the High Representative (OHR)[42] has stated that defence expenditures are bankrupting the Bosnian state. The financial impasse has given the international community new leverage for insisting on reform, also using offers of training and equipment for restructured forces as a 'carrot', and the OHR has taken a strong proactive approach, essentially driving defence reform in Bosnia and Herzegovina. NATO has linked military reform, specifically the creation of a unified state-level defence organisation (command and control system), with Bosnia and Herzegovina's developing closer ties to NATO, including eventual membership of the PFP.[43] As a result, significant reforms were pushed through in 2003 towards the establishment of a unified armed forces command, including the OHR's decision in April 2003 to abolish the Republika Srpska's Supreme Defence Council in order to prevent contravention of the Dayton Peace Agreement and its prohibition against having separate military command structures.[44]

The Defence Reform Commission (DRC) was established in May 2003 by High Representative Lord Ashdown to draft or amend the legislation required for the reform of BiH defence structures in accord with Euro-Atlantic norms.[45] The DRC has endorsed PFP and ultimately NATO membership as goals to guide reform.[46] A key step was the creation of a single, central defence establishment – which became possible once the Muslim nationalist Party of Democratic Action dropped its demands for a single, unified army.[47] Under heavy pressure from the international community, the BiH authorities agreed to the establishment of state-level central command and control of the two armies, which will now have a single flag and uniform, but will remain ethnically distinct.[48] The entities will retain separate armed forces and defence ministries for administrative functions. The BiH state-level defence ministry and general staff will be responsible for 'higher functions' and the supreme command would be the BiH joint presidency, which would make decisions based on consensus.[49]

The BiH Parliament had enacted the 2003 Defence Law and almost all of the DRC's legislative recommendations by the end of 2003.[50] Nevertheless, the pace of reform was still considered too slow to meet PFP targets by the Istanbul NATO Summit of June 2004, prompting a decision to expand and refocus the mandate of the DRC.[51] The DRC is now mandated to oversee implementation of its recommendations, including the filling of new posts established by the Defence Law (especially the state-level defence minister as well as the joint chiefs of staff and their deputies); the establishment of new organs such as the Security Committee of the Parliamentary Assembly; and the drafting, adoption and implementation of BiH defence budgets.[52] In parallel, Bosnia and Herzegovina announced in February 2004 that it would make major reductions in the BiH armed forces, downsizing to 12,000 professional soldiers in three ethnically based brigades with 8,000 in the Federation Army and 4,000 in the Bosnian Serb Army.[53] Agreement has been reached on a draft joint military doctrine and common training standards for all the BiH armed forces, one of the prerequisites for joining the PFP.

Intelligence reform has proven even more difficult than defence reform in Bosnia and Herzegovina, where political parties and figures allegedly control their own intelligence services.[54] These highly politicised services are thought to spy not just on other entities, but also on international actors present in the country, including SFOR troops and researchers at the ICTY. The Republika Srpska Government closed a military intelligence office in April 2003 after it had been caught doing this.[55] The services have also been linked to a broad range of criminal activities, including helping indicted war criminals such as President of Republika Srpska Radovan Karadzic to escape arrest, and recently selling military arms and equipment to Iraq in violation of a UN embargo.[56] Recently, however, pressure for reform in this field has increased because of international concerns about terrorism and organised crime. The EU made intelligence reform a key condition, along with tax system reforms and cooperation with the ICTY, for starting to negotiate any SAA with Bosnia and Herzegovina in 2004. Lord Ashdown set up a seven-member Expert Commission for Intelligence Reform following a number of scandals involving parallel BiH security structures.[57] A draft intelligence law was formulated, revised with international advice, and – after three months of hesitation by the tripartite presidency – sent by Lord Ashdown directly to parliament, thus sidestepping the Council of Ministers. Lord Ashdown indicated that he will enforce reform in the absence of cooperation from authorities in Republika Srpska, and set the deadline of 1 April 2004 for the new single Intelligence and Security Agency to be approved by the BiH Parliament and established.[58] The agency will collect information on threats to BiH security both within and outside the country and will be obliged to forward information about war crimes suspects to the ICTY.

Police reform in Bosnia and Herzegovina has been predominantly driven by the international community through successive international police missions – UNMIBH and the International Police Task Force (IPTF) from December 1995 until the end of 2002, and the EU Police Mission (EUPM) since January 2003. The IPTF achieved the limited goals of an overhaul of local police forces; the retraining of senior police officers and the training of over 1,000 young cadets. The number of police has been cut from 44,000 immediately following the end of hostilities in 1996 to 16,000 in mid-2003.[59] A de-certification process run by the UN identified personnel whose records during the war disqualified them, but many of those de-certified by UNMIBH were re-employed in ministries of the interior, where they could still influence policing.[60] The police de-certification process has recently run into problems, such as the requests by more than 150 individuals dismissed by the IPTF for the courts to review their cases and the reinstatement of some police officers following a court order.[61]

BiH policing suffers from continuing political interference and control over police structures and appointments, with little democratic accountability. The police are poorly paid, perceived as corrupt and not trusted by the public to enforce the law fairly. Politicians, policemen and customs agents are considered to be among the most corrupt officials in the country.[62] Police powers are highly decentralised, with each of the ten BiH cantons having an interior ministry, while central state authorities are responsible only for international and inter-entity policing. The extreme fragmentation and lack of cooperation impede effective policing of organised crime and trafficking, in which local authorities and police are still suspected of being complicit. The creation of the State Information and Protection Agency (SIPA) Programme, a state-level investigative law enforcement agency, is meant to facilitate inter-entity and international police cooperation in combating organised crime, but at the end of 2003 the SIPA Programme still lacked a budget and permanent facilities.[63] Furthermore, there have been persistent efforts to prevent the establishment of an independent, impartial and multi-ethnic judiciary, which is viewed as a key obstacle to further progress in establishing rule of law. It appears increasingly likely that the EUPM, which at nearly 500 police officers is much smaller than the IPTF (1,800), will have to develop closer cooperation with the High Representative so that the latter's discretionary powers can be used to tackle such interference.[64]

In summary, there was progress in 2003 in the reform of BiH security institutions, but it has been critically dependent on international pressure and on the High Representative's use of his powers to impose legislation and dismiss obstructionist officials. The EU and NATO have increasingly used their institutional leverage (including their power as donors) to the same end, and the EU will presumably attempt to do so in an even more focused way once it takes over responsibility for the SFOR peacekeeping force, as well as, the EUPM. This raises the question of how meaningful and durable reforms can be without the sufficient engagement and informed consent of local political institutions. The choice that appears to exist, in a country as dependent on international tutelage and assistance as Bosnia and Herzegovina, is between effective SSR and democratic SSR. As SSR ultimately concerns the ability of national authorities to govern the security dimension effectively, it is worrying that the domestic political process has been side-stepped in engineering some significant structural changes.[65] Questions may be raised about the legitimacy and durability of measures so lacking in truly local 'ownership'.

Croatia

Croatia had to build up its armed forces and security (intelligence) services from scratch in the early 1990s in the context of the 'war of independence' and under the authoritarian rule of President Franjo Tudjman's nationalist Croatian Democratic Union (HDZ). A fundamental change in the regional security environment occurred with the death of Tudjman and the fall of the regime of Slobodan Milosevic in neighbouring Serbia and Montenegro (then the Federal Republic of Yugoslavia) in 2000. The main external threat to Croatia faded and relations with Serbia and Montenegro gradually improved. A pro-reform government set Croatia on a new course for integration with the Euro-Atlantic structures. However, it also faced the challenge of reforming the bloated and politicised security structures, which it inherited from the Tudjman era.

Subsequent security sector reforms have involved mainly constitutional changes (reducing the powers of the president) and new legislation (for example, in 2002, new laws on defence, security services, national security strategy and national defence strategy). Practical reforms have been scarce. For instance, the Security Services Act established a National Security Council, but it has yet to meet, leaving certain ministers in charge of intelligence agencies.[66] The Croatian political system has become essentially semi-presidential, with a sharing of certain key powers, which obscures political accountability and raises the possibility of deadlock when the president and the prime minister are politically opposed (cohabitation).[67]

Because of the outbreak of war at the beginning of the 1990s, existing members of the State Security Service (SDS, the intelligence service inherited by the new government) did not undergo a screening or review process to remove those involved in human rights abuses during the communist era. Following the end of the war, the Croatian intelligence services experienced a 'post-war identity crisis' and became a source of political opposition to the single-party government, while some members became actively involved in smuggling, trafficking and organised crime.[68] After two years of rivalry within the executive, a new legal framework was achieved in the form of the 2002 Security Services Act, which renamed the services and placed them under the shared power of the prime minister and cabinet and the president. However, there has been little effort to implement the new provisions (for example, there is no lustration process to screen personnel).[69] Continuing turf wars among politicians in 2000–2002 blocked badly needed reforms and were aggravated by the failure of the National Security Council to meet and provide strategic guidance. Democratic oversight and control of the services are practically non-existent because the Parliamentary Internal Affairs and National Security Committee has not taken up its duties as defined by the Security Services Act, and other intelligence oversight bodies have not been established.[70] In summary, Croatia's intelligence services still do not function in accordance with democratic principles.

The Croatian armed forces are essentially new, built up in the first years of the independence struggle and composed of civilian volunteers, former militarised police units, local territorial defence forces and a few officers from the former Yugoslav People's Army,[71] where education and training standards were relatively low and the forces highly politicised. Croatia now needs to adapt the armed forces to a new security environment through downsizing. At the same time, there has been a significant decrease in the defence budget. The continuing dependence by parts of Croatian society and specific regions on the military, in a context of high unemployment, makes it politically difficult to downsize, which may explain why the government's declaration of principles on the matter has not been translated into any clear policy plans.[72]

There has, however, been progress in the de-politicisation of the officer corps and increased transparency in the defence budget and procurement process. Still remaining is the need to address personnel management within the armed forces, including the system of promotions. Parliamentary oversight of defence affairs is still largely perfunctory. Members of the Domestic Policy and National Security Committee are responsible for all security-related issues, but lack the expertise to exercise their duties effectively and Croatia has no specific committee to oversee the armed forces.[73] There is a general lack of security expertise in civil society and thus of experts to provide independent advice to parliamentary committees.

Croatia is conducting a strategic defence review, which is due to be completed in 2004. NATO has criticised the over-emphasis in Croatia's armed forces on territorial defence, insufficient mobility of forces, heavy and outdated weapons, and a hollow command structure.[74] The review is expected to advocate a shift towards collective defence within the NATO framework and towards making deployable forces available for NATO operations, specifically in NATO rapid reaction forces.

Policing in Croatia was strongly influenced by the armed conflict in the 1990s and by the decade of nationalist right-wing government under President Franjo Tudjman. The paramilitarisation of police in the 1991–92 war reinforced their bonds of professional loyalty, which made the subsequent tasks of rooting out police corruption or creating internal controls on misconduct more difficult. Nevertheless, the war helped to create a legitimate indigenous police force that was divorced in the public mind from the despised and repressive Yugoslav militia[75] and brought the police much higher public esteem than their counterparts enjoy in many Central European countries. However, that legitimacy was eroded from the late 1990s, probably as a result of the high levels of police corruption. The latter is a key issue for police reform, together with excessive use of force, implementation of community policing, reform of the police organisation and staff policies.[76] Serious problems in the functioning of the judiciary, including inadequately qualified staff, insufficient budgets, long delays and a huge backlog of pending civil law cases, are also undermining the rule of law, effective law enforcement and implementation of decisions.[77]

Thus, while Croatia has made rapid progress and is acknowledged to be ahead of the other Western Balkan states economically and in many of its institutional reforms, numerous problems remain in the security sector.

The Former Yugoslav Republic of Macedonia

During the 1990s, FYROM was seen as an island of peaceful ethnic coexistence in the region. However, this peace was built on the de facto division of the two main communities in the state – ethnic Macedonians and ethnic Albanians – who lived in more or less isolated parallel societies, with a high degree of mutual mistrust. Discrimination against the ethnic Albanian minority was a structural feature of the state, but without the violence and attempts at ethnic cleansing that characterised Kosovo. Albanians had formal minority status in FYROM, with their own political parties, media outlets and education in their own language up to secondary level.

The conflict in the neighbouring Serbian province of Kosovo put greater strains on inter-ethnic relations between the Macedonian and Albanian communities. In February 2001 armed conflict broke out in northwestern FYROM between armed Albanian insurgents and FYROM security forces. The National Liberation Army (NLA), recruiting insurgents from Kosovo and from the FYROM Albanian community, employed guerrilla warfare and terrorist tactics, allegedly in protest against discrimination of Albanians and the slow pace of reform. The FYROM authorities believed that the insurgents sought to split off the north-western part of the country and join it to a 'Greater Albania' (or 'Greater Kosovo'). This guerrilla conflict continued for six months and escalated ethnic tensions until the international community brokered a cease-fire agreement in August 2001– the Ohrid Framework Agreement. The agreement provided greater rights and representation for Albanians and an amnesty for the NLA fighters in exchange for the disarming and disbanding of the NLA.[78]

In September 2001 a 1,000-strong peacekeeping force, Amber Fox, replaced NATO's Essential Harvest missionto protect EU and OSCE monitors who were overseeing the implementation of the Ohrid Agreement and monitoring the 15 September 2002 general election. These forces left in December and were replaced in March 2003 by the 350-member EU Military Operation in the Former Yugoslav Republic of Macedonia (EUFOR), Operation Concordia, patrolling areas mostly around the Kosovo border. Operation Concordia was the first EU military crisis-management operation.[79] The FYROM government requested an extension of the EU mission until 15 December. At that point, by agreement with the government and with support from NATO and the OSCE, the EU military mission was replaced by the EU Police Mission in the Former Yugoslav Republic of Macedonia (EUPOL), Operation Proxima, indicating a shift of emphasis from peacekeeping to internal security tasks, including improving police training, refugee return and anti-crime measures.[80]

According to international observers, the current situation is 'improving', despite sporadic incidents of inter-ethnic and political violence. Others perceive a disturbing succession of security incidents that suggest underlying tensions and a propensity towards violence. One analyst maintains that FYROM is both post-conflict and possibly pre-conflict, given the continuing tensions, the continued existence of Albanian splinter paramilitary groups (the NLA having agreed to disband) and the proliferation of small arms.[81] Other underlying factors of instability include the erosion and collapse of the industrial sector, rural underdevelopment, economic weakness and a flagging private sector – further undermining a state that is neither representative in its structure nor equitable in its distribution of public goods and services.

SSR in FYROM faces the fundamental challenge of improving the efficiency of the security structures in carrying out their basic tasks – both in peace and in conflict. The 2001 crisis revealed confusion regarding the legal authority of key governmental actors over security institutions. A strategic defence review has been under way in FYROM, with adoption by the parliament expected in the spring of 2004. It includes plans for the army to be fully professionalised by 2008, with appropriate representation of ethnic communities, while other reforms (including the modernisation of equipment and downsizing) were initiated ahead of the Istanbul NATO Summit. A total of €14 million is to be spent on modernisation in 2004 and some €16 million in 2005.[82] FYROM will downsize its army of 60,000, including 45,000 reservists, to about 8,300, including a Defence Ministry staff of about 500 employees.[83] The armed forces will be restructured to create a small, efficient and modern force compatible with NATO and EU rapid reaction forces. The review also redefines the role of the Army of the Republic of Macedonia (ARM), which will relinquish control of the borders to the border police after 2005. A limited ARM counter-insurgency capability will be developed now that ethnic Albanian opposition to ARM support for the police during security operations has been removed. In this context Albanian politicians successfully insisted, however, that a specific mechanism for defining and authorising army support in police operations should be developed.[84]

More problematic is the reform of policing in FYROM. The relations between police and the ethnic Albanian community have been particularly troubled. Policing is highly centralised and, before the Ohrid Agreement, it was highly unrepresentative of the population. Mistrust of ethnic Albanians within the Ministry of the Interior is a continuing problem, despite recent efforts to increase Albanian representation in the police and the ministry. Ethnic Macedonian dominance in the police, taken together with underlying ethnic tensions and Albanian distrust of state authority, has made the public security sector a flashpoint for inter-ethnic conflict. In the past, provocative police actions, especially those of the special force of 'Lions' under former Interior Minister Ljube Boskovski, raised the possibility of armed confrontations with ethnic Albanians.

The international community has paid considerable attention to monitoring police and guiding police reform in FYROM since the conclusion of the Ohrid Agreement. The OSCE in particular has played a major role in police monitoring, introducing community policing and providing training and support for multi-ethnic units.[85] This has helped FYROM to achieve the benchmarks set out in the Ohrid Agreement for recruitment of more ethnic Albanians and the spread of multi-ethnic policing in former conflict zones. However, the performance of the police in FYROM is still deficient, notably in terms of their operational effectiveness.[86] Further reforms are needed in the direction of decentralisation of policing and strengthening civilian oversight of police. Moreover, the police have been repeatedly accused of ill-treatment, including indiscriminate arrests and even torture. According to Amnesty International, prosecution of accused police officers on these grounds is 'almost negligible', and most of the cases referred to the Ministry of the Interior by the Ombudsman's Office have been dismissed.[87] The Council of Europe's Committee for the Prevention of Torture and Inhuman or Degrading Treatment or Punishment found in a report based on a visit in 2001 that physical ill-treatment of detainees is a serious problem and that there is no guarantee that an investigation will be carried out.[88]

While ethnic Albanians may be slowly making progress in the police through targeted programmes of recruitment and training, elements within the Interior Ministry and secret police continue to exhibit anti-Albanian sentiments.[89] There is a need for ethnic Macedonians to 'share more state privileges in exchange for greater acceptance by ethnic Albanians of the state's integrity and authority'.[90] Albanians for their part have traditionally not had confidence in state institutions, and efforts must be made to engender greater respect among them for state institutions and state authority – in terms not only of policing, but also of accepting other public services and responsibilities, such as paying taxes.

Serbia and Montenegro

The State Union of Serbia and Montenegro is still struggling to find its path after more than a decade of conflict, defeat, sanctions, international condemnation and isolation. The electoral defeat and ousting of President Milosevic in October 2000 raised hopes for democratisation, but tensions within the successor government and the uncertainty surrounding the constitutional nature of the Yugoslav federation caused reform to stall by late 2002. After the assassination on 12 March 2003 of Serbia's reformist Prime Minister Zoran Djindjic, it appeared that the Serbian Government would finally be galvanised to act against the threat posed by the forces of organised crime, corruption and uncontrolled paramilitaries and their links with politics, business and the security forces. Under a state of emergency, which lasted until 22 April 2003, the government made mass arrests of organised criminals in

Operation Sword. During this period the Serbian police interrogated more than 11,000 criminal suspects, detained 2,700 and indicted almost 4,000 for crimes.[91] However, the crime sweep failed to reach the financial underpinnings of the numerous criminal organisations, many of which have built up legitimate and influential businesses. The government appeared unable to overcome strong obstructionist forces within the armed forces, the police and security services or in its own ranks.[92]

A series of elections over the past two years suggested the resurgence of militant nationalism in Serbia and Montenegro, explanations of this focused on resentment against international demands and the underlying problems of poverty and corruption. Some thirty per cent of the population live below the poverty level, and the country appears to be sliding even further into economic recession.[93] During the parliamentary elections of 28 December 2003, the extreme nationalist Serbian Radical Party of Vojislav Seselj, currently in custody at The Hague for alleged war crimes, received nearly twenty-eight per cent of the votes and almost one-third of the 250 seats in government, followed by Vojislav Kostunica's moderately nationalist Democratic Party of Serbia. The country was left in political stalemate for several months as the main pro-democracy parties bickered over the formation of a government. The new government was finally appointed on 3 March 2004, headed by Prime Minister Kostunica, but this was short-lived as yet another set of elections was forced. Boris Tadic, leader of the pro-Western Democratic Party who enjoys international support, won the 27 June 2004 Serbian presidential elections. Observers are hopeful that Kostunica, who backed Tadic in the last rounds of the election and has again become Prime Minister, will now persist with reforms.

Defence reform in post-Milosevic Serbia and Montenegro was largely paralysed by lingering constitutional uncertainty and opposition to reform by the Milosevic-era military leadership, notably the Yugoslav Army Chief of General Staff and Milosevic appointee General Nebojsa Pavkovic, whom former federal President Kostunica resisted removing until 2002.[94] Constitutional ambiguity was lessened somewhat with the establishment of the new constitutional Charter on the State Union of Serbia and Montenegro, which formally replaced the Yugoslav Army with the Army of Serbia and Montenegro. After Pavkovic's departure the general staff remained a largely autonomous structure until May 2003, when it was placed under the direct command of the Ministry of Defence in an effort to strengthen civilian control over the military.

A number of key documents are now being revised, including, at the federal level, a new version of the Defence Strategy, completed at the end of February 2004;[95] a revised Military Doctrine; and a White Paper on defence sector reform, due in the spring of 2004. National security strategies are also expected to be developed and adopted by the republic parliaments.[96]

Serbia and Montenegro has focused its efforts on membership of the PFP, with unfulfilled hopes for admission at the NATO Istanbul Summit, due in part to the continuing failure to extradite Bosnian Serb military leader Ratko Mladic to the Hague Tribunal. Eventual membership of the EU and NATO is a longer-term foreign policy objective that has an increasing impact on SSR.[97] Democratic civilian control of the armed forces has also become a declared priority. However, momentum stalled with the delay of new defence legislation, and problems remain with the ambiguous constitutional situation, inadequate funding and lack of political consensus.

The loose state union between Serbia and Montenegro provides a special factor of uncertainty. The Agreement on the Union of Serbia and Montenegro of March 2002 transformed the state into a union of two semi-independent entities, with common foreign and defence policies and a federal presidency, but separate economic systems, currencies and customs services.[98] However, both republics are entitled to review the status of the federation within three years and hold the option of withdrawing from the arrangement. Federal institutions are fragile, given the retention of sovereign rule by each republic over its own territory. Moreover, neither the Serbian nor the Montenegrin public wanted to have a state union. It came about after heavy pressure by the EU, which strongly opposed independence for Montenegro on the grounds that it could encourage other independence-minded groups in the region (Kosovo and FYROM), triggering further violence and forcing the international community to deal with Kosovo's status prematurely.[99]

EU pressure has thus created an essentially artificial arrangement between two mismatched republics[100] that lacks popular legitimacy and leaves their relationship unclear. So long as Kosovo's final status remains unresolved, the constitutional composition of Serbia, and hence of the State Union of Serbia and Montenegro, will be uncertain. Support within Montenegro for independence remains high and was strengthened with the resurgence of nationalist parties in recent Serbian elections. There is growing domestic and international criticism of the EU's opposition to Montenegrin independence.[101]

Montenegro shares the serious problems of corruption and organised crime that are typical of the Western Balkans and needs to implement reforms of its criminal justice system. While Djukanovic and the Montenegrin government have taken steps to shut down smuggling rackets and stop other illicit activities, there is still much to be achieved. Criminal justice reforms need to aim at an independent judiciary and at reforming the corrupt, ineffective, highly centralised and politicised police, which has changed minimally in organisation, structure and command since the early 1990s.[102]

In summary, despite some progress in its relations with NATO and the EU, the continuation of security sector reforms in Serbia and Montenegro had been thrown in doubt even before the open violence in Kosovo in March 2004 by such factors as the internal political struggles among members of the new ruling coalition, the worsening economic situation, a hardening in the stance of the former government towards the ICTY, and Belgrade's deteriorating relations with the West. With the leadership of President Tadic in Serbia, there are strong hopes for the resumption of international cooperation and continuation of security sector reform.

Kosovo

The Serbian province of Kosovo has remained under UN control as an international protectorate since June 1999, after the NATO bombing operation ended the 1998–99 crackdown by Serbian-led forces against ethnic Albanian guerrillas of the Kosovo Liberation Army (KLA) seeking independence for the province. The governing framework in Kosovo is UN Security Council Resolution 1244, under which NATO troops were to provide a stable and secure environment for the people of Kosovo.[103] The United Nations Interim Administration Mission in Kosovo (UNMIK) has cooperated closely with the NATO-led KFOR to achieve this goal, including the demilitarisation and demobilisation of the KLA.

Kosovo's unresolved legal status affects security throughout the region. The province's majority, the ethnic Albanians, favour independence, while the minority Serbs and the authorities in Belgrade insist that the territory remain within Serbia or be separated in the same manner as Bosnia and Herzegovina into entities, including the creation of an entity called the Serb Republic. The previous Special Representative of the UN Secretary-General, Michael Steiner, identified eight goals or standards that must be met by Kosovo's authorities in order for the gradual transfer of competence and responsibility to the provisional Kosovar institutions to take place.[104] They include functioning democratic institutions, enforcement of the rule of law, freedom of movement, the return and reintegration of all inhabitants of Kosovo, development of a market economy, full property rights for all citizens, dialogue and normalised relations with Belgrade, and reduction and transformation of the Kosovo Protection Corps (KPC) in accordance with its mandate.[105] The eight benchmarks were reaffirmed and set out in more detail in late 2003 by former Special Representative, Harri Holkeri,[106] and have been backed by the nations of the informal Contact Group for the Western Balkans (France, Germany, Italy, Russia, the UK and the US). These nations have confirmed that the fulfilment of the eight targets is a prerequisite for the international community's efforts to address the legal status of Kosovo, possibly in mid-2005.[107]

The fact that Kosovo remains an international protectorate has significant implications for the process and substance of SSR. Although Kosovo has a president, prime minister and parliament, most decision-making power rests in the hands of UNMIK. In the spring of 2003 Kosovo Prime Minister Bajram Rexhepi attempted to convince the Special Representative to set up ministries to handle the 'reserved' areas, which include defence and foreign affairs. Steiner declined on the grounds that doing so would be in breach of UN Security Council Resolution 1244 and that the Kosovar Albanian authorities had been unable to guarantee the safety of minorities.[108] UNMIK has, however, transferred other specific responsibilities to local provisional institutions (that is the presidency, the government and the Kosovo Assembly) as part of its commitment to gradually introduce self-government in Kosovo under the constitutional framework.

Despite the large international presence, stability in Kosovo is fragile and tensions remain high, with growing incidence of violent crime and attacks against the minority Serb population. According to statistics gathered by the ICTY, 1,192 Serbs were killed, 1,303 kidnapped and 1,305 wounded in Kosovo during 2003,[109] despite the presence of 18,000 KFOR troops and an international police force of more than 4,000. Ethnic Albanian paramilitaries were seen as the primary perpetrators of these attacks, although relatively few people have been investigated and prosecuted. Organised crime groups and paramilitary groups oversee smuggling through the region which, according to Interpol, functions as a transit route for more than eighty per cent of the heroin that flows to Western Europe.[110] It is estimated that 330,000–460,000 illegal weapons, mostly small firearms, are in the hands of civilians in Kosovo.[111]

The Albanian National Army (ANA) emerged in mid-2002 as a militant ethnic Albanian organisation committed to the cause of a 'Greater Albania'. The ANA has claimed responsibility for a number of attacks not only in Kosovo, but also in FYROM and other parts of Serbia. The ANA was outlawed as a 'terrorist organisation', and in April 2003 UNMIK's former chief Michael Steiner made it a crime to be a member of the ANA in Kosovo, after the ANA claimed responsibility for a bomb attack on a railway in a Serb area.[112]

The complicated issues involved in Kosovo's SSR are demonstrated by the experience of the KPC, an unarmed civil protection force responsible for disaster relief, search-and-rescue operations, de-mining and humanitarian assistance, and post-war reconstruction. Ostensibly civilian, uniformed and multi-ethnic, the establishment of KPC was linked directly to the demobilisation of former UCK members, who were offered membership of the KPC on a privileged basis.[113] Of the more than 3,000 full-time members and 2,000 reservists of the KPC, only 131 are not ethnic Albanians and only thirty-one of these are Serbs. The KPC has retained a quasi-military structure, some of its members have been implicated in numerous bombings and confrontations with Serbs and have links to extremist Albanian groups, including the ANA. Many ethnic Albanians, as well as the majority of its own members and the authorities in Belgrade, tend to see the KPC as the de facto army of Kosovo,[114] and its excessive size has bolstered this perception (5,000 active members before it moved to its present strength at UN insistence). An investigatory committee was launched in the spring of 2003 by UNMIK and KFOR to determine whether members of the KPC are involved in the activities of banned extremist organisations.[115] Based on evidence of illegal activities produced in an inquiry into the April 2003 bombing of a railway, Special Representative Holkeri suspended two generals and ten officers in the KPC in December. However, Commander-General of the KPC Agim Ceku, who was a former chief of staff of the UCK, stated that he would ignore the decision.[116]

Many analysts maintain that the absence of a final decision regarding Kosovo's political status feeds the continuing serious threats to public security, the inter-ethnic violence and the emergence of isolated ethnic enclaves. At the same time, the international community has begun a parallel process of disengagement from Kosovo and Bosnia and Herzegovina. The number of NATO troops serving in both regions is planned to be reduced by November 2004 by nearly half from 30,500 to 17,500.[117] Meanwhile, UNMIK and international peacekeepers have increasingly become targets of bombs and explosive devices in Kosovo. In part this is due to local reactions to the role of international police in carrying out arrests of individuals indicted for war crimes[118] (a particularly sensitive issue in Kosovo, where many ethnic Albanians regard the UCK guerrillas as heroes in a war of national liberation). However, it also reflects ethnic Albanian frustration with the UN's insistence on 'standards before status' and the ethnic Serbs' belief that the UN cannot or will not protect them.[119]

Law enforcement is the responsibility of UNMIK through the deployment of an international civil police force and through the recruitment and training of a domestic police force, the Kosovo Police Service (KPS), to which responsibility should progressively be transferred. The KPS has been designed as an apolitical, multi-ethnic civil police organisation with a strength of about 5,185 officers. KPS recruits are trained in the new KPS School (KPSS), run by the OSCE Department of Police Education and Development.[120] As many as half of the recruits, who undergo a vetting procedure, are drawn from demobilised former UCK members. While the KPSS has processed nearly 5,000 new recruits, the fast pace of training (250 graduate every four to five weeks) makes it impractical for UNMIK personnel to provide adequate field training for the graduates.[121]

Conclusion

The complexity of the challenge of transforming security institutions is illuminated by the differences between post-socialist transformation in Central Europe and post-conflict reconstruction in South-Eastern Europe. The experience of recent armed conflict, ethnic cleansing, ethnicisation of security structures and delayed transition bring special challenges for SSR in the latter region. Transformation towards democratic political systems and market economies faces higher and more numerous obstacles than in Central Europe, a challenge sometimes made even more complicated by the plethora of international actors, forms of leverage and programmes of assistance on offer. This chapter draws a picture of the states in the Western Balkans engaged in the activity of nation-building and post-war reconstruction of their fractured states and societies. On one hand they are not yet vibrant democracies, on the other they are not experiencing armed conflict and ethnic cleansing, as was the case a few years ago.

The exceptionally high degree of commitment and engagement by Western donors to this region, and above all the acknowledgement that these states will eventually form part of the EU, has been the main driver of peace building and reform, including SSR. In the absence of a widespread domestic consensus, the sustainability of SSR relies on the leverage that the EU and NATO can bring to bear. The international community's role, however, is ambivalent, not only because it is inclined or obliged to push reforms not fully willed or even understood by the local populations, but also because it is motivated in large part by its own security concerns regarding a region so close to Europe's heartland. Security sector reform in the Western Balkans, then, is not so much the consensual product of a rational process of self-evaluation by national political elites as it is an instrument to serve the interests of external actors and agendas. Its economic base is correspondingly contingent and non-self-sustaining, and in the event of 'donor fatigue' – which may now be a danger, *inter alia* because of competing demands from Afghanistan and Iraq – the maintenance even of the progress made so far becomes moot. It remains to be seen how the shock of renewed violence in Kosovo in March 2004 will affect this equation.

The case of the Western Balkans illustrates particularly well the need for security to be analysed and approached in a broader regional framework. The unsettled final status of Kosovo, notably, provides a potential source of instability for FYROM and the region. A regional dynamic has increasingly been factored into SSR approaches, most notably through the regional programmes of the Stability Pact for South-Eastern Europe to combat organised crime, trafficking and smuggling, and small arms proliferation, and the emphasis of the EU's SAP on regional cooperation between police and judiciaries in the same areas. These approaches have, however, been criticised by certain actors in the region because they implicitly hold each state's progress, in the eyes of EU and NATO, hostage to the willingness of its neighbours to cooperate – in a way that hardly applied in Central Europe.[122] Local states such as Slovenia in the past, and now Croatia and FYROM, have preferred to pursue Western integration on the basis of individual initiatives, rather than as part of the stigmatised 'Balkans'.

Moreover, despite the progress made by the Stability Pact for South Eastern Europe and other strategic approaches, there is still a significant lack of coordination among international actors involved in SSR, especially within individual target states.[123] A degree of competition no doubt contributes to this, and things are made no better by host states which fail to coordinate international assistance to optimal effect.[124] The Stability Pact has also been criticised for competing with and duplicating other efforts by the EU, providing a disincentive for regular EU funding of such projects.[125]

The experience of the Western Balkans also demonstrates that the building and reforming of institutions, which is a core part of SSR, cannot be separated from politics and political settlements. In two instances – the Dayton Peace Agreement in Bosnia and Herzegovina and the Ohrid Framework Agreement in FYROM – the international community used the conclusion of cease-fire agreements to introduce SSR as a priority area for follow-up. Those agreements continue to influence the situation on the ground, not only in terms of regulating relations among formerly warring parties, but also in the institutional and procedural frameworks that govern future developments. The case of Bosnia and Herzegovina also underlines how ethnic and political divisions within the state can frustrate the normative as well as the practical objectives of SSR. If the legitimacy of a state rests on its capacity to provide public goods – security included – to its citizens, it is not surprising that the fragmentation of security in Bosnia and Herzegovina poses a barrier to development of the central authority.

How can local ownership of SSR be cultivated in countries where the international community has played the lead role in initiating reform? Political scientists from the Balkan states have noted the disconnection that exists between their reformist political elites and citizens. The latter, typically less interested in NATO or EU membership, are frustrated with the functioning of their political systems and dismayed by the lowered standards of living and high rates of unemployment, corruption and personal insecurity. In the view of Ivan Krastev, the main risk facing the Balkan countries today is the 'slow death of democracy' or 'the erosion and de-legitimisation of democratic regimes in the institutional framework of democracy itself'.[126] The democratic deficit that has been diagnosed in the integration policies of the current member states of the European Union and now Central European accession states[127] is even more visible in the Western Balkans. The international community must learn that establishing sound and accountable security institutions constitutes part of a wider process of democratisation and that coercing reforms from the leaders of disillusioned and disenfranchised publics will ultimately undermine the political basis for programmes of democratic reform. The challenge of security sector reform in post-conflict societies such as those of the Western Balkans is not only to identify suitable policy content, but also to ensure that the political process by which it is developed, implemented and sold to key stakeholders and the public is one that strengthens democracy itself.

Notes

[1]   'The Western Balkans' is the term which the European Union has used since 1999 to refer to those countries of South-Eastern Europe which are not yet EU members and have not yet received a specific commitment or date for future membership, but which enjoy a credible prospect of membership once political stability in the countries is restored. The region consists of Albania and four successor states of the former Yugoslavia—Bosnia and Herzegovina, Croatia, the Former Yugoslav Republic of Macedonia, and Serbia and Montenegro, including the international protectorate of Kosovo, a province of the Republic of Serbia. Slovenia is not included, as it has joined the European Union (May 2004) and the North Atlantic Treaty Organisation (March 2004).

[2]   The term 'security sector reform' includes the reform of defence policies and forces as well as the reform of other actors in internal security, both governmental and non-governmental, for purposes of efficiency and good governance. See Hendrickson, D. and Karkoszka, A., 'The challenges of security sector reform', *SIPRI Yearbook 2002: Armaments, Disarmament and International Security* (Oxford University Press: Oxford, 2002), pp. 175–201; and Caparini, M., 'Security sector reform and NATO and EU enlargement', *SIPRI Yearbook 2003: Armaments, Disarmament and International Security* (Oxford University Press: Oxford, 2003), pp. 237–60.

[3]   Commission of the European Communities, 'The EU's actions in support to the Stabilisation & Association Process', available at
<http://europa.eu.int/comm/external_relations/see/actions/sap.htm>.

[4]   The FYROM Government submitted its formal application for EU membership on 22 March 2004. Croatia submitted an application for full EU membership in February 2003 and received candidate status on 18 June 2004, marking the onset of negotiations for full membership.

[5]   For the status of each South-East European country's relations with the EU see URL <http://www.seerecon.org/gen/eu-see.htm>. Seselj has been indicted by the ICTY; see 'Vojislav Seselj indicted by the ICTY for crimes against humanity and war crimes', ICTY press release, The Hague, 14 Feb. 2003, available at
<http://www.un.org/icty/pressreal/2003/p728-e.htm>.

[6]   For details of the 2002–2006 CARDS programme see
<http://europa.eu.it/comm/external_relations/see/docs/cards/sp02_06.pdf>.

[7]   Council of the European Union, 'Joint Conclusions', EU–Western Balkans Forum, JHA Ministerial Meeting, Brussels, 28 Nov. 2003, SN 3559/1/03, REV 1, available at <http://www.ueitalia2003.it/NR/rdonlyres/3F0A32BC-C573-4553-8EB7-08ABA8C60CDA/0/1128_JHA_Balkans_jconcl_EN.pdf>.

[8]   For the convention and its protocols, as well as the signatories and parties, see <http://www.pfc.org.uk/legal/echrtext.htm>.

[9]   For the Council of Europe Code of Police Ethics see <http://www.iocoe.org.mk/>.

[10]   Commission of the European Communities, 'Report from the Commission: The Stabilisation and Association process for South East Europe, Third Annual Report', COM(2004)202/2 final, Brussels, 30 Mar. 2004, pp. 20–21, available at <http://europa.eu.int/comm/external_relations/see/sap/rep3/index.htm>.

[11] On the Copenhagen criteria, agreed at the 1993 Copenhagen European Council, see European Commission, 'EU enlargement: a historic opportunity', available at <http://europa.eu.int/comm/enlargement/intro/criteria.htm>.

[12] This is explained in relation to the Central European states in Caparini, 'Security sector reform and NATO and EU enlargement'.

[13] On 1 July 2003 the US suspended $46 million in military assistance to thirty-five states that had signed the ICC Statute, but had not concluded BIAs. Among them were most of the South-East European states: Bulgaria, Croatia, Serbia and Montenegro, Slovakia and Slovenia. A temporary waiver was extended to twenty-two states, including Albania, Bosnia and Herzegovina, FYROM and Romania. Coalition for the International Criminal Court, 'Questions & answers: US Bilateral Immunity or so-called "Article 98" Agreements', Fact Sheet, 30 Sep. 2003, available at <http://www.iccnow.org/pressroom/factsheets/FS-BIAsSept2003.pdf>.

[14] Commission of the European Communities, 'EU and NATO concerted approach for the Western Balkans', Council of Ministers Press Release PRES 03/218, 29 July 2003.

[15] Hagelin, B., Perlo-Freeman, S. and Wezeman, P. D., 'Military spending, armament and arms transfers, eds I. Gyarmati and S. Vesel, *Security Sector Governance in the Western Balkans 2003–2004* (Nomos: Baden-Baden, 2004).

[16] See Dziedzic, M. and Bair, A., 'Bosnia and the International Police Task Force', eds. R. Oakley, M. Dziedzic and E. Goldberg, *Policing in the New World Disorder: Peace Operations and Public Security* (Institute for National Strategic Studies, National Defense University: Washington, DC, 1998), available at <http://www.ndu.edu/inss/books/Books%20%201998/Policing%20the%20New%20World%20Disorder%20-%20May%2098/chapter8.html>; and Partos, G., 'Serbia's "elite" enemy within', BBC News Online, 26 Mar. 2003, available at <http://news.bbc.co.uk/1/hi/world/europe/2888943.stm>; and Ivkovic, S. K., 'Distinct and different: the transformation of the Croatian police', eds. M. Caparini and O. Marenin, *Transforming Police in Central and Eastern Europe: Process and Progress* (LIT: Münster, 2004).

[17] European Commission, External Relations, 'CARDS Regional Strategy Paper 2002–2006', adopted 22 Oct. 2001, p. 8. URL <http://europa.eu.int/comm/external_relations/see/news/ip01_1464.htm>.

[18] On the Stability Pact, established by the EU and subsequently put under the auspices of the OSCE, see URL <http://www.stabilitypact.org/>. See also NATO, *Common Platform of the Ohrid Regional Conference on Border Security and Management*, 22–23 May 2003, available at <http://www.nato.int/docu/conf/2003/030522_ohrid/c030522a.htm>.

[19] Greco, E., 'New trends in peace-keeping: Operation Alba', *Security Dialogue*, vol. 29 (June 1998), pp. 201–12. Operation Alba was mandated by UN Security Council Resolution 1101, 28 Mar. 1997.

[20] Cili, H., 'Security and defence: civil society and the media', eds J. Trapans and P. Fluri, *Defence and Security Sector Governance and Reform in South-East Europe: Insights and Perspectives, A Self-Assessment Study*, vol. 1, *Albania, Bulgaria, Croatia* (Geneva Centre for the Democratic Control of Armed Forces (DCAF): Geneva and Belgrade, 2003), p. 119.

21 Bumci, A., 'Overview of security sector reform in Albania', eds. Trapans and Fluri, *Defence and Security Sector*, p. 25.

22 Gumi, V., 'Parliament and the security sector', eds. Trapans and Fluri, *Defence and Security Sector*, pp. 60–61.

23 Kajsiu, B., 'Transparency and accountability in governance', eds. Trapans and Fluri, *Defence and Security Sector*, pp. 111–14.

24 Bumci 'Overview of security', p. 25.

25 International Organisation for Migration (IOM), 'II Research Report on Third Country National Trafficking Victims in Albania', June 2002, p. 4, available at <www.icmc.net/files/traffalb.en.pdf>.

26 Human Rights Watch, 'Human rights overview: Albania', January 2004, available at <http://hrw.org/english/docs/2003/12/31/albani7270.htm>.

27 US Department of State, 'Albania: country reports on human rights practices – 2002', 31 Mar. 2003, available at <http://www.state.gov/g/drl/rls/hrrpt/2002/18349pf.htm>.

28 OSCE, 'OSCE-facilitated agreement on witness protection signed today in Albania', Press Release, 17 June 2003, available at <http://www.hrea.org/lists/hr-legal-professionals/markup/msg00091.html>. See also OSCE, 'Report to the Permanent Council', Ambassador Osmo Lipponen, Head of OSCE Presence in Albania, 26 February 2004.

29 OSCE Presence in Albania, 'Legal sector report for Albania', 2004, p. 47, available at <http://www.osce.org/albania/documents/reports/>.

30 European Commission , *Albania: Stabilisation and Association Report*, Commission Staff Working Paper, COM (2003) 139 final, 26 March 2003, p. 1, available at <http://europa.eu.int/comm/external_relations/see/sap/rep2/com03_339.htm>.

31 The WEU-led Multinational Advisory Police Element (MAPE) operated in Albania in 1997–2001. An EC Police Assistance (ECPA) project was set up in 2001 to ensure continuity until the Police Assistance Mission of the European Commission (PAMECA) was established in December 2002. See <http://www.mpo.gov.al/PAMECA/Background.htm>.

32 US Department of State, *Victims of Trafficking and Violence Protection Act of 2000: Trafficking in Persons Report*, June 2003, available at <http://www.state.gov/g/tip/rls/tiprpt/2003/>.

33 Human Rights Watch Report, vol. 14, no. 9(D), Nov. 2002, available at <http://www.hrw.org/reports/2002/bosnia/>; Comité européen pour la prévention de la torture et des peines ou traitements inhumains ou dégradants, 'Rapport au Gouvernement de l'Albanie relatif à la visite effectuée en Albanie par le Comité européen pour la prévention de la torture et des peines ou traitements inhumains ou dégradants du 22 au 26 octobre 2001' [Report to the Government of Albania by the European Committee for the Prevention of Torture and Inhuman or Degrading Punishment (CPT) on its visit to Albania from 22 to 26 October 2001], 2003, available at <http://www.cpt.coe.int/documents/alb/2003-11-inf-fra.htm>. See also US Department of State, *Victims of Trafficking*.

34 European Commissio , *Albania: Stabilisation,* p. 6.

35 Human Rights Watch, *The Cost of Speech: Violations of Media Freedom in Albania,* vol. 14, no. 5 (June 2002).

[36] Agreement on Regional Stabilisation, Annex 1-B of the Dayton Peace Agreement, available at <http://www.ohr.int/dpa/default.asp?content_id=380>.

[37] 'US wraps up military program in Bosnia', *Radio Free Europe/Radio Liberty Newsline – Southeastern Europe*, 31 October 2002.

[38] On the MPRi see <http://www.mpri.com/channels/home.html>.

[39] Orsini, D., 'Security-sector restructuring in Bosnia-Herzegovina', *Conflict, Security & Development*, vol. 3, no. 1 (April 2003), p. 81.

[40] By the end of the war in 1995, the armed forces numbered 430,000 troops. By early 2004 they had been reduced to a total of 21,000 regulars, 12,600 conscripts and 360,000 reserves, with further cuts expected in the future. See 'Developments in South-Eastern Europe', Report of the Assembly of the Western European Union, 49th Session, Submitted by Mr. Hancock, Rapporteur, on behalf of the Political Committee, Document A/1820, 4 June 2003, p. 16.

[41] Hagelin, Perlo-Freeman and Wezeman, 'Military spending, armament'.

[42] The position of the High Representative was created under the Dayton Peace Agreement (note 36) to oversee implementation of the civilian aspects of the agreement on behalf of the international community. The High Representative is responsible for coordinating the activities of civilian organisations and agencies working in Bosnia and Herzegovina. See the OHR Internet site at <http://www.ohr.int/ohr-info/gen-info/>.

[43] 'NATO decision-makers urge Bosnia to reform military', *NATO Update*, 10 April 2003, URL <http://www.nato.int/docu/update/2003/04-april/e0410a.htm>.

[44] Office of the High Representative, 'High Representative acts to ensure that military in BiH are under effective civilian control', 2 April 2003, available at <http://www.ohr.int/ohr-dept/presso/pressr/default.asp?content_id=29614>.

[45] The DRC was made up of representatives of Bosnia and Herzegovina and of SFOR, NATO and the OSCE. The goals of the DRC included central command and control, interoperability, democratic control of the defence budget and democratic oversight of forces. Office of the High Representative, 'Decision establishing the Defense Reform Commission', 9 May 2003, available at <http://www.ohr.int/decisions/statemattersdec/default.asp?content_id=29840>.

[46] *The Path to Partnership for Peace,* Report of the Defence Reform Commission, Bosnia and Herzegovina, Sarajevo, 25 September 2003, available at <http://www.ohr.int/archive/drc-report/pdf/drc-eng.pdf>.

[47] Agence France-Presse, 'International High Representative in Bosnia welcomes defence reform', 26 September 2003.

[48] Agence France-Presse, 'Bosnian leaders agree on central command for armed forces', 26 September 2003.

[49] Prlenda, A., 'Defence reform in BiH enters new phase', *Southeast European Times*, 21 October 2003.

[50] 'International community welcomes adoption of crucial defence law in BiH', *Southeast European Times*, 2 Dec. 2003; and 'Law on Defence of Bosnia and Herzegovina', *Official Gazette of Bosnia and Herzegovina*, vol. 43, no. 3 (29 December 2003).

[51] The Peace Implementation Council (PIC) Steering Board, which adjusted the DRC mandate, is chaired by the High Representative and is composed of representatives of Canada, France, Germany, Italy, Japan, Russia, the UK, the US, the Presidency of the EU, the

European Commission and the Organisation of the Islamic Conference. See 'Communiqué by the PIC Steering Board', 11 December 2003, available at
<http://www.ohr.int/pic/default.asp?content_id=31361>.

52 Office of the High Representative, 'Decision extending the mandate of the Defense Reform Commission', 4 February 2004, available at
<http://www.ohr.int/decisions/statemattersdec/default.asp?content_id=31761>.

53 The decision has yet to be formally endorsed by the state presidency. Sito-Sucic, D., 'Bosnia to slash military to boost NATO ties', Reuters AlertNet, 3 February 2004.

54 Kaldor, M., 'Security structures in Bosnia and Herzegovina', eds. G. Cawthra and R. Luckham, *Governing Insecurity: Democratic Control of Military and Security Establishments in Transitional Democracies* (Zed Books: London and New York, 2003), p. 221.

55 Associated Press, 'Bosnian Serb President closes spy agency', 15 April 2003, available at
<http://www.balkanpeace.org/hed/archive/apr03/hed5645.shtml>.

56 Traynor, I., 'Bosnia's arms to Iraq scandal claims top political scalp', *Guardian Unlimited, Special Report: Serbia,* 3 April 2003, available at
<http://www.guardian.co.uk/serbia/article/0,2479,928400,00.html>.

57 Office of the High Representative, 'Decision establishing the Expert Commission on Intelligence Reform', 30 May 2003, available at
<http://www.ohr.int/decisions/statemattersdec/default.asp?content_id=29988>.

58 Office of the High Representative, 'Decision proposing the Law on the Intelligence and Security Agency of BiH to the Parliamentary Assembly of BiH', 17 December 2003, available at
<http://www.ohr.int/decisions/statemattersdec/default.asp?content_id=31403>.

59 Assembly of Western European Union, 'Developments in South-Eastern Europe', WEU document A/1820, 4 June 2003, available at
<http://assembly-weu.itnetwork.fr/en/documents/sessions_ordinaires/rpt/2003/1820.html>

60 Palmer, L. K., 'Police reforms in Bosnia-Herzegovina: external pressure and internal resistance', eds. Caparini and Marenin, *Transforming Police in Central* , p. 179.

61 Office of the High Representative, 'Speech by the High Representative for BiH Paddy Ashdown at the United Nations Security Council', 3 March 2004, available at
<http://www.ohr.int/ohr-dept/presso/pressr/default.asp?content_id=31948>.

62 Transparency International (TI), 'TI: Corruption, bribery drop in Bosnian Federation, rise in Serb entity', BBC Monitoring Service, 11 March 2004, in *TI Daily Corruption News,* 12 March 2004.

63 US Department of State, 'Bosnia and Herzegovina: Country Reports on Human Rights Practices – 2003', 25 February 2004.

64 Orsini, D., 'Case study: EUPM in Bosnia and Herzegovina', International Alert and Saferworld, in association with the European Peacebuilding Liaison Office, *Strengthening Global Security Through Addressing the Root Causes of Conflict: Priorities for the Irish and Dutch Presidencies in 2004* (Saferworld and International Alert: London, February 2004), p. 11.

65 For similar tendencies see Chandler, D., 'Anti-corruption strategies and democratization in Bosnia-Herzegovina', *Democratization,* vol. 9, no. 2 (summer 2002), p. 117.

66 Vesel, S., 'Security sector reform in Croatia: summary of self-assessment studies', eds E. Cole, T. Donais and P. Fluri, *Defence and Security Sector Governance and Reform in*

South East Europe: Self-Assessment Studies – Regional Perspectives, vol. 3, *Comparative Perspectives* (Nomos: Baden-Baden, forthcoming 2004).

[67] Stanicic, M., 'Security sector reform in Croatia', eds. Gyarmati and Vesel, *Security Sector Governance in the Western Balkans 2003–2004.*

[68] Zunec, O., 'Democratic oversight and control over intelligence and security agencies', eds Trapans and Fluri , *Defence and Security Sector,* pp. 384–85.

[69] Zunec, ' Democratic oversight', p. 396.

[70] Zunec, ' Democratic oversight', p. 397.

[71] Edmunds, T., *Defence Reform in Croatia and Serbia-Montenegro,* Adelphi Paper 360, International Institute for Strategic Studies (Oxford University Press: Oxford, 2003), p. 9.

[72] Stanicic, M., 'Croatia, SEE Self-Assessment Study', eds Trapans and Fluri, *Defence and Security Sector.*

[73] NATO Parliamentary Assembly, Sub-committee on Future Security and Defence Capabilities, 'Mission Report on visit to Croatia, 2–4 March 2004', available at <http://www.naa.be/default.asp?TAB=470>.

[74] Stanicic 'Security sector reform in Croatia'.

[75] Ivkovic, 'Distinct and different: the transformation'.

[76] European Commission, 'Croatia: Stabilisation and Association Report 2003', COM(2003) 139 final, Brussels, 26 March 2003, p. 7.

[77] European Commission,. 'Croatia: Stabilisation', pp. 6–7.

[78] For the Ohrid Framework Agreement, 13 August 2001, see <http://www.president.gov.mk/eng/info/dogovor.htm>.

[79] See Dwan, R. and Lachowski, L., 'The military and security dimensions of the European Union', *SIPRI Yearbook 2003*, pp. 213–36.

[80] Dempsey, J., 'EU to beef up police training in the Balkans', *Financial Times,* 8 August 2003, p. 6.

[81] Vankovska, B., *Current Perspectives on Macedonia,* Part IV, 'Problems and prospects of security sector reform: conflict prevention and/or post-conflict reconstruction in Macedonia', 2003, p. 7, URL <http://www.boell.de/downloads/konflikt/vankovska_pt4.pdf>.

[82] 'Macedonian leaders review progress of army reform, relations with NATO', MIA News Agency (Skopje), in English, 2 February 2004, *Global News Wire – Asia Africa Intelligence Wire, BBC Monitoring International Reports,* 2 February 2004.

[83] 'Macedonian Army, Defence Ministry, to employ 8,300 after downsizing', *Urinski Vesnik* (Skopje), (in Macedonian), 19 Jan. 2004, *Global News Wire – Asia Africa Intelligence Wire, BBC Monitoring International Reports,* 22 January 2004.

[84] 'Macedonian Government to define scope for future army intervention', *Lobi* (Skopje), (in Albanian), 28 October 2003, *BBC Monitoring Europe – Political, BBC Worldwide Monitoring,* 29 October 2003.

[85] See OSCE, Police Development Unit, 'OSCE Spillover Monitor Mission to Skopje', available at <http://www.osce.org/skopje/pdu>.

[86] International Crisis Group (ICG), *Macedonia: No Room for Complacency,* ICG Europe Report no. 149 (23 October 2003), p. 4.

[87] Amnesty International (AI), 'Continuing failure by the Macedonian authorities to confront police ill-treatment and torture', AI Index EUR 65/008/2003, 1 June 2003, available at <http://web.amnesty.org/library/print/ENGEUR650082003>.

[88] On this committee see <http://www.cpt.coe.int/en/>. See also 'Council of Europe Anti-Torture Committee publishes reports on "the former Yugoslav Republic of Macedonia"', Press Release, 16 January 2003. The report and press release are available at <http://www.cpt.coe.int/en/states/mkd.htm>.

[89] ICG *Macedonia: No Room,* p. 5.

[90] ICG *Macedonia: No Room,* p. 7.

[91] Matic, V., *Serbia After Djindjic: Can Invigorated Reforms be Sustained?* (Public International Law & Policy Group: Boston, Mass., October 2003), pp. 3–4.

[92] International Crisis Group (ICG), *Serbian Reform Stalls Again,* ICG Balkans Report no. 145, 17 July 2003.

[93] 'Experts say nearly one-third of Serbs live below the poverty line', *RFE/RL Newsline – Southeastern Europe,* vol. 8, no. 5 (9 January 2004).

[94] See Edmunds *Defence Reform in Croatia,* pp. 11–12.

[95] Internet site of the Serbian and Montenegrin Armed Forces, News Archive, 25 February 2004, see <http://www.vj.yu/english/en_aktuelno/vesti/februar2004/v0225-e.htm>.

[96] Ministry of Defence of Serbia and Montenegro, 'Defence sector reform in Serbia and Montenegro', Prepared for the Donors Meeting for Serbia and Montenegro, Brussels, 18 November 2003, see <http://www.seerecon.org/serbiamontenegro/documents/su>.

[97] Edmunds, *Defence Reform in Croatia,* p. 50.

[98] 'Serbia and Montenegro in deal to reshape Yugoslavia', *Financial Times,* 14 March 2002.

[99] Hadzic, M., Geneva Centre for the Democratic Control of Armed Forces (DCAF), 'New constitutional position of the army', DCAF Working Paper no. 112 (February 2003), p. 1, available at <http://www.dcaf.ch/publications/Working_Papers/112.pdf>.

[100] Serbia has a population of about 7 million, while Montenegro has 650,000 inhabitants.

[101] International Crisis Group, *A Marriage of Inconvenience: Montenegro 2003,* Balkans Report no. 142 (16 April 2003).

[102] Sevic, Z. and Bakrac, D., 'Police reform in the Republic of Montenegro', eds. Caparini and Marenin, *Transforming Police in Central.*

[103] UN Security Council Resolution 1244, 10 June 1999, available at <http://www.nato.int/kosovo/docu/u990610a.htm>.

[104] 'Address to the Security Council by Michael Steiner, Special Representative of the Secretary-General', UNMIK Press Release PR719, 24 April. 2002, available at <http://www.unmikonline.org/press/2002/pressr/pr719.htm>.

[105] The KPC was established in 1999 as a multi-ethnic civilian emergency organisation. For the issues surrounding it see below in this section; and UN Security Council, Report of the Secretary-General on the United Nations Interim Administration Mission in Kosovo, 26 January 2004, p. 15, available at <http://www.un.org/Depts/dhl/da/kosovo/kosovo3a.htm>.

[106] 'Standards for Kosovo', UNMIK Press Release 1078, 10 December 2003, available at <http://www.unmikonline.org/press/2003/pressr/pr1078.pdf>.

[107] US Department of State, 'The future of Kosovo', Testimony of Deputy Assistant Secretary for South Central Europe Janet Bogue before the House International Relations Committee 21 May 2003; and Agence France-Presse, 'Kosovo given timetable for democratic reform', 10 November 2003.

[108] B92 (Belgrade), 'Steiner: no chance for speedy Kosovo independence', 3 May 2003, available at URL <http://news.serbianunity.net/bydate/2003/May_03/0.html>.

[109] Vincent, I., 'Crime, terror flourish in "liberated" Kosovo', *National Post*, 10 December 2003, p. A1.

[110] Figure provided by Ray Kendall, former Secretary General of Interpol, in Repa, J., 'Europe's drug gangs', BBC News Online, 15 June 2000, available at <http://news.bbc.co.uk/1/hi/world/europe/792290.stm>. See also the statistics in Council of the European Union, 'Draft Action Plan on Drugs Between the EU and Countries of Western Balkans and Candidate Countries (Bulgaria, Romania and Turkey)', document 5062/203 REV 2 COR 1, Brussels, 3 June 2003, available at <http://europa.en.int/comm/external_relations/drugs/docs/wb.pdf>.

[111] Khakhee, A. and Florquin, N., *Kosovo and the Gun: A Baseline Assessment of Small Arms and Light Weapons in Kosovo*, Special Report (Small Arms Survey for the United Nations Development Programme: Geneva, June 2003), p. 2, available at <http://www.smallarmssurvey.org/SReports/Special%20Report%20Kosovo.pdf>.

[112] Agence France-Presse, 'UN official brands Kosovo Albanian group "terrorist" after railway attack', 18 April 2003, available at <http://www.balkanpeace.org/hed/archive/apr03/hed5654.shtml>.

[113] Cockell, J. C., 'Civil–military responses to security challenges in peace operations: ten lessons from Kosovo', *Global Governance*, vol. 8, no. 4 (2002).

[114] Belgrade's Kosovo Coordination Centre urged the Serbs not to join the KPC until its role was clearly limited to that set out in UN Security Council Resolution 1244 and Kosovo's constitutional framework. See B92 (Belgrade), 'Belgrade urges Serbs not to join Protection Corps', 5 May 2003.

[115] See Mustapha, A. and Xharra, J., 'Kosovo officers under investigation', Balkan Crisis Report no. 472 (11 December 2003), available at <http://www.iwpr.net/index.pl?archive/bcr3/bcr3_2003121_472_1_eng.txt>.

[116] Buza, S., 'UN suspension move angers Kosovo ex-guerrillas', Reuters, 4 December 2003, available on the Internet site of Global Policy Forum at <http://www.globalpolicy.org/security/issues/kosovo1/2003/1203suspension.htm>.

[117] Agence France-Press, 'NATO troop numbers to be slashed in Bosnia, Kosovo: France', 14 January 2004, <http://www.balkanpeace.org/hed/archive/jan04/hed6192.shtml>.

[118] Castle, S., 'KLA link suspected in UN police murder', *The Independent*, 6 August 2003, p. 11.

[119] Kirby, M., 'Police defuse bombs near UN Headquarters', *World Markets Analysis* (World Markets Research Centre), 8 March 2004.

[120] On the KPSS see <http://www.osce.org/kosovo/police>.

[121] Cockell, 'Civil–military responses'.

[122] Woodward, S. L., 'In whose interest is security sector reform? lessons from the Balkans', eds. G. Cawthra and R. Luckham, *Governing Insecurity* (Zed Books: London and New York, 2003), p. 297.

[123] The problems include not only material overlaps but also conflicting advice. Edmunds, *Defence Reform in Croatia*, pp. 56–57.

[124] 'Preliminary Gaps Analysis', Project on Security Sector Reform in South Eastern Europe: An Inventory of Initiatives, Centre for International and Security Studies, York University, Canada, available at <http://ssr.yciss.yorku.ca>.

[125] See the comments by Lamers, K., 'Reform Balkans Stability Pact, German politician urges', *Die Welt*, 23 January 2002, available at

    <http://www.setimes.com/html2/english/020201-SVETLA-001.htm>.
126 Krastev, I., *The Inflexibility Trap: Frustrated Societies, Weak States and Democracy*,
    Report on the State of Democracy in the Balkans (National Endowment for Democracy:
    Sofia, May 2002), available at <http://www.ned.org/reports/balkansFeb2002.html>.
127 Zielonka, J., 'Challenges of EU enlargement', Mungiu-Pippidi, A., 'Beyond the new
    borders', Pehe, J., 'Consolidating free government in the new EU', and Rupnik, J., 'Con-
    cluding reflections', *Journal of Democracy*, vol. 15, no. 1 (2004), pp. 22–85. See also
    Schmitter, P. C., 'Democracy in Europe and Europe's democratisation', and Dahrendorf,
    R., 'The challenge for democracy', *Journal of Democracy*, vol. 14, no. 4 (2003), pp. 101–
    14.

Chapter 8

Governing Insecurity in Post-Conflict States: the Case of Sierra Leone and Liberia

J. 'Kayode Fayemi

Introduction

No aspect of institutional design in Africa has proved more difficult, complex and delicate than that of security sector reconstruction in the rebuilding efforts of states emerging from conflict.[1] Although reform of the security sector after war is not new in Africa since the remarkable experience of Nigeria after the civil war in 1970, most of the security sector reform initiatives undertaken have not been transformative because they have been largely *ad-hoc*, accidental *by-products* of broader reform agenda, or reforms by *stealth*. Hence they have had limited success in shifting power relations and entrenching institutional transformation. More importantly, they pose the question as to whether security sector reform really can be institutionally designed.

If there is any opportunity to test the possibility of institutional design in the security sector, post-conflict Sierra Leone and Liberia offer the best examples. The de-institutionalisation and 'informalisation' of the security sector before, during and in the immediate aftermath of conflict provides that space for altering the relations of power within the sector in the direction of civil/constitutional control. It can transform institutional culture, promote professionalism, improve resource utilisation and operational effectiveness (on the side of the security forces), better policy management (on the side of civil authorities), in tandem with accountability and respect for human rights and international law and involving inputs from a wide-range of stakeholders and role-players. Our choice of the two countries is predicated on this.

Yet, the experience of the two countries reviewed in this chapter is a demonstration of the complex nature of security sector reconstruction programmes that attempt to shift relations of power and not just achieve a return to *status quo ante bellum*. In summary, the chapter argues that security sector reconstruction in the aftermath of conflict is often a product of the nature of transition from war to peace. Moreover, that the extent to which the legacies of conflict have been addressed in the post-war settlement, the commitment of primary actors and the peace guarantors, the scope of the reconstruction plan and the regional security context of conflict are crucial. The paper also argues that for security sector reconstruction to be effective and sustainable, it should be part of a multi-dimensional peace-building construct, stretching from humanitarian relief through transitional rehabilitation to long-term development, often requiring a long-term process. In essence, post-conflict security sector reconstruction must possess the ability for immediate disaster and relief operations, as well as addressing comprehensive *nation-building tasks*. However, for this to happen, the paper suggests that it will require a re-orientation of the relationship between the political authority and the citizenry, revisiting relationships between contending forces, creating a political and civil society that is conscious of its role in security sector reform, promoting reconciliation, and reforming economic policies and institutions that foster long-term security and development.

Context of Security Sector Reconstruction in Sierra Leone and Liberia

Four factors are crucial to the understanding of current attempts towards security sector reconstruction in Liberia and Sierra Leone. These are: a) the legacies of conflict and authoritarianism; b) the decomposition of the state security sector and the simultaneous privatisation of violence; c) removal of the erstwhile imperial umbrella in the wake of the collapse of the Cold War and, finally; d) the regionalisation of conflict in West Africa, all of which are inextricably intertwined.

Legacies of Conflict and Authoritarian Rule

Apart from belonging to the Mano River regional security complex, it would at first appear that Liberia and Sierra Leone had followed different trajectories in their journey towards political independence and self-rule. On the one hand, Liberia technically never experienced colonialism having been founded by ex-American slaves of the American Colonisation Society (ACS), whose 'love of liberty' brought them back to the West African coast in 1822. On the other hand, Sierra Leone also established by returnee ex-slaves, this time from Britain had gained independence from the UK in 1961. So, one country had the uniqueness of permanent black rule, especially of Americo-Liberian domination and the other experienced colonial rule.

Yet, this distinction made no difference when looking at the politics of the two countries from the late 1960s. The politics revealed a consistent streak of authoritarian legacies in which state militarism was legitimised by the rule of law, and regime security replaced national security and well-being of the citizens as public goods, all under the veneer of electoral democracy. In Liberia, the William V.S.Tubman (1945-71) and William R.Tolbert (1971-80) regimes turned Liberia into personal fiefdoms. As part of this process, the leadership extensively encouraged a de-institutionalisation of the armed forces – leaving in its wake a disgruntled and unprofessional military apparatus and a population completely disconnected from the ruling elite. By the time Master Sergeant Samuel Kanyon Doe toppled the civilian regime in 1980 with no agenda for societal transformation, the military was further sucked into the vortex of praetorianism and decomposition, and the stage was set for what was to follow in the next two decades.[2]

In Sierra Leone there was a relatively peaceful transition to independence and a post-independence self-rule in 1961 that broadly mirrored the Westminster model of parliamentary democracy. In the first five years, key state institutions such as the Sierra Leone army, police, the judiciary and the civil service functioned with a relatively high degree of independence and professionalism. However, by 1967-8 when the country experienced its first opposition backed coup d'état, the country began its slide into authoritarian and predatory rule. The inception of the radical Socialist All Peoples' Congress (APC) under the leadership of Sir Siaka Stevens in 1968 led the country in the direction of a one-party state, which was declared in 1971. This marked the beginning of oppressive and predatory rule, an increasingly centralised system of government and the concentration of power in the capital.[3] To consolidate the personalised rule, the Siaka Stevens regime deliberately embarked on a state security-weakening project. In 1972, not fully confident of the loyalty of the professional military, Sir Stevens established an alternative power centre in the Internal Security Unit (ISU) and an ISU offshoot, the Special Security Division (SSD). Over the next twenty-four years of

APC rule in Sierra Leone until it was overthrown in a military coup in 1992
(by which time a rebellion had started in the diamond region), the APC pre-
sided over the most systematic de-institutionalisation of the Sierra Leonean
state. This left Sir Steven's successor, General Joseph Momoh with little or
no capacity to confront the rebellion that eventually removed him from office.[4]

Decomposition of Security Institutions and Privatisation of Violence

Although the decomposition of the security institutions was engineered by
the authoritarian legacies of the post-independence autocrats, the economic
stagnation of the 1980s in several West African countries, coupled with the
eventual removal of imperial security umbrellas in the wake of the Cold
War, saw the flowering of people driven to challenge militarisation and authoritarianism. Ironically, given the sharp deterioration in the security environment that had been encouraged by insecure leaders these two processes
were somewhat inextricably intertwined. With the collapse of the Cold War
and the increasing availability and privatisation of the instruments of violence, the stage was set for the transformation of the military balance between state and society. Massive retrenchment and a growing surplus of
military assets globally, simultaneously with a breakdown in supply and
demand side controls on global arms markets and (locally) recycling of de-
commissioned weaponry ended up proliferating West Africa with small arms
and light weapons.

This resulted, for the most part in contradictory phenomena. On the
one hand, the 1990s West Africa benefited from the upsurge in democratisation with the Benin republic leading the way in 1990. On the other hand, the
shift from coups to democratic change was also accompanied by a shift to
ill-defined conflicts which encouraged new forms of violent national and
transnational conflicts, promoted the psychology of militarism, implanted a
culture of violence, and discouraged peaceful conflict resolution and processes of change. West Africa, Liberia and Sierra Leone quickly became the
poster countries for this new wave of state transformation and this continued
throughout the 1990sas local ethnic militias like the Kamajors and external
non-state actors like Executive Outcomes, Sandline and the Gurkha Security
Services further deepened the de-institutionalisation of mainstream forces.[5]

The Loss of the Imperial Security Umbrella

The shifts in global and geo-political power relations, in particular the end of the Cold War and the retraction of the imperial security umbrella, allowed former client regimes to be challenged in ways unimaginable in the past. Whilst some of these responses took the democratic path, there also emerged new forms of political consciousness and identity, which was often structured around religion and ethnicity. This replaced the extant 'universalistic' debates between 'capitalism' and 'socialism' that had underpinned the Cold War, reinforcing the erosion of a sense of common citizenship fostered by state contraction and encouraged popular disillusionment with politics. At the same time, a simultaneous activation of civil society dawned and the increasing power and resources controlled by the non-governmental sector, including the 'uncivil' society, produced mixed results. For example, it soon resulted in the loss of centrality of the state as a consequence of its lack of capacity to deliver essential services, with various implications for its ability to act as the centre of social cohesion as well as for perceptions of citizenship. So, by 1989 rebel forces of the National Patriotic Front of Liberia had taken up arms against Samuel Doe's government in Liberia and by 1991, the Revolutionary United Front forces had unleashed terror in Sierra Leone against the government of Major General Joseph Momoh. Both paved the way for the eventual removal of the two autocrats, but it did not quite result in a democratic transformation for the two countries.

Regionalisation of Conflict and its Impact

It was in the above context that regionalism was revived in West Africa, both in the positive and negative sense. On the one hand, the retreat of the superpowers encouraged the strengthening of the regional collective mechanism – the Economic Community of West African States (ECOWAS), albeit on an ad-hoc basis – especially given the reluctance of the United Nations to respond to the Liberian carnage in 1990. In this regard, the regional organisation was compelled to develop an autonomous capacity to respond to local conflicts and played a critical role in peacekeeping, peacemaking and peace enforcement and developed an integrated strategy with the United Nations in responding to conflict. Equally, and in the negative sense, the conflicts in the two countries contradicted the view that post-Cold War conflicts are mostly intra-state. They revealed the regional character and dimensions of the conflicts in the *Greater* Mano river region (including Côte d'Ivoire and Guinea) and why any reconstruction effort must also have a regional dimension. Although each conflict retained specific local and/or national dimensions and causes, including those described above, there are specific cross-border interventions and links between political elite and rebel groups. This is connected with the illicit flow of goods and resources like timber, diamonds, trafficking in weapons, providing soldiers of fortune and the involuntary flow of migrants, to create a 'regional political economy of war'. The above paints a sobering picture of the options open to the sovereign state in the quest for security sector reconstruction in situations where a regional conflict has emerged as part of the problem, as well as a potential solution to the crisis of insecurity in post-conflict states.

The Nature of Security Sector Reconstruction in the Transition from War to Peace in Liberia and Sierra Leone

Given the context outlined above, the transition from war to peace in Liberia and Sierra Leone presented two immediate challenges with respect to security sector reconstruction. First, the need to establish effective and accountable security agencies that can provide the base for broader socio-economic reconstruction and are capable of protecting the security not only of the state, but also of its citizens. Second, the need to establish effective civilian oversight of the emergent armed forces and security agencies. Among the war belligerents and the broader public in general, there is a clearer recognition that settling the question of the composition, disposition, and oversight of the force structure in the security institutions is central to any political settlement and, ultimately, democratisation itself.

Consequently, post-conflict negotiations in Liberia and Sierra Leone clearly focused on security sector reconstruction in an immediate sense for a number of reasons. With the lack of functioning security institutions after a decade of war, as well as the lack of the most basic institutions capable of undertaking humanitarian tasks, peace negotiators had no other choice than to use the opportunity of cease-fire agreements to re-order priorities in the direction of providing basic security and basic needs in the two countries. In terms of scope, the focus of this immediate restoration of order was understandably short-term. At the end of 1998, 600,000 people were internally displaced in Sierra Leone with 450,000 refugees in both Guinea and Liberia.[6] In Liberia at the end of 2003, there were at least 500,000 internally displaced persons, and 280,000 Liberian refugees in neighbouring countries of

Guinea, Côte d'Ivoire and Sierra Leone.[7] Without a measure of security established in the first place, it will be near impossible to deliver humanitarian aid and restore some order in the countryside beyond the capitals, Freetown and Monrovia.

It is too early at the time of writing to comprehensively assess the scope and impact of the demobilisation, disarmament and reintegration efforts in Liberia given the delay in commencing these set of activities.[8] Almost four years after the cessation of conflict in Sierra Leone, however, considerable progress had been made in terms of the short-term goals of demobilisation of ex-combatants and the re-integration activities across the country. Between 1998 and 2002, some records show that '72,500 combatants were disarmed and demobilised and 42,300 weapons and 1.2 million pieces of ammunition were collected and destroyed'.[9] By the end of 2002, nearly 57,000 ex-combatants had registered for re-integration exercises with the intention of undergoing skills training and receiving assistance to find jobs.[10] In spite of the progress made, enormous challenges remain.[11] The most pertinent problem is the challenge of unemployment that faces the demobilised young men and women that have received skills training in Sierra Leone. The employment market is generally bleak and the nature of the resettlement and reintegration programme is skewed, especially in the remote parts and diamond regions of the country.[12] This effectively links the immediate search for security with the need for development. There is legitimate fear that the exit of the international peacekeeping force, the United Nations Mission in Sierra Leone (UNAMSIL) might re-ignite the passions of the frustrated and volatile youths in Sierra Leone if some comprehensive plan is not developed to address the lingering problem of post-DDR activities.

The above clearly underscores why security sector reconstruction is a long-term and deeply political issue, not just a technical one and why to be deemed successful, *peacebuilding* must aim to seamlessly merge with *nation-building*. It also brings into clear relief why the reconstruction of the security sector can only work if pursued as part of a more comprehensive restructuring agenda aimed at improving governance and promoting democratisation. Security sector reconstruction in a post-conflict setting is therefore also a discussion about the development of an effective and overarching governance framework. For this reason, we seek to review the peace agreements and examine the extent to which they integrate security and development issues within a broader governance framework.

It would appear that the agreements struck in Sierra Leone and Liberia have been enriched by the experience of agreements produced in the aftermath of previous conflicts in their *comprehensiveness*, preventing any hasty generalisation about the nature and quality of peace agreements as a conflict management tool.[13] For example, the Lome Peace Agreement of 7 July 1999, which provided the basis of current reconstruction in Sierra Leone, was primarily limited to armed parties with the most direct culpability for the carnage and violence that had attended the civil war (the Government of Sierra Leone and the Revolutionary United Front). There was little or no provision for civil society forces advocating peace. Thereby producing agreements with narrow concepts of rehabilitation and reconstruction since priority was placed on addressing the problems of ex-combatants, rewarding violence, rather than taking a holistic approach that focuses on the range of stakeholders affected by conflict. The fact that the Accra Peace Agreement of August 2003 embraced the notion of a multi-stakeholder peace agreement, with civil society and political parties not only having a place at the table (not as observers only as was the case in Lome), but also actively represented in the power-sharing arrangements is a striking departure from the Lome peace agreement. It could still be argued that the Accra agreement rewarded violence by awarding the bulk of the positions in government to Government of Liberia (GoL), Liberians United for Reconciliation and Democracy (LURD) and Movement for Democracy in Liberia (MODEL) - the three warring factions - hence undermining any prospects of altering power relations. It is still credible, however, that these external forces can act as equilibrating mechanisms in the quest for realising the objectives of the agreement, especially with the commitment of the guarantors: ECOWAS, the International Contact Group on Liberia and the United Nations.

Other relevant differences between the two agreements relate to how they respond to atrocities and human rights violations. The Lome Peace Agreement provides guaranteed amnesty for offenders, but there are no amnesty provisions in the Accra Peace Agreements. Although both contain provisions for Truth and Reconciliation Commissions, it was the inclusion of the amnesty provision in the Lome Peace agreement that constituted the first difficult point in the immediate aftermath of negotiations. Especially after the United Nations withdrew its support for the agreement as a result of this provision. Finally, the Accra Peace agreement was more holistic in its recognition of the steps that needed to be taken to achieve security and development and in its recognition that reconstruction of society after war requires a long-term process in a continually conflictual, complex and resource-intensive environment. To this end, there are detailed provisions with time-lines and benchmarks for monitoring progress on both the short-term objectives (like DDR) and the longer-term issues around elections, rebuilding of the armed forces and promotion of long-term structural reform and institution building.

Some of these differences have been highlighted in Table 8.1.This is to show that despite the gaps in peace settlements, which recently have been the subject of some academic attention, significant lessons have been borne in mind by negotiators, even if gaps remain between the letter of the peace agreements signed and the implementation of such agreements.[14]

Table 8.1: Provisions of the Lome and Accra Agreements

Lome Agreement (Sierra Leone, 1999)[15]	Accra Agreement (Liberia, 2003)[16]
1. Signed between GoSL & Revolutionary United Front. Select civil society – Inter-Religion Council witnessed.	1. Signed between GoL, LURD, MODEL, Political Parties & Civil Society representatives.
2. Power sharing agreement between major parties to conflict – 4 Cabinet positions, 4 non-cabinet positions to each and Chairmanship of Strategic Minerals Commission to RUF.	2. Power sharing agreement – 5 cabinet positions each to GoL, LURD & MODEL and 6 cabinet positions to political parties and civil society.
3. Elected President continues in office with vice-presidency to Rebel Leader, Foday Sankoh.	3. Elected president replaced with an Independent Chairman of Transitional Government and no key position for rebel leaders.
4. Existing Legislature remains in office.	4. New Transitional Legislative Assembly with 76 members with 12 each for the factions and 18 seats to political parties and civil society.
5. Amnesty provision	5. No amnesty provision.
6. Sketchy SSR agenda	6. Detailed SSR provisions
7. Transitional justice provisions	7. Similar transitional justice provisions
8. No implementation timetable	8. Timetable for implementation

Unlike Sierra Leone (1996) and Liberia (1997) where elections served as conflict triggers for those excluded from the process, the Accra agreement also took account of this and decided to pursue a transitional government option.[17]

The above lessons may have been partly due to the fact that the Accra Peace Agreement was driven largely by Liberians and the regional body – ECOWAS. This is a pertinent lesson that wholly foreign brokered peace processes as an approach to building stable and democratic civil security relations remains inherently problematic.[18] The assumption that every post-conflict situation must produce agreements that follow a set pattern of actions – humanitarian relief, elections, 'disinvestment' of state sector companies and reduction in security expenditures, or a shift from the military to policing is too generic.

Thus, there is a need for post-conflict security sector reconstruction to move away from the current donor focus on short-term objectives, based on the interpretation of peace as a mere absence of war, (securing an early end to hostilities, followed by demobilisation) to a recognition of the post-conflict rebuilding process in a continuum. This includes the reintegration of ex-combatants, re-professionalisation of the armed forces and policing, and building of institutions of democratic oversight, all necessarily longer-term, more complex and resource-intensive processes. Experience has shown that where the 'demand' for security sector reconstruction is not 'owned' by indigenous forces or grounded in local norms or culture, external influence has been much more limited in shaping security sector reform outcomes and virtually irrelevant in determining the nature of the post-conflict regimes. This is demonstrated by the subsequent analysis of security sector reconstruction in Sierra Leone and Liberia. Beyond DDR processes where there seems to be general consensus, even if limited, but ultimately unsustainable gains, the next section examines the state of the security institutions and the nature of restructuring experienced in the post-conflict reform agenda.

Beyond DDR: Scope of Security Sector Reconstruction in Sierra Leone and Liberia

We have argued elsewhere that the most hospitable political environment for 'full-scale' security sector reconstruction in Africa has been post-conflict situations – also precisely the kind of context that (for better or worse) facilitates unfettered donor interventions.[19] A key reason for this is that fact that conflict forces greater attention to issues of security sector reconstruction. This is manifest in four ways:

(a)   There is a clearer recognition that settling the question of the composition, disposition and control of force structures is central to any political settlement, and ultimately, to democratisation itself;

(b)   Support for more holistic approaches to dealing with force structures, formal as well as informal;

(c)   Presence of leaders who tend to be much more savvy in negotiating both political and military issues;

(d)   The fact that conflict has often given rise to new institutions, social and economic relations, and forms of consciousness that seek to enhance social capital.

However, these are also the precise contexts that pose the most formidable challenges to security sector reform, owing to:

- Lack of functioning security institutions, as well as the most basic civil institutions capable of undertaking complex tasks of designing and implementing reform;
- The proliferation of both formal and informal armed formations, requiring complex and demanding DDR processes;
- The need to eliminate both the embedded legacies of violent conflict (for example, militaristic values and a culture of impunity), and the material and economic supports for continued violence (for example, arms proliferation, illicit resource extraction, and so on);
- The need to resettle displaced populations and marginalised youth;
- The need to restore some form of economic normalcy and long-term development.[20]

Mindful of the above challenges, we believe it is still possible to examine the scope and processes involved in the reconstruction of the security sector in Sierra Leone and Liberia. This will be achieved by looking at the details of steps taken in relation to international support, the reform of the armed forces, police, justice sector, youth reintegration and broader governance framework.

International Support for Post-Conflict Reconstruction in West Africa

West Africa currently has the world's largest contingent of UN peacekeeping forces distributed in the United Nations Mission in Sierra Leone (UNAMSIL), the United Nations Mission in Liberia (UNMIL) and the United Nations Mission in Côte d'Ivoire (MINUCI). Given the robustness and size of the missions in Sierra Leone and Liberia, with the comprehensive Chapter VII mandate, the question is not whether the capacity is there to restore security and enforcement of the agreement. The question now revolves around the ability of the two states to regain legitimacy and capacity before the missions' mandate expires. Although the UN has responded positively to concerns expressed by West African leaders on a planned withdrawal of UN troops from Sierra Leone, by acknowledging that an exit will be based on a careful assessment of regional and internal security concerns including completing the re-integration of ex-combatants; re-establishing and consolidating government authority throughout the country; and re-establishing government control over diamond mining.[21] Nevertheless, UNAMSIL's withdrawal of troops has continued.[22] So, while the restructuring of Sierra Leone's armed forces and police is underway, there is clearly little evidence to suggest that Sierra Leone's authorities are presently in a position, or will be by December 2004, to govern insecurity and consolidate democracy. In neighbouring Liberia, the United Nations Mission was approved under Resolution 1509 on 19 September 2003 – two days after the peace agreement was signed in Accra. It outlines a planned roll-in of 15,000 peacekeepers and 1,115 international civilian police, of whom at least 200 will be armed to assist in the maintenance of law and order. As of April 2004 though, only 10,000 peacekeepers were in place, the bulk of which came from ECOWAS countries, and from among the forces withdrawn from Sierra Leone.

The combined impact of withdrawing troops in Sierra Leone and inadequate troops in Liberia is the uncertainty it poses for regional stability and restoration of order. Given the fluid situation in Liberia and the continuing crisis in Côte d'Ivoire, confidence is bound to ebb for the prospects of reconstruction even as many commend the United Nations Missions in both countries for effectiveness. There is fear that warring factions might exploit the situation and re-ignite the conflicts. With ECOWAS's increased capacity, the relationship with the UN has evolved since the reluctance to get involved in the Liberian crisis in 1991. The current situation is significantly better than the first UN mission in West Africa. The UN eventually approved the United Nations Observer Mission in Liberia (UNOMIL) under a Chapter VI mandate with an observer mission of 368 peacekeepers to back-up the Economic Community Monitoring Group (ECOMOG) force of 7,269 troops in 1997.[23] Even so, the challenge of re-ordering the relationship between the UN, regional and sub-regional organisations in managing post-conflict arrangements remains a key issue in the UN operations in Sierra Leone and Liberia. Particularly since Western countries continue to show increasing reluctance to send troops and back UN missions in Africa.[24] Although cooperation between the UN and sub-regional organisations has greatly improved, division of responsibilities is still fraught with difficulties.[25]

Another issue of immediate concern is the role of nodal countries – Britain in Sierra Leone and the United States in Liberia in the reconstruction of the security sector. In Sierra Leone, Britain has taken a frontline role in security and governance reconstruction since 1998 and the success of its African Conflict Prevention Strategy is hinged on the impact of its work in Sierra Leone. For now, Britain's role in the rebuilding of the army and through the British led International Military Assistance Training Team, which is still ongoing, is deemed to have been somewhat successful. The army appears more professional, disciplined and robust and according to Comfort Ero, 'all of this suggests that notions of civilian control have taken a foothold in the new army.'[26]

Although it is early days in Liberia, the United States has picked up an increasing interest from its erstwhile slower pace of engagement.[27] Given the historical links to Liberia, the spectacle of the US' reluctance to commit itself to supporting the peace process in Liberia came to a head as West African Defence Chiefs met in Dakar in July 2003. When the US eventually committed $10 million to airlift ECOMOG troops into Liberia, it refused to send troops to support the peace process on the ground, apart from the small force sent to protect embassy staff.[28] It would appear that that the latest interest has come as a result of complaints in American civil society about the lopsided support focused on Iraq and Afghanistan and it is not clear how long this support will last.[29] However, the fact that the situation in Liberia is being linked to the anti-terror campaign might strengthen the justification for sustained engagement and increased resources.[30] It would appear, however, that this response is bound to be caught in an opportunistic, unfocused and reactive response and the challenge remains to ensure America's engagement in response to an objective need. Many expect the US to react positively to requests for involvement in security sector reform.[31]

In terms of the overarching international involvement in the restoration and sustenance of governance and development, the joint appeal spearheaded by the United States and the United Nations in February 2004 on Liberia surpassed the target of $500 million. While this is reassuring in terms of ensuring that the activities of the United Nations can be accomplished over the next eighteen months, it provides little relief for the long-term challenges of security restructuring and reform of the devastated economic and social infrastructure in the country.

What is also worrying is that there seems to be little evidence that the elected government of President Kabbah in Sierra Leone and the National Transition Government in Liberia headed by businessman, Gyude Bryant really play critical roles in directing the governance and security situations in their countries, yet the political authority reside with them. Instead, the Special Representative of the United Nations' Secretary General in Liberia, General Jacques Klein, behaves like the Viceroy in Liberia, eliciting mixed reactions from stakeholders. There is a feeling that Mr Klein is keen to transpose his Bosnian/Kosovar experience to Liberia with little or no sensitivity to the local dynamics. Although the situation in Sierra Leone is more consensual and unobtrusive, the UN still wields the central authority, yet the sovereign powers are still reposed in the elected authority. This clearly raises questions of accountability, ownership and coordination with the constituted authorities in the short and medium term, given the fact that the local authorities will ultimately be responsible for the security and development agenda.

Restructuring of the Armed Forces

Since security remains the big issue in the reconstruction of the post-conflict states, considerable attention has been paid to the sector since 1998 in Sierra Leone, and 2003 in Liberia. It is also true that it was the deliberate decomposition of the armed forces by the authoritarian rulers in the two countries that led to the de-professionalisation of the military. In the case of Sierra Leone, Britain has been at the forefront of the restructuring initiative, as indicated above. Prior to Britain's involvement, the Sierra Leonean government had toyed with the idea of doing away with the military altogether following a proposed initiative under the auspices of former Costa Rican president, Oscar Arias, but the government changed its mind.[32] Subsequently, the government approached ECOMOG Headquarters to come up with a restructuring plan for the Sierra Leone armed forces.

In addition to the broad plan, which the ECOMOG team had started to implement in 1998, the team encountered critical challenges to the plan in terms of the integration of the Civil Defence Forces into the mainstream armed forces. This was due to the difficulty of re-orienting the Civil Defence Forces' (CDF) leadership into the military command and control system. Also, funding the restructuring programme and providing at least 3,000 housing units were highlighted by the ECOMOG team as challenges that they needed to overcome.[33]

The plan that emerged after the 1999 Lome Peace Agreement simply failed to take the above into account, partly because of the need to bring into the Republic of Sierra Leone Armed Forces (RSLAF) some of the rebel troops who had turned themselves in for re-integration. However, the general impression, in spite of recent worrying developments,[34] is that the RSLAF has imbibed 'a more democratic ethos, that most now understand their role in a democracy and are no longer interested in being involved in the internal affairs of the country'.[35] Yet problems persist about military professionalism and readiness in the wake of UNAMSIL's planned departure from the country in December 2004. The International Military Assistance Training Team (IMATT) has been at the forefront of this reform agenda, but there are still indications that questions of size, force structure, order of battle, legislative oversight, salary, housing, communications, heavy armour and rapid deployment equipment and inadequate military vehicles continue to inhibit the performance of the military. Popular confidence remains low about the building of a professional military, but the government seems keen to do this given the likelihood of UNAMSIL's departure from Sierra Leone.

Unlike the vague and sketchy provisions contained in the Sierra Leone agreement, the Accra Peace Agreement devotes the whole of Part Four of the agreement to security sector reform. The section stipulates: i) the disbandment of all irregular forces; (ii) the restructuring of the Armed Forces of Liberia with a new command structure and forces 'which may be drawn from the ranks of the present GOL forces, the LURD and the MODEL, as well as from civilians with appropriate background and experience'.[36] The agreement also outlines the principles that shall be taken into account in the formation of the restructured Liberian Armed Forces, namely:

(a) Incoming service personnel shall be screened with respect to educational, professional, medical and fitness qualifications as well as prior history with regard to human rights abuses;

(b) The restructured force shall take into account the country's national balance. It shall be composed without any political bias to ensure that it represents the national character of Liberia;

(c) The Mission of the Armed Forces of Liberia shall be to defend the national sovereignty and in extremis, respond to natural disasters;

(d) All Parties shall cooperate with ECOWAS, the UN, the AU, ICGL and the United States of America.[37]

While these elaborate provisions set the standards for what to expect, it is too early to reach any definite judgement about security sector reconstruction in Liberia. Although some success has been achieved in the DDR process, questions have arisen as to who is really in charge – the transitional authority or UNMIL. There is a growing perception that the reintegration work ought to be more inclusive given the experience available in Liberia and the need for legitimacy and ownership.[38] Equally, there is also the need to acknowledge that re-integration is simply not a stopgap measure between conflict and development, but a long-term process that must be linked to strengthening the economy and offer concrete prospects to demobilised soldiers.

Reconstructing the Police and Demilitarising Public Order

As noted earlier, the post-conflict environment offers an appropriate space for eliminating the embedded legacies of violent conflict, for example the psyche of militarism that is etched in the ethos, values and actions of ordinary people in society. There is a belief that the best way to 'demilitarise the mind' and at the same time ensure safety is through the strengthening of civilian policing. Yet, the Sierra Leone and Liberian Police were almost non-existent both in the government's order of priority and in the popular hierarchy of organisations that retain public trust. It is not surprising, therefore, that the police forces continue to suffer tremendous shortfalls in personnel, training and resources in spite of considerable efforts to improve their conditions.[39]

The Sierra Leone Police now number 6,500 to 7,000 men and the goal is to increase the force to its pre-war level of 9,500, with recruitment of at least another 3,500 – 4,000 men by 2005.[40] Even if this pre-war status is achieved, it is still going to be a far cry from the UN stipulated police-citizens ratio of 1:400. Added to the gross personnel shortage are inadequate accommodation and transportation; a poor communication network; poorly funded training institutions; and insufficient criminal intelligence gathering capacity.[41]

Notwithstanding the above, the police has undergone a complete reorientation of its mission and objectives. It has also moved out from the capital to the provinces and attempts are currently being made to expand the training centre in Hastings as well as to rebuild the regional centres in Bo, Kenema and Makeni, all of which were destroyed during the war. The reform process had been led by the Commonwealth and UNAMSIL Civilian Police Unit, but questions have been raised about the competence of the reform team and the lack of ownership of the reform process by the Sierra Leone Police.[42] Continuing challenges in the police reform programme include: (1) expansion of recruitment in the police; (2) codification of procedures and new doctrine, improvement of training and standards especially to prevent human rights abuse recurring, increase in the resources available to police, reduction of redundant officers and expansion of its role in intelligence and security information gathering and injecting new blood into the force; and (3) increasing the size of the police and pay of its operatives thus improving its estimation in the eyes of the public.[43]

There is no telling if this could be achieved in the short-term. However, the question of engaging civil policing for democratic governance is central to the issue of exorcising militarism from the body politic as it is relevant to the issue of returning security and safety to the local communities, and ensuring accountability in Sierra Leone. The challenge is to achieve this before the departure of UNAMSIL from Sierra Leone.

Equally in Liberia, the issue of how best to restructure the police organisation, structure and operations has been particularly central in the post-conflict environment given the problems that attended the centralised control of the police force and how it had been used under previous regimes, most recently, President Taylor's. To create a service *culture,* and not a regimented force arrangement, accountability to the ordinary citizens is central to public order. The police cannot be trusted within the community if it retains a structure that is only accountable to the President. To this end, Article VIII of the Accra Peace agreement focuses on the restructuring of the Liberian National Police, the Immigration Force, Special Security Services, Custom Security Guards and such other statutory security units. Article VIII (5) disbands 'The Special Security Units including the Anti-Terrorist Unit, the Special Operations Division (SOD) of the Liberian National Police Force and such paramilitary groups that operate within the organisations as the National Ports Authority (NPA), The Liberian Telecommunications Corporation (NTC), the Liberian Refining Corporation (LRPC) and the Airports'. In its place, an Interim Police Force shall be created, which will be monitored by the United Nations Civil Police components (UNCIVPOL) within the International Stabilisation Force(ISF).

Serious as the problems of policing are, the problems cannot be seen in isolation from the criminal justice system since the police is only an implementing agent of the criminal justice system – especially the prisons and correctional facilities and the justice sector. Yet, in both countries reforms in the prisons and the judicial system have been much slower than reforms in the military and the police, although there is now a recognition that these issues must be taken together. The ad-hoc approach adopted so far will not bring change, a comprehensive approach to justice and law enforcement is

needed. A comprehensive approach will necessarily involve addressing existing gaps in law reform, accountability, oversight, access, due process,
effectiveness, efficiency and representation at the level of the judicial, prosecutorial, correctional and policing institutions. Moreover, it will ensure the
necessary linkages in the justice and security sector community – the police,
correctional services, the judiciary and prosecution services etc.[44] Equally
important is the degree to which decentralisation will aid access to justice
and the building of trust in the justice sector. [45] Although some progress has
been made on superficial reforms and restoration of infrastructures, the challenge is to have a comprehensive overhaul of the justice sector, aligning the
common law with the customary court system and clearing the huge backlog
of cases currently unattended.

Tackling Impunity and Egregious Violations of Human Rights

Addressing questions of impunity has proved to be a tough challenge of
post-conflict security sector reconstruction anywhere in the world. Yet, ignoring the past and rushing to reconciliation will certainly produce a
counter-productive result since it is crucial for post-conflict societies to
maintain an appropriate mix of remembering and forgetting in order to stop
future occurrence.[46] In the case of Sierra Leone and Liberia, both countries
agreed to clear provisions for addressing human rights violations. Article
XXVI of the Lome Peace Agreement stipulates that a Truth and Reconciliation Commission shall be established and Part Six, Article XIII of the Accra
Peace Agreement amongst the Liberian parties also established a Truth and
Reconciliation Commission (TRC).

In addition to the above, a Special Court was also established for Sierra Leone under the UN auspices with the mandate to try 'those who bear
the greatest responsibility' for the civil war. The key challenge in the cases
of Sierra Leone and Liberia is how to strike the right balance between ob-
taining justice and not unravelling the fragile peace. This tricky balance has
already been tested with the indictments against the ex-Liberian leader,
Charles Taylor, the Kamajor leader, Hinga Norman who was the former
Deputy Defence Minister and two key leaders of the Kamajor, Allieu Kon-
dewa and Moinina Fofana. Since reconciliation processes are often context
specific, many found it shocking that any indictment against Charles Taylor
could be released on 4 June 2003, the same day that West African leaders
were working on his voluntary resignation in Accra, Ghana. To this end,
ECOWAS leaders immediately rejected the process of indictment and this

has somewhat put the work of the Special Court in the balance. Equally, the arrest of the Kamajor leaders had elicited similar responses among their allies and supporters prompting fears that it might undermine the fragile peace process that had worked so far, especially given the likelihood of UNAMSIL's departure. Although there is limited appetite for a return to war, the perception is now rife that the Special Court is a witch hunting exercise, rather than a justice-seeking vehicle. The fact that the Chairperson of the Court did not recuse himself, even after his well-publicised views on the Revolutionary United Front cadres, further damaged the reputation of the Court. In spite of this, there remains a groundswell of support for a truth telling and reconciliation process, one that is linked to the reform of the judicial system and restoration of basic human rights in the conduct of government and other stakeholders in Sierra Leone and the region.

Liberia's situation with regards to Truth and Reconciliation clearly mirrors Sierra Leone's. In fact, there is often a connecting thread in many of the atrocities that were committed in Liberia in the fourteen years of war and there is a demand for a truth and justice exercise. It is too early to say if Liberia will also have its own UN backed Special Court, but various institutions have been exploring the possibilities of such a Court in Liberia, including the UN Office of the High Commissioner for Human Rights (OHCHR). Other institutions like the Open Society Justice Initiative and the International Centre for Transitional Justice have conducted exploratory missions to Liberia. For such outside interest to make a difference on the entrenchment of security sector reconstruction, coherence must be achieved on timing, sequencing, resources and structure, and commitment of the political leadership (many of whom are recycled and are themselves probably guilty of such egregious violations) assured.[47]

What is worrying in all of the current post-conflict transitional justice arrangements so far is the absence of any informal (traditional) justice mechanisms, or at least the utilisation of both formal and informal mechanisms toward a long-lasting achievement of truth, justice and reconciliation.[48]

The Place of Irregular Forces and the Crisis of Youth Culture

Herein lies, in the author's view, the greatest threat to security sector reconstruction in both Sierra Leone and Liberia, and probably in the rest of the region. Any attempt to design security sector reconstruction without an understanding of the sociological underpinnings of the youth culture and a carefully constructed strategic response runs the risk of undermining all other aspects of this institutional design project that we have examined above.[49]

This chapter deliberately links the question of irregular forces or de-mobilised ex-combatants with the crisis in youth culture because of the continuing tendency to focus, even after years of post-conflict reconstruction, almost exclusively on dealing with one without addressing the other. In both Sierra Leone and Liberia, priority is still placed on narrow concepts of rehabilitating and reintegrating the ex-combatants, making them 'economically viable' and independent in the genuine, but naïve expectation that this is enough to address the crisis of youth culture. There are many reasons for this – the first is the lack of interest in a transformational agenda on the Sierra Leonean and Liberian authorities' side. The second factor is development assistance's obsession with humanitarian assistance (which privileges project cycles). Third is the proclivity for the short-term in post-conflict reconstruction and, finally the reluctance to embrace a regional response to an issue that has become largely cross-border.

On the side of irregular forces and ex-combatants, the forces that have been focused on are the civil defence units popularly known as Kamajors and the RUF cadres (which has Africa's largest youth contingent), and the GoL, LURD and MODEL forces in Liberia. The CDFs and RUF rebels have participated in the demobilisation exercise. In fact, according to ICG records, 37,000 Kamajor militia members took part in the exercise, but the report also cautions that demobilising troops in a force that is largely community based is suspect. It is believed that the Kamajor still has the capacity to wreak havoc and their frustrations with the government of Sierra Leone seems to have increased due to the ongoing trials of the Kamajor leadership as indicated in earlier sections. The same may be true of the other disillusioned ex-combatants within the RUF and the various rebel entities in Liberia even if they have all benefited from the DDR initiatives in both countries. Collectively, they constitute a threat to post-conflict reconstruction and it is a threat that can only be addressed if treated as part of a comprehensive reform agenda. As Ibrahim Abdullah eloquently argues,

> '...the major challenge in post-war Sierra Leone...is to channel youth energy and creativity towards a constructive agenda. The coalition of different youth experiences suggests the necessity for a coherent national strategy that will speak to their collective interest as a group. A project that addresses the needs of youths in general with built-in sensitivity to the different categories of

youth is more likely to succeed than one that is designed for a particular group of ex-combatants'.[50]

Sierra Leone has done precisely this by developing a National Youth Policy in 2003, which focuses on six strategic areas namely job creation, skills training, information and sensitisation, community development projects, presidential award for excellence and youth consultation/participation. However, even this effort has been criticised for excluding young people in its formulation. Youth unemployment has not abated and skills training is still an issue with a largely illiterate youth population. It is also no surprise that the country's leadership continues to believe that consultation with the youth should only be limited to issues affecting young people, and not broader issues of governance and economic reform. Yet, it is estimated that 'youth' will constitute fifty-five percent of the country's population by 2005.[51] The net result is an idle youth population ready to be mobilised by any opportunistic segment of the political elite and the likelihood of a security sector reconstruction that is susceptible to unravelling. The Liberian crisis is the exact replica of this.

Even if these issues are tackled within a strategic and broad national framework, they are not problems that can be resolved on a state by state basis. Hence the need for regional responses in tackling cross border issues that has developed with dangerous links to networks of small arms proliferators, resource exploiters and mercenaries from the Gambia to the Congo. Although ECOWAS established a Child Protection Unit in 2002 and has been trying to develop a coherent policy framework that its member nations can adopt, there is little evidence to suggest that the regional body recognises the enormity of this problem.[52]

This requires a far greater radical response by all the intervenors and international development assistance agencies, regional actors and national players. This must be seen as key to the future of security sector reconstruction and overall national governance stability if progress is to be made on the post-conflict agenda in the medium and long-term.

Conclusion

This chapter proceeds from the premise that Sierra Leone and Liberia in the aftermath of conflict offer a genuine opportunity to test the possibility of comprehensive security sector reconstruction. Although we argued that security sector reconstruction in post-conflict states hold a greater potential for altering relations of power, from the foregoing discussion, security sector reconstruction in Sierra Leone and Liberia, tentative as our conclusion maybe, have not managed to overcome the deficiencies of past experience.

In spite of this general conclusion, some specific lessons could be drawn that are useful for an agenda that is, at best, too early for hasty dismissal. For example, Sierra Leone was the test case for UK's new SSR policy and has thus far been the country where SSR thinking has been most fully applied by donors anywhere in Africa. The kind of reforms that the UK government has supported in Sierra Leone are certainly consistent with the effort at improving civilian oversight and civilian input into security sector decision making processes by: a) rebuilding the Ministry of Defence, and making it a joint civilian-military entity, with a new headquarters; b) publication of a defence white paper; c) efforts at broader security sector review that is currently underway; d) establishment of a new office of National Security as well as the creation of the National Security Coordinating Committee representing all intelligence agencies.[53]

Yet, what the experience of Sierra Leone and Liberia also brings into clear relief is the place of the modern nation-state in Africa and the importance of consistently generating regional responses. The responsibility to prevent, manage and transform conflict should not be hobbled by the Westphalian logic of state sovereignty. Regional institutions have emerged as critical actors in this chain, and now is the time to reflect a lot more coherently on the political and institutional requirements that will place such organisations at the forefront of security sector reconstruction in Africa.

In spite of all the efforts that are underway in Sierra Leone and Liberia, sustainability and ownership issues will continue to persist unless security sector reconstruction is fully integrated into the wider institutional reform agenda. As currently conceived in these states, security sector reconstruction attempts to re-engineer and resuscitate often decrepit and discredited institutions and to re-centre the state in the security game, not initiate fundamental rethinking of security/strategic concepts and frameworks, governance institutions and relations of power. With UK influence in Sierra Leone what has also been clear has been the manner ownership issues have been relegated to the background because of the influence wielded by the British advisers and IMATT officers on the powerholder. This became more pronounced following the role played by these officers in directly advising the President of Sierra Leone during the crisis period of May-June 2000. It was not uncommon for these officers to always take their views directly to the President, bypassing normal decision-making procedures within the Ministry of Defence, a situation which led to Sierra Leoneans being excluded and undermining the very purpose of SSR programme, which was to help build local management capacity.

Yet precisely because the decay in the security sector in the two states inevitably springs from the dynamics of weak states, and the often severely deteriorated character of their security establishments, the thread running through this paper is that security sector reconstruction is neither an a-political project, nor is it a purely technical programme that can be carefully designed with expected outcomes. It must be undergirded by an overarching governance framework, one that reconstitutes power relations in a process oriented, participatory and accountable manner. This approach has at its core the need for rights based development that promotes an organic link between peace agreements primarily concerned with simply guaranteeing compliance among belligerent parties, and a broader constitutional framework that legitimises power structures and relations based on a broad social consensus on the values of a diverse society. It also requires an arrangement that holds donors accountable to both the local constituency and the wider international community.

Quite clearly, questions of a donor driven agenda, lack of local ownership, the under-funded nature of post-conflict security sector reconstruction that are ill-adjusted to domestic institutional and resource needs, as well as the non-holistic and ad-hoc nature of current reconstruction efforts and their sustainability, are issues that will have to be fully addressed if security sector reconstruction is to retain any relevance to the countries it seeks to serve. Whether the lessons learned in Sierra Leone will fully inform developments in Liberia remains to be seen, but the extent to which security can be institutionally designed remains in doubt. Particularly if it continues to be characterised by lack of political will, weak government leadership and inter-agency collaboration, lack of transparency and participation, and weak (or non-existent) policy and strategic framework.

Notes

[1] For a recent analysis of security sector governance in Africa, see Ball, N., Fayemi, J. 'K., Olonisakin, F. and Williams R., 'Governance in the Security Sector', in N. Van de Walle, N. Ball & V. Ramachandran (eds), *Beyond Structural Adjustment: The Institutional Context of African Development* (New York, Palgrave, 2003).

[2]   For details of Liberia's descent into autocracy, see Sawyer, A., *The Emergence of Autoc-racy in Liberia: Tragedy and Challenge* (San Franscisco: Institute for Contemporary Studies Press, 1992); Dunn, D.E., and Tar, S.B., *Liberia: National Polity in Transition* (New Jersey: Scarecrow Press, 1988); Sawyer, A. 'Foundations for Reconstruction in Li-beria: Challenges and Responses' in J. 'Kayode Fayemi, (ed), *Security, Democracy & De-velopment in Post War Liberia*, (London: CDD, 1998) and Liebenow, J. G., *Liberia – The Quest for Democracy* (Bloomington: Indiana University Press, 1987).

[3]   See Abraham, A., 'The Quest for Peace in Sierra Leone', in 'F. Olonisakin, *Engaging Sierra Leone: Roundtable on Reconciliation and State-Building* (London: CDD, 2000).

[4]   For details of Sierra Leone's progressive decline into chaos, please see Abdullah,I., 'Lumpen Youth Culture and Political Violence: Sierra Leoneans Debate the RUF and the Civil War.' *African Development* 22: 171-215, 1997; Abdullah, I. 'Bush-path to Destruc-tion: the Origin and Character of the Revolutionary United Front', *African Development*, ibid; Richards, P., *Fighting for the Rain Forest: War, Youth and Resources in Sierra Leone* (London: James Currey, 1996); Bangura, Y., 'Understanding the Political and Cul-tural Dynamics of the Sierra Leone civil war: A critique of Paul Richard's Fighting the Rain Forest', *African Development*, op-cit. and Reno, W., *Corruption and State Politics in Sierra Leone* (Cambridge: Cambridge University Press, 1995).

[5]   See Abdel-Fatau Musah & J. 'Kayode Fayemi (eds), *Mercenaries: An African Security Dilemma*, (London: Pluto Press, 2000) for an extensive treatment of this development.

[6]   Francis Kai-Kai, 'Reintegration and Rehabilitation of Groups', in Funmi Olonisakin (ed), *Engaging Sierra Leone*, op. cit.

[7]   ICG, *Liberia: Security Challenges*, Africa Report no. 71 (Freetown/Brussels: November 2003), p. 5.

[8]   For a useful assessment of the early stages of DDR in Liberia, see ICG, *Rebuilding Libe-ria: Prospects and Perils*, Africa Report no. 75 (Freetown/Brussels, 30 January 2004).

[9]   GFN-SSR, *Security Sector Reform Policy Brief* (London: HMG, 2003).

[10] ICG, *Sierra Leone: State of Security and Governance*, Africa Report no. 67 (Free-town/Brussels, 2 September 2003).

[11] For a review of the DDR programme in Sierra Leone, see 'The DDR Programme: Status and Strategies for Completion', a report to the Consultative Group Meeting, Paris, 13-14 November 2002.

[12] See Victor Kamara, 'Accelerated Dynamics of Resettlement Emerging from Conflict in Sierra Leone: Field Study Report for the Conflict and Stability in West Africa Pro-gramme', *Club du Sahel Secretariat*, (OECD Paris, December 2003).

[13] There is the view in the security field that a war that results in the defeat of one party holds out a greater promise for security sector reconstruction. The African experience of conquest states like Uganda, Ethiopia, and Rwanda does not show any correlation be-tween a conquest state and democratically governed and professional security sector.

[14] For a useful critique of peace negotiations, see Stephen Stedman, et al., *Ending Civil Wars: The Success and Failure of Negotiated Settlements in Civil War* (Lanham, MD: Lynne Rienner, 2002).

[15] There were previous peace accords that aimed to resolve the conflict, namely the Conakry and Abidjan Peace Accords, but the accord that provided the basis of current settlement was the Lome Peace Agreement signed between the Government of Sierra Leone and the Revolutionary United Front in 1999, even though this quickly unravelled after the crisis of

January 2000. For details of this Agreement, please see, Funmi Olonisakin, (ed), *Engaging Sierra Leone.*

[16] The Accra Peace Agreement provided the basis for the current reconstruction of the security sector in Liberia. Equally, earlier agreements including the Abuja Accord 1996, which provided a framework for the reform of the armed forces foundered at the altar of electoral politics in 1997.

[17] Other options like a hybrid ECOWAS-UN Trusteeship or an outright UN trusteeship were also seriously considered, but the national transition government arrangement was the option settled for.

[18] With regard to the Lome Peace Agreement, Sierra Leone government officials have spoken about how they were pressured by the United States into signing an agreement that they objected to. See Ryan Lizza, 'The Clinton Administration and Sierra Leone: A Betrayal', in *The New Republic* (Washington D.C., USA), 24 July 2000. Also see the reflections of one of the key technical experts that worked on the Lome Peace Agreements, Georges Nzongola-Ntalaja, 'Unpacking the Lome Peace Agreement' in Abdel Fatau Musah (ed), *Sierra Leone: One Year after Lome,* (London: CDD, 2000).

[19] See 'Kayode Fayemi & Eboe Hutchful, *Security System Reform in Africa – An OECD-DAC Study,* forthcoming.

[20] Ibid.

[21] 'Fifteenth Report of the Secretary-General on the United Nations Mission in Sierra Leone', S/2002/987, 5 September 2002.

[22] ICG, *Sierra Leone: The State of Governance and Security,* p.5. Although the number of troops was meant to have been drawn down from its original size of 17, 398 to 13,100 by May 2003, a revised plan following protest by ECOWAS has been developed with planned completion of a phased withdrawal now put at December 2004.

[23] For an excellent account of the politics of UNOMIL and ECOMOG, see Clement E.Adibe, 'Muddling Through: An Analysis of the ECOWAS Experience in Conflict Management in West Africa' in Liisa Laakso (ed), *Regional Integration for Conflict Prevention and Peace Building in Africa Europe, SADC and ECOWAS* (Helsinki: University of Helsinki, 2002).

[24] See 'UN Peacekeeping Chief warns of 2004 Troops Shortage' *Financial Times,* 18 December 2003. In it, the UN Peacekeeping Chief, Jean-Marie Guehenno expressed concerns about the likely competitition for troops in Afghanistan and Iraq.

[25] Adibe, 'Muddling Through'.

[26] Comfort Ero, 'Sierra Leone: Legacies of Authoritarianism and Political Violence', in Gavin Cawthra and Robin Luckham (eds), *Governing Insecurity: Democratic Control of Military and Security Establishments in Transitional Democracies* (London, Zed, 2003), p.250.

[27] The United States has committed $200 million for non-peacekeeping efforts, targeting community based re-integration of ex-combatants, refugees and IDPs with the remainder used to fill gaps after the responses from other donors. Source: ICG, *Rebuilding Liberia,* p.7.

[28] The author was in Dakar during the series of meetings held by ECOWAS Foreign Ministers and Defence chiefs aimed at convincing the United States to commit troops to Liberia.

[29] Discussion with Nancy Lindborg, Executive Vice President, MercyCorps in Virginia, USA, May 11, 2004.

[30] See Report of House of Representatives' International Relations Sub-Committee on Africa - Public Hearing on African Terrorism, April 1, 2004. See also Douglas Farah, 'Islamic Fundamentalism, Terrorism and al-Qaeda in Africa', American Enterprise Institute, April 13, 2004 and Mahmood Mamdani, *Good Muslim, Bad Muslim: America, the Cold War and the Roots of Terror* (New York: Random House, 2004) for insights on terrorism and alleged links to Africa.

[31] See ICG Report, op. cit. There is likelihood that if such support comes from the US, it will be routed via private military contractors.

[32] This initiative followed a UNDP sponsored conference in Arusha, Tanzania in 1998 and the Sierra Leonean delegation led by erstwhile Internal Affairs Minister, Albert Margai seriously considered the 'no-military' plan and called President Kabbah in the middle of the conference to discuss the Arias Plan.

[33] Ibid.

[34] Discussions with Mr Joe Blell, Deputy Defence Minister of Sierra Leone, 19 June 2003. The worrying developments relate to concerns that had been expressed about the loyalty of some in the military especially in the aftermath of erstwhile military junta leader's disappearance after the May 2002 election.

[35] ICG, *Sierra Leone.*

[36] Article V11 (1).

[37] Article V11 (2).

[38] Interview with Professor To gba Na Tipoteh, Director of Sisukku – a local demobilisation and reintegration initiative posted on web. See <http://www.allafrica.com>.

[39] See Osman Gbla, 'Security Sector Reform in Sierra Leone,' Paper presented at the Network on Security Sector Reform in Africa: Comparative Perspectives hosted by the African Security Dialogue & Research, Accra, Ghana, October 2002.

[40] ICG, *Sierra Leone*, p. 8.

[41] I owe this assessment to Mr Kandeh Bangura, Deputy Inspector-General of Police, Sierra Leone Police, October 2002, Abuja, Nigeria.

[42] ICG, *Sierra Leone*, p. 9.

[43] DIG Kandeh Bangura, see above.

[44] The World Bank and DFID have started some work in this regard, but they are concerned about the government's practical commitment to the reform of the judicial sector and the Anti Corruption Commission.

[45] For the first time in twenty-seven years, local government elections took place in Sierra Leone amid claims of election malpractice on the government side. The Accra Peace agreement also acknowledges the need to rapidly extend governance to the countries as a way of arresting disillusionment and legitimacy.

[46] David Bloomfield, Teresa Barnes and Luc Huyse (eds), *Reconciliation after Violent Conflict: A Handbook* (Stockholm, IDEA, 2003).

[47] It has been argued that the core of the leadership of GoL, LURD and MODEL should be held responsible for war crimes. Many in civil society had objected to the choice of Daniel Chea to continue as Defence Minister in the Transition Government and George Dweh as Speaker of the Legislative Assembly on the strength of alleged atrocities committed under Presidents CharlesTaylor and Samuel Doe respectively.

48   The Gacaca justice system in post-conflict Rwanda has received mixed reviews, but what cannot be denied is its legitimacy amongst the people and it's efficacious, even if rudimentary steps.

49   The literature on youth culture and child-soldiers is large. Among the most impressive for the purpose of this paper are: Ibrahim Abdullah, 'Lumpen Youth Culture and Political Violence: Sierra Leoneans Debate the RUF and the Civil War.' *African Development* 22: 171-215, 1997; Donald B. Cruise O'Brien, 'A Lost-Generation? Youth Identity and State Decay in West Africa,' in Richard Webner and Terence Ranger (eds), *Postcolonial Identities in Africa* (London: Zed Books, 1996); Paul Richards, *Fighting for the Rain Forest: War, Youth and Resources in Sierra Leone* (London: James Currey, 1996) and William Murphy, 'Military Patrimonialism and Child Soldier Clientelism in Liberian and Sierra Leone Civil Wars', *African Studies Review*, Volume 46, Number 2 (December 2003), pp. 61-87.

50   Ibrahim Abdullah, 'Youth Culture and Violent Change', in Funmi Olonisakin (ed), *Engaging Sierra Leone*, pp. 101-107.

51   'Sierra Leone National Youth Policy', Ministry of Youth and Sport, (2003), p. 5 quoted in ICG Report, *Sierra Leone.*

52   The CPU office in ECOWAS continues to perform sub-optimally and there is enormous scope for it to work with the United Nations' Office of the Children affected by Armed Conflict and UNICEF on this issue whilst integrating its activities with state policies on child soldiers, trafficking and youth culture. See *Learning for Change: Report of Conference on Youth and Conflict Avoidance in West Africa* by the Centre for Democracy & Development, CODAC & PADEAP, November 17-20, 2002 in Otta, Nigeria.

53   I am grateful to Dylan Hendrickson for these useful comments.

Chapter 9

Consolidating an Elusive Peace: Security Sector Reform in Afghanistan

Mark Sedra

Introduction

With the end of the Cold War came a new global security 'problematique'. Failed states and the array of transnational threats that they unleash – including terrorism, organised crime, and population displacements – emerged as the most profound challenge to international order. As the number of cases of post-conflict reconstruction multiplied over the 1990s, it became apparent that 'winning the peace' in failed and war affected states posed as much of a challenge as the initial military intervention. Securing and stabilising post-conflict settings necessitated a new model of security assistance that diverged from Cold War realist logic. Security sector reform (SSR), a model of security assistance that assembles the doctrines of security and development under one conceptual roof, was designed to meet that need. SSR is rooted in the premise that an accountable, equitable, and rights respecting security sector is a prerequisite for development and stability. Although the concept has been widely embraced by development and security actors across the globe, its record of implementation can best be described as mixed. Afghanistan's SSR programme, two year's after its launch, appears to have fallen into this pattern.

In Afghanistan, SSR is widely viewed as the lynchpin upon which the success of the entire state-building process depends. Transformation rather than reform is the most apt word to describe the process since after twenty-three years of civil war the country's security institutions are in a state of disarray. Afghanistan has not had a professional national army and police since the Najibullah period in the early 1990s and its judicial system, which has been at the centre of a struggle between Western reformers and Islamic extremists for decades, is largely dysfunctional. The process faces a conspicuous and ominous paradox that will be difficult to overcome. SSR is invariably a long-term process, yet in Afghanistan it has been presented as a means to confront the country's immediate security woes. The process has been thrust in this position due to the absence of conflict management mechanisms, notably a countrywide peace-support mission, to fill the security vacuum in the aftermath of the Taliban's fall from power. The SSR model requires a minimum level of security to function, a base line currently absent in Afghanistan. Relying on SSR to restore security and stability in the short-term has precipitated an acceleration of the process, forcing stakeholders to make dangerous compromises on some of its core democratic principles.

This chapter will provide a thorough examination of Afghanistan's SSR process, from the design to the implementation phase. As the first case of SSR in the post-September 11th era, the importance of this case transcends Afghanistan. Many of the flaws of the Afghan process, notably the ambivalence of donor motivations and objectives; the lack of local ownership and coordination; and funding shortfalls, cut across security sector reform programmes ranging from Sierra Leone to Cambodia. The chapter argues that the underdeveloped nature of the SSR concept, aptly characterised by Jane Chanaa as the 'conceptual-contextual divide', explains its modest record of implementation.[1] As the Afghan case shows, the model is ill-suited to meet the challenges of complex post-conflict environments, marked by adverse security conditions and ethnic and political fragmentation.

This chapter is divided into four sections. The first will offer an analysis of the conditions that led to the formation of the current SSR agenda in Afghanistan. The context in which the process is being implemented will be discussed in the second section, with particular attention paid to the security situation. Section three will offer an in-depth analysis of each of the five pillars of Afghanistan's SSR process. The final section will offer lessons from the experience of implementation with insight on how the process can be made more effective. The chapter will end with some broad recommendations on how the process can be set on the right path.

Setting the Agenda

Acutely aware of the importance of the security sector reform enterprise, Hamid Karzai, the President of the Afghan Transitional Administration (ATA), has described it as 'the basic prerequisite to re-creating the nation that today's parents hope to leave to future generations'.[2] President Karzai made this statement in his opening address to a conference on security sector reform held in Kabul in July 2003. The conference, which assembled all of the relevant domestic and international stakeholders in the SSR process, was held during a period marked by rising insecurity, emerging signs of donor fatigue, and lacklustre rates of development. It was convened to jumpstart an SSR process that was perceived to be faltering. The inability of SSR to ameliorate these adverse conditions compelled many to pessimistically call for a shift in course for the programme.

Nineteen months earlier, in January 2002, when the international donor community met in Tokyo, only one month after the signing of the Bonn Agreement, the seeds of the programme's future tribulations were laid. Perhaps it was the air of optimism that reigned over the gathering, hopeful atmosphere, coupled with a needs assessment[3] that was prepared in 'a great hurry, without first-hand data or experience of Afghan costs or conditions,' which contributed to the formulation of pledges and support structures that grossly underestimated the reconstruction needs of the country, particularly in the security sector.[4] Although a general outline of the security sector reform agenda was sketched at the Tokyo donor conference, it was not formalised until two security donors' conferences held in Geneva in April and May 2002. The Geneva conferences resulted in the establishment of a multi-sectoral donor support scheme, in which individual donors were allocated responsibility for overseeing each of the five pillars of the process: Military Reform (US lead); Police Reform (German lead); the Disarmament, Demobilization, and Reintegration of Ex-Combatants (Japan lead); Judicial Reform (Italy lead); and Counter-Narcotics (UK lead). From its outset the process has been hindered by a security environment that has proven counterproductive for reform. As the Afghan National Security Council has affirmed in a recent report, 'the 2001 assessments on which plans were based perhaps naively assumed an improvement in security which has not yet materialised'.[5]

Afghanistan's Security Dilemma

The fall of the Taliban regime in November 2001, followed by the international community's commitment to reconstruct the country, aroused great hope that Afghanistan was entering a period of unprecedented security and stability. Deteriorating security conditions on the ground quickly tempered such expectations. Insecurity has grown steadily across the country since the collapse of the Taliban regime, obstructing development and reconstruction efforts and preventing the central government from asserting its authority in many areas. Fuelling this wave of insecurity has been a rejuvenated criminalised economy, dominated by the burgeoning opium trade. Overcoming what Barnett Rubin describes as the 'nexus of insecurity and the criminalised economy' is the principal challenge facing security sector reform.[6] Demonstrating the tenuous nature of the security situation, between October 2003 and April 2004, over 550 people were killed in violent incidents across the country, making it the most violent period since the fall of the Taliban.[7] A number of factors, summarised below, have contributed to the upsurge of insecurity.

Anti-Government Spoiler Groups. Afghanistan's spoiler groups, which include remnants of the Taliban; former Prime Minister Gulbuddin Hekmatyar's Hizb-i-Islami faction;[8] and al-Qaeda, are determined to undermine the authority of the new central government and bring about the withdrawal of the international community, particularly the US-led coalition forces. The Taliban, which appears to be operating at the head of a loose alliance comprising the three groups, is not in a position to unilaterally overthrow the central government. The Taliban movement 'has evolved into a decentralised guerrilla group that has portrayed itself as a vehicle for Pashtun nationalism'.[9] At a Senate Hearing in Washington in late February 2004, Vice Admiral Lowell Jacoby, the head of the US Defence Intelligence Agency, claimed that attacks had reached 'their highest levels since the collapse of the Taliban government'. [10] Operating primarily in the southeast, spoiler groups have gradually adjusted their tactics from targeting coalition forces to focusing on 'soft targets', including aid workers and government employees. The new strategy has borne fruit, as the UN and major international organisations, including the International Committee for the Red Cross (ICRC), have scaled back their operations in the south and east, depriving up to one third of the country of development assistance.

Warlordism. After the fall of the Taliban regime, regional military commanders across Afghanistan proceeded to establish mini-fiefdoms within their spheres of influence. In many respects, this represented a return to the status-quo ante of 1994, just prior to the Taliban's rise to power. This group of predatory elites operates with impunity in the areas under their control, preventing the government from establishing its authority. They collect taxes and customs duties, maintain their own private armies and exploit the criminalised economy. Their power is rooted in the military assets at their disposal, the 'clientelistic' personalised networks that they maintain and, to a lesser extent, support from external actors. These networks are not limited to the periphery, but extend deep into the government, giving them a de facto veto over the state building process. Inevitably, conflicts between warlords, over territory and resources have erupted at various flashpoints around the country, resulting in hundreds of casualties and an inhospitable environment for development.

Narcotics Trade and the 'Shadow Economy'. Afghanistan's criminalised or 'shadow' economy, a hub for criminal networks stretching from Russia to the Gulf States, is one of the principal engines of insecurity in Afghanistan. It comprises a range of illegitimate economic activities including smuggling of consumer goods and trafficking in gems, timber, archaeological artefacts and even humans. However, it is the production and trafficking of opium that forms its largest and most profitable element. In 2002, Afghanistan returned to its position as the foremost supplier of opiates to the world market, accounting for approximately seventy-five per cent of world production. The drug trade in Afghanistan generated $2.3 billion in income in 2003, more than fifty per cent of Afghanistan's legal GDP. Most indicators show that the problem will only worsen in the years ahead. A survey of farmers' intentions conducted by the United Nations Office on Drugs and Crime (UNODC) in late 2003, found that sixty-nine per cent of farmers surveyed intend to increase poppy cultivation in 2004 and more than thirty per cent of farmers intend to double production.[11] The impact of the growth of the trade has been far-reaching. It has channelled resources to spoiler groups and warlords, it has undermined the growth of the legitimate economy, and it has led to a sharp increase in Afghan drug use and addiction.

The SSR process cannot be implemented in a security vacuum – a security buffer is required to facilitate its operationalisation. In the case of Mozambique, government security forces filled that role, while in the Balkan states of Kosovo and Bosnia, NATO insulated the process. In the South African case, widely regarded as the most successful example of SSR implementation, the security environment was largely stable. In sharp contrast, Afghanistan faces a plethora of external and internal threats. While individually they may not be robust enough to unravel the Afghan Transitional Administration and the nascent political process, cumulatively they present a fundamental obstacle to change.

Deconstructing the Process

In October 2001, a US-led coalition intervened in Afghanistan to overthrow the Taliban regime. Motivated by the September 11th terrorist attacks, the intervention was intended to remove the Taliban from power and prevent the country from being utilised as a sanctuary for terrorists. As Barnett Rubin states, 'the main goal of US policy in Afghanistan was not to set up a better regime for the Afghan people. If the United States had wanted to do that, it could have done it much more easily and more cheaply earlier'.[12] This ambivalence towards the reconstruction of Afghanistan extends to the security sector reform process, which, from its very outset has lacked the necessary resources, leadership and security support to succeed. This adverse situation can be partially attributed to the multi-sectoral donor support scheme established to advance and underwrite the process. The rationale behind the scheme was logical – by giving the principal donors a direct stake in the process their long-term attention and support would be secured. In practice, this framework has encouraged donor rivalries and competition, hindered the exploitation of synergies across the sector and increased Afghan suspicions of the process. Global tensions stimulated by events such as the Iraq war have been superimposed on the Afghan stage creating a hostile environment for consensus building and coordination, vital prerequisites for the process.

While elements of the process, such as the counter narcotics pillar, are surely unique to the Afghan context, overall it represents the application of a general SSR formula. Steps are gradually being taken to reorient the process to meet Afghanistan's particularistic needs and complex social and political context. However, the inability of the process to stray beyond the Euro-Atlantic understanding of the security sector, hardly applicable in Afghanistan, continues to hinder implementation. The following section provides an analysis of developments in regard to each of the five pillars of the security sector reform process.

Military and Ministry of Defence (MoD) Reform

The military reform process, led by the United States with assistance from a number of donor countries, including Britain, France and Turkey, has two components - the creation of an Afghan National Army (ANA) and the reform of the Afghan Ministry of Defence (MoD). In spite of resolute US commitments to oversee the process to its fruition, progress has been slow.

Afghan National Army (ANA). The establishment of an effective and politically reliable Afghan National Army (ANA) is widely viewed as a precondition for security and stability in Afghanistan. The primary task of this force will not be to defend Afghanistan from foreign invasion, a capability that would take decades to develop at a massive cost, but to insulate the state from internal spoiler groups. The US military began training the first intake of Afghan recruits on 14 May 2002 at the country's former military academy on the outskirts of Kabul, renamed the Kabul Military Training Centre (KMTC). The US programme was originally based on a ten-week training cycle with two classes being trained simultaneously, but this was reduced to eight weeks in the fall of 2003 in order to expedite the process. The original aim of the programme was to train 18,000 troops by October 2003, however, as of June 2004, only 11,000 ANA recruits had graduated. High desertion rates accounted for the programme's inability to meet its force targets. In the summer of 2003, the desertion rate reached a high water mark of ten per cent per month, corresponding to seventy-two per cent on a yearly basis. The US was able to gradually reduce desertions from a rate of six per cent in November to a respectable one-point-eight per cent by May 2004.[13] There are numerous reasons for the high desertion rates:

• *Recruitment*: The US initially relied on the Ministry of Defence and regional military commanders to provide recruits for the ANA programme who submitted unqualified candidates while maintaining their most loyal and best-trained troops. In an effort to reconfigure the recruitment process, the US has established National Army Volunteer Centres (NAVC) in several provincial capitals staffed by specially trained ANA officers, and will provide recruits with food and accommodation until they are deployed to the KMTC.

• *Ethnic Imbalance*: The issue of ethnic representation, which cuts across the entire SSR process, has complicated efforts to build a national army. At the beginning of the training process the pool of recruits featured a disproportionately large number of Tajiks, particularly at officer level, a result of interference by the Tajik dominated Ministry of Defence. This fostered suspicion of the institution among other minority groups and had a deleterious effect on morale, as reports of abuse perpetrated by Tajik officers on recruits of other ethnic groups surfaced. The US has taken a number of steps to address this inequity, primarily through improvements in the recruitment process and have indicated that, as of spring 2004, it was roughly representative of the wider population.

- *Low Pay*: The issue of pay was the principal cause of the high ANA desertion rates. This problem was systematically addressed in mid-2003 when salaries were raised. In spite of these advancements, US sources estimate, on the basis of a survey of ANA troops, that the salary level required to keep soldiers in the ranks is approximately $150 per month. When operating in the field, ANA troops earn close to this figure, but the yearly average still falls short, at about $110.[14]

ANA units have reportedly performed extremely well in their initial limited deployments and have been largely welcomed by Afghan communities where they have served. Units of the Central Corps, which reached full strength in March 2004, have been deployed on combat operations against the Taliban and al-Qaeda in the southeast; to support the ISAF-led heavy weapons cantonment program in Kabul; to quell regional disturbances in Herat, Mazar-i-Sharif, and Faryab; and will be called upon to support the country's first election in September 2004. Regional expansion envisages four commands beyond the Central Corps giving a total of ten brigades outside Kabul. The ONSC estimates that at the current rate of output, the ANA will be able to field a force of approximately 23,000 by June 2006.[15]. It is important that in light of the government's limited degree of internal revenue, a final force size is chosen on the basis of its economic sustainability. Already, shortfalls in equipment, particularly in transportation, have emerged. The US has committed itself to fund the capital and recurrent expenditures of the force for the foreseeable future, but in the coming years the MoD will be expected to cover an increasing portion of the ANA's budget.

Ministry of Defence (MoD) Reform. The Ministry of Defence, Ministry of Interior and the security services are dominated by one faction of the Northern Alliance, the Panjsheri Tajiks led by Defence Minister Fahim. This faction was able to assert control of the security organs of Afghanistan at the Bonn conference where its position as the military partner of the Coalition allowed it to dictate the contours of the post-war political order. In the aftermath of Bonn, Minister Fahim worked assiduously to consolidate his control over the security sector. Illustrating this concerted effort, of the one hundred generals appointed by Fahim during the interim administration, ninety were Panjsheri Tajiks.[16] In the Defence Ministry, two attempts have thus far been made to implement institutional and personnel reforms. The first, in early 2003, resulted in some new appointments within the general staff, however, it did not significantly alter the balance of power within the Ministry. The second, launched in September 2003, saw twenty-two new appointments created, affecting all the senior positions within the Ministry, including five deputy ministers. The reforms installed a Pashtun, General Abdul Rahim Wardak, as the first deputy for the Army Chief of Staff and three additional deputies representing the Hazara, Uzbek, and Pashtun ethnicities. Although the appointments are significant, two of the three top posts within the ministry remained in the hands of the Panjsheri faction. The next phase of the reform process will be the appointment of 309 mid-ranking officials at the Ministry, the first one hundred of which were announced in December 2003. The recent creation of a recruitment board, which will determine new appointments, should enhance both the speed and accountability of the process.[17]

Police and Ministry of Interior (MoI) Reform

The bulk of the country's police officers have not received any form of police training, lack basic equipment, including firearms and transportation, and is chronically corrupt. Most are former mujahidin fighters that bring a militiaman's mentality to the job that is not conducive for effective policing. Afghanistan's police reform process was set in motion on 14-15 March 2002 when Germany, as the designated lead nation, introduced a comprehensive plan to create a national police service, dubbed the 'German Project for Support of the Police in Afghanistan'. Since March 2002, the project has launched a number of initiatives including the re-establishment of the central command in Kabul and the initiation of a reform programme for the Ministry of Interior; the rehabilitation of the Kabul Police Academy, responsible for training the officer and the non-commissioned officer (NCO) corps of the police services; and the provision of equipment to enhance police communications and mobility.

In early 2003 the US, in an effort to expedite the formation of a professional national police service, established a centre in the capital to rapidly train rank-and-file police. The US commitment was subsequently expanded to include the construction of eight Regional Training Centres (RTC), mirroring the CTC. As of June 2004, six of the RTCs in Kabul, Paktia, Jalalabad, Kunduz, Mazar-i-Sharif, and Kandahar had begun operation and two more in Bamiyan and Herat were scheduled for construction by the end of 2004.

Although the training process is progressing at a satisfactory pace, the overall police reform process has been slowed by a number of factors, including a lack of equipment notably in the areas of communications and transportation, crumbling infrastructure, poor pay, corruption and problems with recruitment. Training is a means to an end not an end to itself. If the newly trained police are merely deployed to existing police posts throughout the country, often consisting of decrepit buildings with little equipment and grossly inadequate pay, they will be drawn into previous patterns of corruption. If the process is to be sustainable, reforms must reach down to the district level.

Ministry of Interior Reform. In spite of the appointment of a progressive and forward-thinking Minister, Ahmad Jalali, Afghanistan's Interior Ministry has been shown to be a largely dysfunctional institution, rivalling only the Defence Ministry in terms of corruption and mismanagement. According to available personnel statistics, the Ministry employs 93,000 people throughout the country, yet it lacks a coherent salary payment system, basic equipment and coherent organisational structures. Germany and the US have developed parallel schemes to reform the Ministry. Germany has contributed a senior advisor to the Minister of Interior while the United States has embedded a team of eight policing experts within the Ministry to carry out reforms at the operational level. Ensuring that the Ministry is governed in an efficient and accountable manner is the lynchpin for police reform. Interior Ministry officials are considering a number of options to overhaul the institution to ensure it is operated in accordance with international standards of good governance, including the establishment of a Civil Service Academy and the launch of in-service training. However, neither of these initiatives has begun due to funding difficulties.

National Security Directorate (NSD). The NSD is one of the largest institutions in the country, consisting of 15,000-20,000 employees. It is rife with corruption and unrepresentative of the country's ethnic make-up. The US Central Intelligence Agency (CIA) and the Government of Germany are currently spearheading reform efforts, but the process has been characterised by a lack of transparency and coordination. The goal of the programme is to create a non-political, non-partisan and accountable security service. Among the significant accomplishments made have been the establishment of a merit based appointment system and the promulgation of a charter that circumscribes the wide powers of arrest and detention that it previously held. Plans have been made to create an Intelligence Academy that will train 5,000 new officers within five years. Shortfalls in resources for logistics, communications and transportation have hindered efforts to professionalise the force.

Counter-Narcotics

On 17 January 2002, in an attempt to halt drug production, the Afghan Interim Administration (AIA) banned poppy cultivation and the consumption of heroin and introduced, with British support, an aggressive poppy eradication programme. From the outset, the programme was plagued by inefficiency and mismanagement. The abject failure of this $34 million programme, prompting UK and ATA officials to shelve it, was evinced by the fact that poppy cultivation actually increased in the targeted areas. Despite the failure of this programme, a number of important steps have been undertaken to confront the problem, including the establishment of a Counter-Narcotics Directorate within the ONSC to provide technical support and advice to relevant Ministries and to ensure the timely implementation of national drug control objectives; the adoption of a National Drug Control Strategy (NDCS) aimed at eliminating the production, consumption, and trafficking of illicit narcotics into, within, and from the country; the inauguration of a Counter-Narcotics Police of Afghanistan (CNPA) within the Ministry of Interior, to spearhead interdiction efforts; and the promulgation of a National Drug Law on 20 October 2003.

Judicial Reform

Afghanistan's long civil war shattered the country's judicial system. To alter this untenable situation, a judicial reform process, under Italian supervision, has been established to revitalise the country's legal system. The process has been spearheaded by a Judicial Commission established by the Bonn Agreement to rebuild Afghan justice institutions and re-establish the rule of law. It has overseen the implementation of the following initiatives – the redrafting of legal codes covering a number of subjects, the ratification of an Interim Criminal Procedure Code, the completion of law collection, the establishment of a training programme for judicial personnel including judges, magistrates and defence counsellors, the inauguration of infrastructure rehabilitation activities, and the launch of administrative reforms. In spite of these initiatives, judicial reform has lagged far behind the other pillars of the security sector reform process. It has been hindered by insufficient resources, insecurity, a lack of human capacity, insufficient coordination between the permanent Afghan Judicial institutions, the Supreme Court, the Attorney General, and the Ministry of Justice, a lack of adequate correctional facilities, the limited availability of legislation, legal texts, and jurisprudence collections, and poor infrastructure.

Disarmament, Demobilisation and Reintegration of Ex-combatants (DDR)

Afghanistan's DDR programme is more than just disarmament or targeted job creation. The overarching objective of the programme is to dismantle active military formations in order to foster an enabling environment for reconstruction. It is a means to sever internal dependency and patronage relationships and facilitate the transition from a war to peace economy The Afghan New Beginnings Programme (ANBP), introduced in February 2003 at a donor's conference in Tokyo, was created to assist line Ministries to advance DDR under the auspices of the United Nations Assistance Mission for Afghanistan (UNAMA) and the United Nations Development Programme (UNDP), with support from Japan, the lead donor for DDR.

A demobilisation and reintegration programme targeting children has also been established by the United Nations Children's Fund (UNICEF). The UN agency has determined that there are 8,000 child soldiers that require special demobilisation and reintegration assistance in Afghanistan. In light of Afghanistan's recent history of foreign intervention and internecine strife, during which it became a sanctuary for terrorists and mercenaries and a dumping ground for arms, the two DDR initiatives have set an ambitious goal, to complete the demilitarisation of the country in three years.

The ANBP and the UNICEF child soldiers programme were launched in late 2003 and early 2004 respectively. In light of the incessant delays, which have plagued the DDR process, their mere commencement should be celebrated. However, the early results of implementation have shown that the core preconditions for DDR – a minimum level of security, a broad-based consensus among key powerbrokers and commanders, further reforms of the Ministry of Defence, and the availability of labour-intensive employment opportunities – are not yet in place.

The initial, disappointing results of the pilot phase of the ANBP show that the programme's design is at variance with the prevailing conditions on the ground and does not adequately address the main challenges to DDR implementation that exist. The lack of mechanisms to entice and co-opt commanders to submit to the programme coupled with its overemphasis on active AMF soldiers, ignoring irregular tribal forces, exemplify the programme's inherent limitations. The ANA is taking steps to rectify these deficiencies, notably the establishment of a scheme to profile and devise targeted incentive packages for commanders. It is important that further steps are taken to reorient the programme for its failure will have far-reaching implications for the ongoing political process.

The Office of the National Security Council (ONSC)

The Afghan National Security council was established by presidential decree to provide the President with advice on security related issues and to develop and coordinate Afghan security policy, acting as a bridge between the line security Ministries and the executive branch of government. It was intended to act as a coordinating umbrella for the security sector reform process, harmonising the competing agendas of donors and Afghan stakeholders and serving as a focal point for government policy and strategy. The ONSC can also be viewed as a bulwark for good governance within the security sector as it is responsible for oversight of policy implementation by the line Ministries and security forces. It is mandated to monitor and analyse the implementation of executive orders and cabinet decisions to ensure the integrity of the chain of command. Despite the urgent need for such a body, few of the principal stakeholders in the SSR process have accepted its authority. It has been sidelined on many of the principal issues and has yet to fully establish its legitimacy. By the summer of 2004, this situation had begun to change due to shifting donor policy and pressure from President Karzai, but it has yet to fully realise its mandate.

Lessons Learned

When analysing Afghanistan's ongoing SSR process a number of general obstacles can be discerned, including insecurity, inadequate coordination, insufficient administrative capacity and resource shortfalls. Rising levels of insecurity spurred by spoiler groups and regional warlords have, in the ab-

sence of an international or local security buffer, severely complicated reforms. The lack of coordination among donors, other external actors, and
Afghan stakeholders has undermined efforts to erect a unified strategy. The
anaemic capacity of the Afghan government has slowed change and the unwillingness of donors to make long-term and durable commitments of funds
to the process has cast a shadow of uncertainty on the process. Although the
SSR process in Afghanistan remains at an early stage, a number of important
lessons can drawn from its experience with implementation that may help
narrow these gaps.

Local Ownership and Consensus

For SSR to be successful and sustainable it must be built upon a consensus
among local actors. As UNDP has stated, SSR 'programmes must be locally
designed, locally implemented, and locally evaluated, for what may appear
to be productive from the perspective of the international community may
have significantly different connotations and effects when judged by domestic actors.'[18] Most of the SSR programmes implemented over the past decade, Afghanistan included, could be characterised as 'donor driven'. This
denies the process legitimacy and makes it susceptible to attack from spoilers and extremists.

    The form that local ownership takes is also very important. As wide a
consensus as possible must be achieved for SSR to be sustainable. The international community must be circumspect when choosing local partners to
implement SSR. In Afghanistan, the Bonn political process favoured a narrow ethnic-based faction of the Northern Alliance, the Panjsheri Tajiks, facilitating its assumption of control over the principal power ministries of the
government. This served to factionalise the SSR process along ethnic lines.
Luckham asserts that 'when ethnic patronage is built into military, police
and security bureaucracies, it corrupts them, weakens discipline, reinforces a
sense of impunity and fosters public (and especially minority) distrust of the
state itself.'[19] In selecting local partners on the basis of military and political
expediency—the Northern Alliance represented the only coherent military
power in the country after the fall of the Taliban, primarily due to US supplies of money and arms – the international community institutionalised a
destructive ethnic imbalance in the security ministries that has delegitimised
SSR and undermined efforts to establish democratic accountability.

Coordination

Inadequate coordination is a common dilemma afflicting SSR processes. There are four distinct levels of coordination that can be identified in the Afghan SSR process with coordination deficits experienced at each level in the process:

Donor-Donor: At the donor-donor level, the nature of Afghanistan's multi-sectoral donor support scheme has complicated coordination efforts. The rationale behind the scheme, which divided responsibility for each of the five pillars of the SSR process among the five main donor states for the security sector, was that providing donors with a direct stake in the process would deepen their commitment to it. In actuality, it has fragmented reform efforts and triggered 'turf wars' among the donors. The various institutions of a security sector are highly interconnected. Reforming them relies on the exploitation of synergies between reform programmes. The SSR framework in Afghanistan has obstructed the formation of such relationships. For example, although relations between the German and US police reform programmes are cordial, levels of collaboration and joint planning are surprisingly low. The two policing programmes have established separate schemes to reform and reorganise the Ministry of Interior that feature a large degree of duplication. Such situations are common across the SSR agenda.

Donor-Government: Communication and coordination between donor agencies and the relevant Ministries of the Afghan government could be characterised as inconsistent and of generally poor quality. For instance, in the area of military reform, the process to train the ANA has been pursued independently of the Afghan Ministry of Defence. The US forms policy for the fledgling ANA, covers its capital and recurrent expenditures, and utilises fledgling ANA units to support Coalition military operations in the southeast. The Afghan MoD has little influence over the ANA, seen in many quarters as a US militia. There are clear reasons why the MoD has been sidelined in the process, notably that it has obstructed the ANA training process on numerous occasions. Nevertheless, it highlights both the lack of Afghan ownership of the process and the absence of civilian control over the newly created security forces.

Intra-Governmental: Afghanistan's line security ministries are highly fragmented, a product of the Bonn Agreement, which, in the words of one analyst, created a government 'that rested on a power base of warlords'.[20] Exemplifying the problem of intra-governmental coordination is the justice sector. The three principal Afghan justice institutions, the Supreme Court, the Attorney General, and the Ministry of Justice are highly factionalised and deeply divided. The failure of these Ministries to develop a unity of effort and purpose has stalled the judicial reform process and precipitated the collapse of the first government appointed Judicial Commission intended to spearhead reform.

Inter-Agency: Coordination problems are not limited to donor states and the Afghan government, but have also taken place at the sub-national, agency and programme level. For example, two programmes have been created to advance the demilitarisation of Afghan ex-combatants, the ANBP, which targets adult ex-combatants and UNICEF's child soldiers programme, which targets underage combatants. In spite of the two programmes' shared objectives, they are operated independently with separate sources of funding. There is little communication, let alone collaboration, between the programmes, despite the fact that there is a significant degree of overlap in their administrative structures. It is difficult to discern a rational reason for the separation. Methodological differences between the planners of the two programmes appear to have provoked the split. Moreover, in terms of indigenous coordination the Office of the National Security Council (ONSC) has encountered significant difficulties in asserting its authority, due to intra-governmental rivalries and the reluctance of certain donors to recognise its authority. Key ongoing priorities remain namely the compilation of a National Threat Assessment; the formulation of a comprehensive National Security Policy Framework; and the creation of a high level SSR steering group, assembling all of the relevant stakeholders.

Local Capacity

In post-conflict settings, state institutions are likely to be dysfunctional and state capacity limited. This problem is particularly acute in Afghanistan, where after twenty-three years of civil war most of the machinery of the state has collapsed and indigenous capacity has been severely depleted. The current government is beset by problems of bureaucratic inefficiency, disorganisation, corruption and nepotism. This illustrates a contradiction in regard to the implementation of SSR, for 'the ability to implement the principles of good governance in the security sector is reliant on the existence of well-functioning institutions and capable human resources.'[21] It is difficult to forge democratically accountable security structures in very weak states suffering from deficits in institutional and human capacity and the only way to resolve this contradiction is the application of robust institutional reforms and capacity development programmes across the government during the first phase of the political process. A number of specific measures should be applied to create a solid foundation for SSR - salaries of all security forces must be raised to a level commensurate with the costs of living and paid on a timely basis; a comprehensive training and re-training programme for civil servants and security forces must be designed and launched; unqualified personnel must be redeployed or removed, a severance scheme should be introduced to remove employees who are politically unreliable or who lack applicable skills; and succinct recruitment procedures and guidelines should be introduced.

Investment in Traditional Structures

SSR programmes should be tailored to fit the social and political context where they are applied and should aim to build upon traditional security structures. External actors must recognise that 'while new security structures are established to resemble more formal 'acceptable' security and state institutions, personal, informal security networks continue to flourish and may even become more politically and economically viable at the expense of reform efforts'.[22] Supplanting organic structures with external ones can serve to disrupt communities rather then provide stability.

In Afghanistan, the notion that all traditional security systems have been destroyed, are dysfunctional, or incompatible with international norms of human rights is incorrect. Not only are traditional structures intact and functioning, but also they present the most viable option to promote security and stability in some areas. This does not obviate the need to introduce Western practices and principles, it merely demonstrates that a mixed approach that respects exiting traditions is most appropriate. An important caveat to this argument is that traditional structures deemed to conform to international norms must be fully integrated into the wider security sector and subjected to strict standards of accountability. If permitted to remain outside the formal security sector, such structures could erode the authority and legitimacy of the entire system.

Donor Funding

The burden of funding the Afghan SSR process over the next five to seven
years will inevitably fall on the shoulders of the international community. A
report presented by the Afghan government at a Donor Conference in Berlin
on 20 March - 1 April 2004, offered a detailed plan for the reconstruction of
Afghanistan's security sector over the next seven years. According to the
report, entitled 'Securing Afghanistan's Future: Accomplishments and the
Strategic Path Forward', $2.6 billion will be needed to implement the proc-
ess over this time period (see Table 9.1 for funding breakdown). It is imperative that the donor community meet this funding request.

Table 9.1: Overall Security Sector Needs (2004-2007) [23]

Sub-Sector	2004-2006 (in millions of US$)	2007-2010 (in millions of US$)
National Police and Law Enforcement	504	140
Counter Narcotics	98	66
National Army	754	289
Justice	73	20
Disarmament, Demobilisation, and Reintegration of Ex-Combatants (DDR)	117	100
Mine Action	224	196
TOTAL	1770	811

The lack of government capacity in Afghanistan to handle funds in a
transparent manner has compelled donors in such settings to allocate security
sector funds directly to donor agencies and programmes, circumventing government institutions. While donor justifications for such practices are valid,
it has a number of deleterious implications – it divests the government of
ownership over the process, diminishes popular perception of the role of
government in driving reform, hinders donor coordination, and arouses suspicion of donor intentions among the local population. A more effective
policy would be to transfer aid to national government institutions through
internationally administered trust funds. This would permit robust international oversight of donor aid while giving the government authority over its

disbursement. Several trust funds have been established to facilitate the de-livery of donor aid to the security sector in Afghanistan. The most notable of these is the Law and Order Trust Fund for Afghanistan (LOTFA), created in December 2002 to cover the recurrent budgetary expenditures, most impor-tantly salaries, of the police. The establishment of the trust fund was hailed as a watershed in the police reform process, however, it has been hindered by fund-raising difficulties. As of November 2003, only $ 45.5 million of the $115 million funding target for that fiscal year had been collected.[24]

Regional Security Framework

In Afghanistan the involvement of regional and international states, notably Pakistan, Iran, India, and Russia, is viewed by many Afghans as the princi-pal cause of the country's seemingly interminable instability. Foreign inter-ference in Afghanistan has commonly taken the form of external support for sub-national proxies, often with linguistic, ethnic or religious ties. Although most states with a history of intervention in Afghanistan have supported the US-led Operation Enduring Freedom and the subsequent state-building ef-fort, most continue to provide covert support for various warlords, an effort to hedge their bets in the event of a US withdrawal from the region.

To create an environment conducive for SSR, external interference in Afghanistan must be halted. A significant step towards achieving this goal was achieved with the signing of the Kabul Declaration on Good-neighbourly Relations, a pledge of non-interference by Afghanistan's imme-diate neighbours: Pakistan, Uzbekistan, Turkmenistan, China and Iran, on 22 December 2002. The United States and the international community must build on this achievement by guaranteeing Afghanistan's external security. Some observers have even suggested that Afghanistan be declared a neutral state, like Austria or Switzerland. SSR will be difficult to advance if such profound external threats to the process persist.

International Security Assistance

During the period needed to complete basic structural reforms and form ade-quate security, it is advisable that international forces fill the prevailing secu-rity gap. As Nicole Ball states, 'it is very important to have effective forces available to raise the cost to local stakeholders of choosing violence over dialogue and compromise in war-affected countries.'[25] In Afghanistan, an expansion of the International Security Assistance Force (ISAF) from Kabul to outlying areas could bridge the prevailing security gap. NATO, currently in command of ISAF, has pledged to do so through the establishment of Provisional Reconstruction Teams (PRT), small units of soldiers and civil affairs officers mandated to provide a security umbrella for reconstruction activities and to carry out small-scale development projects at key locations across the country. The concept was originally devised by the Pentagon to win hearts and minds in the southeast of the country, where anti-American sentiment was growing exponentially due to continuing US operations against the Taliban. However, the alliance has encountered difficulties in gathering the necessary resources from its member-states to carry out this limited expansion.

Conclusion

The reality of the current situation in Afghanistan is that despite modest achievements made since the fall of the Taliban, conditions in the country are simply not conducive for security sector reform. SSR is widely portrayed in Afghanistan as a panacea for the country's immediate security woes, a task it is inherently ill-equipped to confront. It has been thrust into this unfortunate role due to the international community's reluctance to deploy a significant peace support operation, but regardless it represents a fundamental obstacle to the process. Expediency has forced compromises and delays on some of the core principles of democracy and good governance. The adverse implications of this situation are clear, for as Luckham points out, 'democratic accountability and the rule of law are not luxuries that can safely be postponed until order and security are restored; they are inseparable from it.'[26]

Other issues that have encumbered the process include the ambivalence of US motivations in the country, the lack of stakeholder consensus, and shortfalls in funding and weaknesses in the SSR model. The Bonn Agreement itself has paradoxically been an obstacle to reform. It institutionalised inequality, led to an ethnicisation of the government, and failed to adequately address security sector reform, missing a seminal opportunity to legitimise the process. While the agreement was supposed to inaugurate a new democratic path for Afghanistan, in effect, it re-established a form of warlord government, entrenching the country's most powerful commanders and their 'clientelistic' networks at the heart of the new political order. This has created the untenable situation in which some of the most powerful ministers of the government are adversaries of the process, as it threatens their vital interests.

To place the security sector reform process in Afghanistan back on track, a number of core issues must be addressed. The contradictions in the policy of the US, by far the most important donor in the country, must be resolved. US strategy in Afghanistan has two distinct dimensions: The war against the Taliban and other spoiler groups in the southeast of the country and the support for President Hamid Karzai's regime and the concomitant state building process in Kabul. Unfortunately, these two arms of US policy have worked at cross purposes, generating friction between the US agencies that oversee them. For instance, the US military, under the auspices of Operation Enduring Freedom, has allied itself with several regional powerbrokers, providing them with money in return for the use of their militias in anti-Taliban operations – individual commanders receive up to $10,000 per month in cash grants from the US. The relatively small number of US troops deployed in this theatre of operations has prompted the Pentagon to rely heavily on local forces, strengthening and emboldening some of the very warlords the central government is endeavouring to bring to heel. This adverse situation is representative of the broader ambivalence of US policy towards Afghanistan. Is the US aim to democratise Afghanistan and meet the security needs of the population, or is it merely to contain the security threat Afghanistan may pose to the outside world? If the former is correct, a much more robust US commitment will be needed in Afghanistan.

It is vital that the NATO-led International Security Assistance Force (ISAF) fulfil its pledges of limited countrywide expansion under the auspices of the Provisional Reconstruction Team (PRT) framework. NATO has pledged to do so through the establishment of eight additional PRTs, bringing the total to twenty-one throughout Afghanistan. However, four months after NATO's governing council authorised expansion, member states have yet to commit the requisite troops. Although NATO Secretary General Jaap de Hoop Scheffer has repeatedly referred to Afghanistan as the alliance's 'top priority', he has been unable to convince its reluctant member states to commit the needed resources. With the security situation in Afghanistan clearly worsening the need for NATO expansion, both to demonstrate international resolve and provide a security buffer, is crucial.

The process must be owned, directed, and coordinated by the Afghan government. Afghanistan surely faces an acute capacity deficit, yet it has successfully established a policy development and coordinating body, the National Security Council, that can oversee reform, and has put forward a competent strategic framework, the Securing Afghanistan's Future Report, that charts a course for the process. Both the ONSC and the SAF are fully Afghan owned and should be endorsed by the international community. Only by doing so can the unity of effort and purpose required for the process to succeed be achieved.

The Afghan SSR experience provides a vivid depiction of the challenges that face SSR implementation in the ever-shifting security landscape of the post-9/11 era. To bridge the gap between planning and implementation or concept and context, the lessons learned in areas like Afghanistan must be understood and absorbed. Afghanistan's SSR process is not without major achievements, yet it is clear that a fundamental reappraisal of the programme's goals and the resources needed to achieve them must be undertaken. In many respects, the Afghan case illustrates the grave challenges to SSR in a complex and hostile security environment. The success of the state-building process is intricately tied to the success of SSR, however, with the international community unwilling to commit the necessary political, economic and military resources to ensure its success, its margin for error has been reduced considerably. In light of Afghanistan's broadening security dilemma, the need for a shift in course on SSR has never been more apparent. The reorientation of the process would set an important precedent for other SSR programmes such as Iraq, which face a similar array of threats.

Notes

[1] See Chanaa, J., *Security Sector Reform: Issues, Challenges and Prospects* (Oxford University Press, New York 2002) p. 61.

[2] As quoted in Sedra, M., 'Introduction', *Confronting Afghanistan's Security Dilemma: Reforming the Security Sector*, BICC Brief 28, (BICC, Bonn, 2003), p. 8.

[3] The needs assessment was prepared by the World Bank, the Asia Development Bank (ADB), and the United Nations Development Programme (UNDP).

[4] See Rubin, B., et al., *Building a New Afghanistan: The Value of Success, the Cost of Failure, Center on International Cooperation* (New York University, New York, 2004), p. 14.

[5] Office of the Afghan National Security Council (ONSC), Security Sector Paper, Government of Afghanistan, Kabul, p. 15.

[6] See Rubin, B., '(Re) Building Afghanistan: The Folly of Stateless Democracy', *Current History* (April 2004) , pp. 165-170, p. 4.

[7] Sedra, M., 'Are the Taliban Really Gone'? *Foreign Policy In Focus* (Silver City, NM & Washington, DC, 2004), p. 1.

8   On 2 May 2004, a delegation of ten senior members of Hizb-i-Islami, claiming to represent the group's executive council, pledged their support to the Karzai government and the ongoing political process. The announcement was made after several months of negotiations with government officials. However, the delegation did not represent the leader of the organisation, Gulbuddin Hekmatyar, who, with the support of a hardcore group of followers, continues to oppose the government.

9   Sedra, M., 'Are the Taliban', p. 3.

10   As quoted in Rubin, 'Rebuilding Afghanistan', p. 4.

11   United Nations Office on Drugs and Crime (UNODC).), *The Opium Problem in Afghanistan: An International Problem* (United Nations, New York, 2003), p. 10.

12   Rubin, 'Rebuilding Afghanistan', p. 167.

13   Giustozzi, A. and Sedra, M., *Securing Afghanistan's Future:*Accomplishments *and Strategic Pathway Forward* – Afghan National Army Technical Annex, Islamic Transitional State of Afghanistan (ITSA),(Kabul, 2004), p. 6.

14   Ibid.

15   ONSC, 'Security', p. 11.

16   See Manuel, A., and Singer, P. W.,"A New Model Afghan Army." *Foreign Affairs*, 81: 4, (2002), pp. 44-59.

17   Giustozzi and Sedra,, '*Securing'*, p. 3.

18   United Nations Development Programme (UNDP), Security Sector Reform and Transitional Justice: A Crisis Post-Conflict Programmatic Approach, (UNDP, New York, 2003), p. 15.

19   Luckham, R., 'Democratic Strategies for Security in Transition and Conflict', *Governing Insecurity: Democratic Control of Military and Security Establishments in Transitional Democracies*, (Gavin Cawthra and Robin Luckham eds. Zed Books, London, 2003), pp. 3-28, p. 22.

20   Rubin, 'Rebuilding Afghanistan', p. 167.

21   Ball, N., *Democratic Governance in the Security Sector*, Paper prepared for the UNDP Workshop on 'Learning from Experience for Afghanistan', 2002, p. 13.

22   See Chanaa, J., 'Security', p. 41-42

23   ITSA, 2004, p. 83.

24   Sedra, M. *Securing Afghanistan's Future: Accomplishments and Strategic Pathway Forward* – National Police and Law Enforcement Technical Annex, Islamic Transitional State of Afghanistan (ITSA), (Kabul, 2004), p. 8.

25   Ball, N., 'Democratic', p. 7.

26   Luckham, R., 'Democratic', p. 21.

Chapter 10

Iraq's Special Challenge: Security Sector Reform 'Under Fire'

*Walter B. Slocombe**

Introduction

The war that resulted in the fall of Saddam Hussein's regime, the occupation of the country by the US-led Coalition and the ongoing process of transition back to Iraqi sovereignty is, and will likely remain, controversial. However, the practical issue facing both the US and its coalition partners, on the one hand, and the Iraqi people on the other, is not whether the war was right (much less the quality and subtlety of American planning and leadership before and since the major fighting), but how to meet the challenges of converting the opportunities the war created into the reality of a secure, stable Iraq. The stakes are very high, most of all for the Iraqi people, but also for the US and the rest of the world. Success means an Iraq that offers its people a decent life under a system of ordered government that respects both majority rule and minority rights and that offers individual Iraqis personal security and personal liberty, in a nation and a region that has seen too little of either. Moreover, success means, for the region, an Iraq that is a force for stability and peace and an example of successful reform in an Islamic Arab nation. Conversely, failure means a risk of civil war, another authoritarian regime with the potential to destabilise the region and to acquire weapons of mass destruction, and, in general, a huge set-back for the security, economic, and

---

* From May to November 2003, the author worked in the Coalition Provisional Authority (CPA) for Iraq as Director for Security Affairs (National Security and Defence), and, as of the preparation of this chapter, he remained an unpaid consultant to CPA and the US Office of the Under Secretary of Defence for Policy and a member of the US Department of Defence's Defence Policy Board of outside advisors. However, the views expressed in this chapter are his own and not necessarily those of the CPA, the Department of Defence or any other element of the US Government.

moral interests of the nations of the Coalition, the region, and the world, and to hopes for peace in the area.

In the overall effort in Iraq, security is critical. In the immediate aftermath of the destruction of the Saddam regime, and for a considerable time afterward, outside security forces necessarily have played a major security role, but in the long run, that security must come from Iraqi organisations. Moreover, genuine transformation of Iraq from a totalitarian state to one based on the rule of law and representative constitutional government requires that the country's security organisations be fundamentally rebuilt, or, in some cases, constructed entirely anew. It is not unusual that nations in such a transition need basic security sector reform; what makes Iraq's case almost uniquely challenging is that its reform must be carried out 'under fire'. Iraq must build its security sector (like other sectors needing reform) in the face, not just of the inevitable conflicts and uncertainties of a political transition in a society with deep ethnic, sectarian, and cultural divides, but of active armed attack from a variety of enemies, united only in their determination to frustrate the transition and their willingness to use any method necessary to that end.

This chapter outlines the basic strategy for that reform that is being pursued as of the mid-2004 transition from occupation to interim sovereign Iraqi government. The strategy is essentially that of fostering the creation and restructuring of Iraqi security institutions and turning over increasing responsibility to them. The chapter begins by noting the relationship of efforts in other critical areas, notably provision of basic services, economic reform, and political construction. Turning to security issues as such, it describes the principal elements that are fostering insecurity; the continuing role of outside security forces; the various parts of the Iraqi security sector that need to be made effective; and the need to ensure that those organisations are not only effective in the short term, but structured and managed so as to be consistent with the political objective of a limited, constitutional government in which the security services are the servants of the state, not, as so often in Iraqi history, its masters. Finally, the chapter identifies some of the lessons from experience to date, lessons which seem likely to be relevant not only to the continuing effort in Iraq, but also to security sector reform efforts in general.

Security Sector Reform in Combat Conditions

To succeed in the national reconstruction that is needed for recovery from decades of tyranny and corruption, Iraqis, with the support of the Coalition, of such other members of the international community as choose to help, and of international organisations, notably the United Nations, must accomplish four different, but related, tasks:

- Provide basic services;
- Build the economy;
- Set up a government that is both representative and legitimate;
- Establish the level of security necessary for the other goals to be achievable.

It is on security, narrowly defined as the maintenance of order and the suppression of violent attacks, that this chapter concentrates. Security is not, however, simply, or even primarily, a technical military, intelligence, or police problem. Progress on the other goals is equally essential, not just for its own sake, but for security as well and although much remains to be done, much progress is being made.

Basic services – such as electricity, water, fuel supply, transportation, communications, healthcare, and education – are, for the most part, back at or above pre-war levels, and a start has been made on making up for the decades of Saddam-era deterioration in infrastructure and public services.

Economic development – essential for long term political and security success – faces obstacles inherent in Saddam's creation of a truly Stalinist economy, characterised by state control, corruption, and inefficiency, exacerbated by the de facto protectionism of sanctions. This has left a legacy of bloated and uncompetitive state-owned industry, a baroquely complex patchwork of costly and inequitable subsidies, very high unemployment, corruption and favouritism, and a culture of dependence on government support at both the individual and enterprise level. However, in contrast to places equally in need of economic reconstruction, like Bosnia, Kosovo, East Timor, Sierra Leone, and Afghanistan, Iraq has not only a critical 'cash crop' in its massive oil reserves, but abundant water, fertile land, a relatively well-educated and enterprising population, and a comparatively advanced, if badly dilapidated, infrastructure. Starting immediately after the fall of Saddam, a vibrant retail sector has sprung up, basic living standards have been sustained by expensive, but socially critical food distribution programmes and income subsidies, a single national currency introduced, and basic legal reform has begun.

The *political process* in Iraq faces real pitfalls, deriving ultimately from the difficulty of a divided nation, with only rudimentary political leadership structures and acting in the face of maximalist demands from extremists of all descriptions, reaching compromises on a system of law-based federalism and representative government that will allow the diverse elements of the country to live together and build their society and economy. Nonetheless a political and constitutional process is underway, building on a degree of political and press freedom and an emerging civil society virtually unprece-dented not just in Iraq, but in the whole Arab world. An interim constitution – the 'Transitional Administrative Law' – has been agreed, which guarantees basic human rights, provides for elections for an interim government and constitutional assembly, and starts the building of a federal, representative, and democratic structure. At the time of writing, the immediate task was agreement on the structure and powers of the provisional government set to assume sovereignty on 1 July 2004 and administer the country pending the elections to be held before February 2005. The emerging greater UN role should facilitate compromises that Iraqi leaders would find difficult to make if the effort continued to be managed primarily by the Coalition, or if it were left entirely to the Iraqi leaders.

It cannot plausibly be doubted that the *security situation* in Iraq in mid-2004 would be unacceptable in the long run. If narrowly based, but well-organized violence succeeds in turning the mass of the population against not just the occupation, but also the prospects of political compromise and establishment of law-based security, the prospect will be grim. The individual incidents of violence – whether ambushes of Coalition soldiers and civilian workers, mass killings of Shias gathered at religious observances or the efforts of the extremist Shia leader Muqtadr al Sadr to establish control of Shia-dominated-cities – are all too real. However, in most of the country streets and stores are full of people, basic services are improving, schools and universities are open, crime is down, employment is up, the currency is stable, and civil society is beginning to function. Even in terms of physical danger, for ordinary Iraqis not personally involved in government or the security services the most important security issue is that of ordinary crime, not politically motivated violence.

The ultimate issue is whether the forces opposed to success can manage, not so much to drive the Coalition out, as to stop Iraqis being willing to work together in building a new and different Iraq. Casualties to American and other Coalition military forces and civilian workers understandably generate the greatest concern outside Iraq. However, from the point of view of the prospects for success, the critical vulnerability is not attacks on foreign forces or personnel, but those aimed at Iraqis who cooperate with the Coalition and are working to build a new Iraq. These attacks could severely hamper the building and reform of the security sector if they make it impossible to recruit and maintain the necessary personnel, at both leadership and rank and file levels. Accordingly, building security is absolutely essential. In the short to medium term foreign military forces will retain a significant security role, but the critical task is to build Iraq's capacity to take care of its own security. This is the goal of most Iraqis, every bit as much as it is of the Coalition nations. Self-sustaining security will require that Iraq have competent police, intelligence services, border patrols, and other security organs, as well as military forces and local paramilitary reserves. The pre-war equivalent security institutions were, at best deeply compromised, and, at worst, pillars of the old regime. Building security capability, therefore, requires fundamental reform and rebuilding, changing leadership, training, control and oversight, and basic institutional culture.

The many challenges to Iraq's internal security require that its security institutions are highly effective. Yet, the new Iraq's security forces must also be truly compatible with a law-based, democratic and representative system of government for an ethnically and religiously diverse nation going through a very difficult social and economic transformation. Reaching that goal will require security sector reform on a grand scale. Iraq is far from unique in needing such far-reaching security sector reform. In the past twenty years, a surprising number of nations casting off authoritarian regimes have faced similar demands for creating new, or at least fundamentally reformed, security institutions – not just in the former Soviet empire, but in places as different as South Africa, Latin America, Bosnia, East Timor and Taiwan.

However, Iraq faces a special misfortune. In contrast to almost every other case, except arguably Afghanistan, Iraq must accomplish security sector reform under conditions of active direct attack by internal and external forces using terrorist methods to frustrate the process. Iraq's new security institutions must be both immediately effective and permanently democratic and law-abiding – not an easy combination. In short, it must accomplish security sector reform 'under fire,' that is in conditions of daily violence and well-supported, skilled campaigns to undermine security.

The Sources of the Threat to Reform

The security challenge is compounded by the multiple and overlapping dimensions to the threats Iraq faces. The distinctions among the groups threatening security are real, but not always sharp. Broadly, all the threat groups share a common goal of undermining progress by making the country too dangerous for outsiders and too fearful for Iraqis. Very disparate groups are prepared to cooperate tactically, and sometimes to masquerade as one another, making it difficult to attribute specific incidents to specific sources. All use terrorist methods, and even those with the strongest indigenous roots take advantage of porous borders and foreign financial and physical havens. Moreover all, if they succeeded, would establish regimes that would be most unlikely to respect basic human rights, individual and collective, or pursue a peaceful foreign policy.

However, for all their similarities, the threat groups differ in composition, motivation, and tactics – and therefore in the responses that will be effective against them. The security challenge comes from these sources:

The Saddamite Returnists. For most of the period since the fall of Saddam, the most numerous and militarily significant group has been the surviving, non-reconciled core of Saddam's support; and this group continues to be a major element in the violence. Likely to number no more than a few thousand out of an Iraqi population of some twenty-eight million and a former Baath Party membership of well over a million, these elements have been responsible for most of the 'military' style attacks on Coalition forces and on Iraqis who cooperate with the Coalition. The actual operations sponsored by these elements are often carried out not by the core Baathists, who need to survive personally to succeed, but by hired thugs and dupes. The capture of Saddam badly damaged the reputation and cohesiveness of the old Baath Party leadership, nonetheless, the Returnists retain a strong, tightly knit organisational structure. They have access to considerable personnel, financial, and weapons resources both inside and outside the country, a deep presence in certain areas heavily Sunni populated, and the motivation of deeply felt fears of what a successful Iraqi transformation would mean for their past special privileges. The Returnists have no overarching value but power, however, they are quite prepared to espouse in name the causes of Iraqi nationalism, Islamic fundamentalism, or Sunni sectionalism and to work operationally with other groups with whom they have essentially no ideological affinity.

Indigenous Sunni extremists. The second major threat element is composed of various Iraq-based Islamist terrorist groups, mostly with some element of a radical Sunni Islamic agenda. They are typified by – but not limited to – the Ansar al-Islam organisation, which operated in Iraq before the war, and has sought to expand its activities since. These Sunni elites and their clients have no great loyalty to Saddam or his Baathist clique, but they fear the loss of past ethnic privilege and the prospect of an Iraq where the Shia majority has real power. With their strong radical Islamist foundation, these groups are in a better position than the Returnists to recruit suicide bombers and other Islam-motivated operatives and to exploit Sunni fears and resentments. It is likely that these people are largely responsible not only for much of the fighting in Sunni communities, but also for the several massively destructive attacks on Shia religious sites and leaders, if only because those attacks are consistent with their objective of fomenting a Shia-Sunni civil conflict. However, they lack the organisational base of the Baath Party leadership or its hidden resources of funds and weaponry. Moreover, as the Zarqawi appeal to al-Qaeda to strike at Shia to arouse a conflict with Sunnis demonstrates, they appear to doubt the strength of their support even within the Sunni community and their ability to sustain the struggles without broader support.

Shia extremists. For the most part, the majority of the Shia community has not been a major source of violence. Over most of the occupation period, it is remarkable how relatively little Shia-based disorder occurred, particularly in regard to Shia groups striking back at their past tormentors. Despite the massive atrocities committed in the past decade costing literally millions of Shia lives and untold hardship, there has been strikingly little spontaneous or organised revenge. A series of murderous attacks on Shia religious leaders and holy sites failed to produce much in the way of a Shia backlash. However, from the start of the occupation a group of Shia extremists, centred around Muqtadr al-Sadr, have stood ready to challenge the moderate Shia leadership and to periodically carry out violent attacks on Coalition personnel. Small in numbers and still with only very limited support in the broader

Shia community, this group seeks to mobilise Shia resentment, to displace the traditional leadership, centred around Grand Ayatollah Sistani, and to turn the Shia community initially against the Coalition and, in all probability, thereafter against the more traditional leadership and any possibility of power sharing or respect for minority rights. The critical determinate will not be the immediate tactical success of the Coalition forces in fighting Sadr's militia, but the willingness and ability of the established Shia leadership to maintain its position and stand up to the extremists. In this contest, the prestige of the traditional leadership is a substantial asset, but it will also be essential to address the underlying concerns of the Shia population, in particular its understandable determination not to again be denied the influence its majority status implies.

External terrorist groups. It is appropriate to be somewhat sceptical of claims – whether from outsiders eager to equate the struggle in Iraq with the global war on terrorism or from some Iraqis, especially Sunnis, eager to blame the problems strictly on outsiders – that the primary source of the violence in Iraq lies outside the country. Much, probably most, of Iraq's security problem is internal. Nonetheless, there is evidence of individual foreign fighters joining essentially indigenous Iraqi groups. Moreover, it is clear that outside terrorist groups, al-Qaeda being the leading one, potentially find Iraq a congenial environment, because of general disorder, easy access across porous borders and some support from elements of the population. Even more than the indigenous Sunni radicals, these groups are able to organise spectacular suicide bombings – and are also inclined to strike at Shia targets. Nonetheless, the pleading tone of Zaqawi's appeal for al-Qaeda to attack Shia targets suggests that al-Qaeda, whatever might be its ambitions, is not the main, or perhaps even a major, source of the attacks in Iraq today.

Local criminals. Finally, and far more important than most outsiders realise, is the fact that Iraq faces an acute problem of ordinary, greed-based criminality. For example, the sabotage of transmission lines, which has seriously impeded restoration and expansion of electricity supplies, appears to be attributable at least as much to the surprisingly profitable criminal enterprise of stealing and selling the copper in the lines as to political motivations. Some of the crime that plagues Iraq is the normal street-level criminality that all societies, to a greater or lesser degree, face. Some is an incipient organised crime network, nurtured by the general weakness of the forces of law and order and the opportunities that a more open society unfortunately creates for such activities. All of it creates serious problems for ordinary people and the government's ability to get this 'regular' crime under control will be an important test of whether the security situation is improving in ways relevant to the general population.

Score-Settling and General Discontent. Some significant incidents and some individual attacks may well reflect ethnic or tribal feuds, or score-settling, for example, taking revenge on individuals or communities thought to be responsible for outrages during the Saddam period. Still more clearly, some incidents, especially of initially orderly protests that spiral out of control, undoubtedly reflect discontent at practical problems such as electricity blackouts or low incomes or employee firings – exacerbated by a culture of dependence and an over-developed sense of entitlement that is quick to blame the current authorities for any practical problems.

The different sources of threat reflect very different – and often deeply opposed – interests. They have in common, however, a determination to stop not just the occupation, but also the transformation of Iraq to a democratic, federal system with a legitimate place for all its diverse communities. As a consequence, there is only a very limited scope for compromise with most of the active opposition elements. In some cases, particularly for the rank and file, they can be offered as individuals de facto amnesties – and even a place in the new system. However, as organised, armed opposition movements, compromise that involves surrendering significant areas to their control is unacceptable. They must be defeated if political and social objectives are to be attained. Yet, that defeat will require more than just effective security responses. Both the emerging Iraqi authorities and their outside supporters will need to be ready to reach out to the communities on which the threat groups depend and win the competition for their support.

Reforming the Security Sector: Capabilities and Resources

Corresponding to the complexity of the challenge, there are many, mutually supporting elements to the response. These include what outside supporters of the process will need to continue to contribute, and the steps necessary to bring into being Iraqi security institutions capable of gradually taking over responsibility for security. Moreover, in the long run, it includes providing the nation with security forces that are capable of being both effective in meeting what are likely to be serious continuing security threats and finding their place in a broad political system that, among other things, controls its security services rather than being controlled by them.

Intelligence

Central to all security is better intelligence. Especially since the capture of Saddam, there has been important progress, particularly in securing information from ordinary Iraqis who understand that their interests lie with the Coalition and the Iraqis who work with it, and that in any event this is more likely to be the winning side in the end. The US and other Coalition intelligence efforts have been adjusted and refined to increase the ability to understand the threats, both strategically and tactically. The development of indigenous Iraqi intelligence capabilities will be an increasingly important element in this effort. However, all the enemy groups remain extremely difficult intelligence targets, because they are small in number, based on multifold and longstanding personal connections, and possess extraordinarily effective counterintelligence methods.

Continuing Importance of Coalition Military Operations

Once adequate intelligence is in hand, robust Coalition military operations can strike effectively to pre-empt and disrupt the opposition forces. The responsibility for security operations will increasingly devolve on Iraqi organisations. Some of these, like the growing Iraqi armed forces capabilities, will operate as part of an overall Coalition-directed effort, while others, like specialised Iraqi police units, will operate independently, but in coordination with Coalition agencies. However, effective Coalition military operations will remain critical for success on the security front until Iraqi security forces are substantially better trained and led, as was demonstrated in the spring of 2004 by a series of failures of Iraqi security forces to engage effectively against serious opposition.

A significant challenge in this connection will be the transition from a military occupation to arrangements that will be, in effect, a security partnership between the provisional Iraqi government and the US and other coalition forces who will have to remain flexible and effective for a significant period after restoration of sovereignty. In this connection, it is significant that the interim constitution provides explicitly that Iraq's military forces will come under the overall operational command of the coalition military authorities, and that the agreements between the US authorities and the interim government, referenced in the June 2004 UN Security Council resolution 1546, provide for both operational flexibility for Coalition forces and a coordinated Coalition-Iraqi security effort as well as meaningful consultation on politically sensitive operations and ultimate Iraqi authority to determine how long the Coalition's role will continue. The test will be how those arrangements work in practice.

Iraqi Security Forces

Iraqis assuming a steadily increasing share of the burden of providing for their own security is central to the security effort. To that end, a range of security forces are being developed, spanning a number of capabilities.

(a) The Iraqi Civil Defence Corps

A key element – and, in an important sense, a bridge between Coalition and Iraqi capability and responsibility – is the creative initiative of the American military leadership to establish on a very rapid timetable an Iraqi Civil Defence Corps (ICDC) to work closely with the Coalition military forces. The personnel are recruited locally and live and work in their own communities. They receive a few weeks initial training and then operate and, in effect, continue to train, as an integral part of US and other Coalition military units. They bring special skills including familiarity with the country and with the communities in which they operate. The ICDC is well on its way to the ultimate objective to have some 35-40,000 members. These ICDC units are not full-scale, independent military units – and efforts to use them as such are likely to fail. They depend on the associated coalition units for most of their support. However, funds are being provided to give the ICDC units basic equipment and an administrative management structure that will reduce their dependence on Coalition military units, and prepare for their separation from them, although at a sometimes unrecognised significant additional financial cost. The ICDC – renamed the National Guard – will administratively come under the control of the Iraqi Ministry of Defence. As the Coalition military's direct internal security role declines, the ICDC, or at least selected elements of it, will, having received more equipment and institutional independence and strengthened also by the invaluable training of close work with

experienced coalition units, transition into a local reserve, under the Ministry
of Defence.

(b) Police and Armed Forces

Both the Coalition's military presence and auxiliary efforts like the ICDC in
its present form are necessarily transitional in nature. In the long run, Iraq's
internal security must be within the capabilities of its police, while its armed
forces, possibly in continued associations with outside allies, see to its external security (as well as those aspects of its internal security that require
high-end military capacities beyond what can reasonably or prudently be
expected of any police force). Accordingly, among the most critical elements
of building the long-term self-sustaining security of Iraq are the major programmes to create professional, highly trained, well-equipped police and
military forces. Those programmes will reach their peak in the coming
months.

The New Iraqi Armed Forces. The current military programme, which is
largely on track as of mid-2004, is to train and bring on line, by late 2004,
nine brigades of light infantry, a small coastal defence force, and a small air
transport unit – totalling something like 35-40,000 personnel. The new
armed forces will include some specialised units, geared to meeting the more
exacting security tasks, as well as units for more general missions. A critical
feature of the new armed forces is that they are to be truly national. The units
that are being trained will be representative – at both officer and enlisted
levels – of the demography of the country as a whole. Armed forces units are
being deployed around the country, without regard to the original homes of
the individual soldiers. The emphasis in the training is on creating a new
leadership, bringing into being of a cadre of Iraqi officers and NCOs who
will then train and lead their units. In practice, most of the 'new' officers
will have prior military experience, either in the old military or in the Kurdish *Peshmerga* (and, to a limited extent, other militias), but they will be only
a tiny percentage of the former totals, and rank and promotion will depend
on performance in the new system, not past status. As units begin to deploy,
they, like the forces contributed by the thirty-plus outside nations that have
troops in Iraq, will be under the operational command of the Coalition central military command (which will gradually include Iraqi officers in its staff
structure, as it now includes officers from coalition contributor countries)
and they will work with Coalition units under arrangements that provide for

consultation on policy decisions while preserving effective military command. Consistent with the arrangements for other national contributions to the Coalition military command, the individual Iraqi units will be under the command of Iraqi officers and under the administrative control of the Iraqi Ministry of Defence. Moreover – and somewhat in contrast to the ICDC – the Iraqi armed forces units will, from the beginning, have their own full suite of equipment, their own base and support structure. The force currently being trained and equipped, mostly with American funding, will be less than a tenth of the old military establishment in numbers. Although much more capable man-for-man than its predecessor, the units will almost certainly not be the full extent of the armed forces of the new Iraq, but they will form the core of the independent Iraqi military. The new Iraqi armed forces will be overseen and managed by the Iraqi Ministry of Defence. The Iraqi armed forces will, like all armies, be primarily oriented toward the defence of the nation against external threats, but they will be available to supplement police and other security units in dealing with internal threats where necessary.

Regular Police. On the police side, US and other international efforts will, by mid-2005, have trained some 25,300 new entrant policemen, who will then work in operational assignments with international trainer-mentors to complete their preparation. The immediate target complement is some 75-80,000 working police personnel. Gradually replacing the existing police forces is a key part of the plan. In the immediate aftermath of the collapse of the Saddam regime, there was no alternative but to make the best of the old police forces. However, experience has demonstrated that the Iraqi police, to be effective, will have to be at least as thoroughly reformed as the army or the intelligence services, especially at senior levels and in terms of operating principles. Short term retraining of current police officers and leaders and provision of proper equipment can produce some improvements, and, as with the army, many of the 'new' police will be drawn from former security organisations. However, it is necessary that new, professionally trained policemen, complemented by thoroughly screened and retrained current officers, join and gradually supplant the current force. Critical specialised police units are also being created. As with the military, the emphasis is on training leaders and creating a force that is appropriate in its professional standards, integrity, systems of discipline and leadership, and technical skills and equipment for a democratic and diverse society. The police – a national force subordinate to the Ministry of the Interior – will have the primary responsibility for dealing with ordinary crime, but they will also have capabilities to fight political violence and terrorism.

(c) Facilities Protection Units

At the lower end of the spectrum of capabilities (and costs), are site security guards with training sufficient for their limited, but important, role. This so-called Facilities Protection Corps will number some 80-100,000, mostly subordinate to the individual ministries whose facilities they will protect. However, the Ministry of the Interior will have overall responsibility for setting standards and certification of the individual ministry security units.

(d) Specialised Security Forces

A substantial number of specialised security forces are being trained to fill other parts of the required range of capabilities. These include border patrols and specialised police and security units for key infrastructure systems, notably oil production, electricity and transportation.

(e) Judicial and Penal Systems

Essential to dealing with the criminal side of the security problem – and to some degree, with the 'political' terrorism side as well – is the continuing progress in getting the Iraqi judiciary, prosecutorial, and penal systems working. All these elements of the criminal justice system come under the Ministry of Justice. The plan has long been to handle the great majority of detainees through the Iraqi criminal, judicial, and penal system. The scandal of mistreatment of prisoners under coalition control at Abu Ghraib prison and elsewhere has made this task even more important. Success will require, not only indignation at past abuses, but also substantial resources and commitment – as well as international support.

Iraqi security forces are steadily growing in capability and responsibility, as well as in numbers. Although all crime statistics are uncertain, and especially so in a context as complex as Iraq's, it appears that ordinary crime rates are down as police conduct regular patrols and develop capacity to investigate crimes and apprehend offenders. Almost all routine guard duties are now performed by Iraqi facilities protection units. The ICDC is serving as a crucial supplement to American and other Coalition military forces. Moreover, the initial 'high end' professional, national police and army units are coming on line, as battalions of newly trained army troops are deployed to operate with Coalition military units, from newly rehabilitated bases in different regions of the country, and the capabilities of local police forces are augmented by newly trained recruits and specialised units.

In many cases, these emergent Iraqi security forces have shown both courage and skill in difficult circumstances, but there have been enough incidences of serious failures by Iraqi police, army, and ICDC units to underscore that it will take time and resources before Iraqi security units can be counted on to routinely perform the more challenging security tasks. There have been pressures, and they are likely to continue, from some Iraqis and some Americans, to meet the schedule by compromising on standards, or to imagine that initially trained Iraqi units can take over difficult missions before they are really ready. The long run necessary to transfer the great bulk of the security tasks to competent Iraqi units requires a continued willingness to pay the costs, in money, time, and, complications, to create the properly trained, fully equipped, and, most important, effectively-led military and police forces that are critical to that transfer. Just as important, during this time, Iraq must develop political institutions that command the loyalty of the bulk of the population and of the security services.

The Problem of Militias

In Iraq the task of assuring that the government has the monopoly on armed force is complicated by the existence of a variety of 'militias' established by regional, sectarian, and political groups. The total number of members in these party-based militias and other extra-governmental security organisations is estimated – with great uncertainty – at around 100,000. Of these the largest – perhaps 70,000 – and best known are the Kurdish *peshmerga* units (organised by the two leading political groups in Kurdistan). There are also Shia-oriented paramilitary formations controlled by community leaders, notably the Badr Corps numbering some 20-30,000 (organised by SCIRI, one of the leading Shiite political groupings that historically has had close ties to Iran), and 'Mahdi's Army', organised by Muqtadr al Sadr, a Shia leader. Other political and tribal groups have smaller armed elements – rationalised either as 'personal security' for the groups' leaders or as ad hoc community protection organisations for their supporters, and, in some cases, for tribal or religious communities.

In many respects, it is easy to understand the desire of these groups to have such forces at their disposal. Both the Kurds and the Shia (as well as other groups, particularly traditional tribal organisations) believe that these forces played a role in maintaining their communities during the Saddam era and that their continued existence in one form or another provides some assurance against unfavourable developments as the political structure evolves. The large, but not overwhelming, Shia majority has a justifiable sense of having long been mistreated and deprived of its rights, not just by Saddam, but also, arguably, ever since the Turkish conquests centuries ago. Similarly, the Kurdish communities have a strong desire to protect the *de facto* autonomy they have enjoyed since 1991 and to avoid a repetition of the terrible history of oppression to which they have historically been subject by too many of their neighbours. At the same time, the Sunnis not only regret the loss of their former powers, but fear retribution and oppression by other groups. The smaller Turkoman, Yazidi, Assyrian, Chaldean, and other minorities also have their fears and claims.

With the important exception of Sadr's militia, 'Mahdi's Army', which has clearly crossed over the line dividing a potential from an urgent threat to order, the problem of militias falls in the category of the important, but not immediate. Virtually none of the present violence can reasonably be attributed to any of the militias other than Mahdi's Army. In fact, in some areas, organisations like the Kurdish Peshmerga and the Badr Corps of SCIRI, one of the mainstream Shia groups, make a positive de facto contribution to containing the terrorist threat. For example, Badr Corps units have apparently resisted Sadr's militia operations, some tribal units have been engaged to protect transmission lines and pipelines passing through their communal areas, and ad hoc 'religious police' provide local security for some Shia religious sites where Coalition forces, and perhaps even official Iraqi security units, would be unwelcome.

In summary, the militia problem is difficult, but by no means hopeless. Both Kurdish and Shia leaders realise that there need to be real changes in the current system and they accept (and have embodied in the interim constitution and agreed with the interim government) the principle that their militias – a term they resolutely reject as failing to acknowledge their positive past historical roles – have to be reduced and the residue transformed into elements of the established security system (although they want that security system to reflect their local interests and avoid past over-centralisation). A plan for such integration of part of their forces and the demobilisation of the rest was agreed between the major factions controlling the forces and the interim government in June 2004. That agreement envisions the transformation of large parts of the existing units into regionally-based security organisations. Inevitably, those units will reflect the demography of the regions – and, in all probability, retain a strong relationship with their former sponsors. Provided those organisations can be brought within the overall control of the legitimate national and regional political authority, it is not necessarily a bad thing in a nation previously characterised by over-centralisation of security responsibility that there are some potential counter-weights to abuse of central authority.

Governance Mechanisms and Ethos of Leadership

The challenges of creating security institutions for Iraq go beyond the concrete tasks of creating competent security services, phasing out those armed groups that lie outside the regular system, and coping with the immediate security threats. Success requires that the security services that will serve the governmental order not only be strong enough to manage the nation's security, but must also be fully responsive to Iraq's new legal and constitutional order and respectful of the rights of its people. This is of special importance in the historical context of Iraq, where – long before Saddam – the military and other security services have been powers unto themselves, dominating the political system and operating outside the law. Moreover, the security organisations have traditionally been instruments of sectarian politics – dominated by Sunnis (and, to some degree in the pre-Baath era, Kurds) and actively excluding Shia. Success, certainly in the long-term, and quite possibly even in meeting immediate security challenges, will require both transforming the ethos and culture of the security services and bringing them within a system of legal and constitutional control.

Ensuring that the security organisations of the country serve the state requires effective constitutional control and respect for human rights. Besides reform of the security organs' internal structure, ensuring that Iraq's new security organisations are congruent with its goal of a representative and constitutional federal democracy requires assuring that the legitimate political authority has full control of the security organs. Conversely, establishing a government that is seen to be legitimate and representative will be crucial to building public support for the fight against the terrorists and for maintaining the loyalty and discipline of the security forces. A critical part of preparing for, and executing, the transfer of full authority to a sovereign government of Iraq is, therefore, setting up the constitutional and legal framework for setting and conducting Iraq's national security policy and for commanding and overseeing its military, intelligence, police, and other security forces. As already noted, a Ministry of Defence is in the process of being created – with civilian leadership, significant civilian staffing, and clear authority over budgets, personnel, policy, and ultimate control over operations. The charter for the new Iraqi intelligence service sharply limits its powers and places it under the control of responsible civilian leaders. A Ministry of the Interior already exists, but there will need to be a formal legal structure, defining its powers and relationship to other institutions.

Specific areas where decisions will be needed include setting Iraq's national security objectives, identifying the significant threats to its internal and external security, and establishing institutional structures and operating principles for Iraq's security policies and institutions – reflected in constitutional, legal, and administrative frameworks. Some of the critical standards to be defined relate to the internal distribution of power and authority – in particular that the military and other security institutions should be under the control of the civilian government, accountable to the public and parliament, free from political involvement, defensively oriented, reasonably representative of the population as a whole, financially affordable, respectful of human rights, and subject to clear rules, both substantive and procedural, in the use of extraordinary measures (such as use of military forces for internal security). Others look more toward Iraq's relations with the outside world, including renunciation of weapons of mass destruction, territorial claims against Iraq's neighbours and the use of force except in self-defence. Moreover, in addition to dealing with issues of respect for rights and subordination of legal authority, a reformed system must end the pervasive corruption and abuses of power for personal gain that have characterised Iraqi military institutions (and much of the rest of the government) in the past. Similar requirements will exist for the police, intelligence agencies, and other security institutions.

Given the historical context of the Iraqi military, it is important that the armed forces of the new Iraq be national in character (not dominated by, or excluding, any groups), and focused on external defence, not internal security. Establishing the military as a genuinely *national* institution will be particularly important because most of the other security organisations – notably the police – are likely to be essentially local and regional in orientation, for both practical and policy reasons. A national armed forces, under the control of the national civilian government, will be an important element in an overall system where central and regional, even local, powers are balanced so as to preserve national unity while protecting against abuse of central power, even when that power is based on an electoral majority.

In all parts of the security sector, effectiveness and accountability both require – even more than professional training and adequate modern equipment – fundamentally reformed, re-oriented leadership. New principles of leadership are needed, not just for democratic and constitutional control and accountability, but also – and perhaps even more – for effectiveness in the field. Even in the past, the Iraqi solider and the policeman on the beat were reasonably competent at a basic technical level. What was lacking – or even counterproductive – was leadership.

Correcting these long-established dysfunctional patterns requires not just excluding those police and military commanders from the era of the old regime who remain actively loyal to the old regime or who were involved personally in abuses, but moving to a transformed ethos of discipline, integrity, and leadership. Replacing the old habits in security sector institutions – which were characterised by a mixture of brutality, passivity, politicisation, and corruption – will not be easy. Fortunately, however, there are a large number of Iraqis – some from the old institutions, some new to the field – who accept the need for these changes. One of the most hopeful signs for the future of the country is the willingness of many Iraqis to run great risks and learn new skills and styles to be part of the new security institutions they know their country needs.

In this development of institutional structures for national security policy, the Coalition can provide advice and support as needed, but these decisions will have to be made by Iraqis – both as part of the process of setting up an interim government and as part of establishing the permanent constitutional order thereafter. This process is already well started. The experience of decades of oppression has made all groups, and many in the leadership of the new security organisations, fully conscious of the need for a whole new approach.

Security Sector Reform and Iraq's External Security

For the immediate future, the problem of purely external threats is distinctly secondary. So long as there are some hundred thousand American and other Coalition forces in Iraq, no neighbour is likely to launch any sort of conventional military challenge. However, an independent, democratic, constitutional Iraq adhering to a constructive foreign policy will find itself living in a dangerous neighbourhood, potentially made the more dangerous by precisely the characteristics of its internal and external policies. A free Iraq will be a model and a beacon in the region, but for those and other reasons, it will likely also have potential enemies. Moreover, even on the most optimistic economic predictions, Iraq will have many competing demands for available resources, besides security forces.

In the longer-term context of Iraq's external security after the immediate internal security situation has adequately been dealt with and foreign forces are no longer needed for internal security, a key issue will be defining Iraq's security relationship with the United States, other coalition states, and its regional neighbours. Specifically, both Iraq and the US and other concerned countries in the region and elsewhere will need to address the issue of a possible mutual security arrangement, where Iraq is not left entirely to its own resources for its own defence. Obviously, whether such an arrangement is possible depends, not just on Iraqi preferences, but on decisions in the US and in the region, and, in particular, on the acceptability on all sides of any significant continuing US or other foreign military presence in Iraq. However, at least until there is a general amelioration of the relationships between Iraq and its principal neighbours – especially Iran – it would appear that both Iraq and those nations, including the US and the Gulf states, that have an interest in Iraq's continued security (and in its not having to devote excessive resources to its military) would benefit from an arrangement in which Iraq's security was a shared regional and international responsibility, with Iraq contributing to the extent of its ability, but backed by guarantees – similar to those for other nations – that it would not have to face external threats entirely alone.

Lessons Learned for Iraq and Beyond

It is far too early to draw definitive lessons since the process is still on-going. However, even at this point it is appropriate to make certain tentative conclusions, based on experience to date – both good and bad – in the process in Iraq.

Effectiveness is a value that has to be taken very seriously into account. A constitutional order that cannot defend itself against ongoing assaults will, by definition, not survive. The greatest challenge to Iraq's security so far is the continuing inability of the Iraqi security forces to handle the challenges themselves, the continued dependence on coalition forces, and the danger that effective 'security' roles will devolve, not on forces responsive to the emerging government, but on various militias, contractors, and actively oppositionist groups. For Iraqi forces to do the job, they must be much more capable at a purely technical level than at present. The plans are in place, and, for the most part, the resources are committed. The task is to implement the plans. In that implementation, professional competence and effectiveness have to be the top priority.

Quality counts. In the immediate context of daily murderous attacks, there are understandable pressures for quick results, and some short-term measures (like relying initially on the inadequate and deeply compromised former regular police) are necessary. However, for long-term success, the nation needs properly trained, properly equipped police and security forces and that takes time and money. 'Low-end' security institutions like the Facilities Protection Services can make an important contribution, and individuals from the old institutions can be retrained and brought up to an adequate standard. Organisations that, like the ICDC, are closely integrated with, but also dependent upon, coalition forces have a high potential to assist in the transition. However, in the long run, it will be success in creating fully competent, self-sufficient, 'high-end' institutions – especially in the police and armed services – that will determine the outcome.

The national unity principle is fundamental. Iraq will be a diverse nation if it remains a nation at all. Necessarily, and rightly, many of its security institutions, notably the police, will reflect local conditions and local populations. Yet, it is also critical that the security organisations of the country do not become the preserve of particular power groups, whether local or national. Not only the army, but other security institutions that are more locally based, must be inclusive of minority groups, and in their operations, security forces – emphatically including those like the police that are necessarily locally based and reflective of the composition of the local community – must respect both minority rights and central authority.

Partition is not a realistic option. Given the divisions of Iraq, it may seem that dividing the country along ethnic/sectarian lines would be the wisest course, rather than persisting in attempting to preserve security in a unified state. However, short of total disaster, partition would be no answer and particularly not to the security challenge. The communities are so intermixed that any line of division would be arbitrary and lead, not only to massive compelled population transfers, but also to endless revanchist/revisionist challenges. However, it is equally true that absolute majoritarianism, with the risk that one group would dominate, is unacceptable. Some constitutional order must be found that will accommodate these conflicting interests. Fortunately, there are strong elements in all communities that recognise that compromise is essential. Despite all the conflicts within Iraq, there is no strong tradition of popularly based ethnic or sectarian violence. A considerable group of moderates, both the formally secular and the more religious who are willing to tolerate other faiths and other branches of Islam, recognise the necessity of finding mechanisms whereby Iraq's diverse population can live together peacefully.

The emphasis must be on reconciliation. The process has real enemies, who must be resolutely, even ruthlessly, prevented from destroying the process and seizing power, but the emphasis must be on reconciliation and 'a second chance'. Among the most difficult tasks for both the occupation authorities and the sovereign Iraqi governments, both interim and permanent, will be dealing with the issue of the role of those who held powerful and privileged positions in the old regime. Some – especially those who were at the top of the old Baath Party or who served in the old regime's inner circle of security organs, intelligence, and repression – are so tainted by the past that, even if they are not subject to formal criminal punishment, they cannot responsibly be given a future role in the public service. However, for most Iraqis, even some at quite senior levels in the old regime, service to the old regime was less a matter of affirmative enthusiasm than at worst opportunism and in most cases, the price that had to be paid to have a professional life. Except for relatively few at the very top of the old system, a 'second chance' – dependent on real acceptance of the new order – is the appropriate course. At the same time, the issue is non-exclusion, not inherited entitlement; there will have to be measures to affirmatively recruit new blood, particularly from communities excluded in the past on ethnic, sectarian, or political grounds.

Corruption is a key issue. For most Iraqis, 'security' primarily means not safety from political attacks, but protection from ordinary crime. No police or security system is entirely free from corruption, but the tempering of generations of despotism with endemic corruption has left a corrosive legacy throughout Iraq. Principles of merit promotion, law-based decision, and rejection of use of public office for personal gain are nowhere fully realised in practice, but Iraq has a long way to go to reach even minimum standards.

Leadership is critical. In the army, in the police, and in the government as a whole, the quality of the leaders will determine the performance of the rank and file. There will be competition for quality people from a growing economy and from opportunities abroad. The targeting of security personnel, particularly in police and local government, acts as a further deterrent to effective service. The new security organisations must give their people, and particularly their leaders, adequate salaries and, where necessary, protection for their families and property.

The key decisions have to be made by Iraqis. To the degree that Iraq will need external help, foreign states and international institutions will have interests and requirements. However, the basic political decisions on how Iraq deals with its security challenges must have the support of the leading political forces in the country and that support must come in the context of agreement on basic constitutional arrangements and political structure. Without such agreement, there will be no government able to command – or perhaps to deserve – the loyalty of security forces committed to success against dangerous and determined enemies.

Conclusion

The fact that Iraq confronts active armed insurrection colours every aspect of the security sector reform agenda, and makes the need for effectiveness far more critical than in the case of nations with a relatively benign security environment. Moreover, some special factors of Iraqi demography or history shape Iraq's reform priorities. For example, the political imperative of a relatively decentralised federal system to accommodate the competing desires of the Shia majority and the Sunni, Kurd, and other minorities, shapes the balance of institutions between a national army and a localised police and national guard. The experience of abuse of security organisations' power, not just under Saddam, but also earlier, puts special emphasis on the need for effective mechanisms of constitutional control. Iraq also has a few special advantages – substantial indigenous financial resources, a strong international commitment to its success, and, so far at least, a very broadly shared public desire not to revert to past abuses.

It is important for its own population, the region, the coalition, and the international community that Iraq should be a success. For that success, security sector reform is vital. Unless security improves, neither economic nor political transformation can fully succeed. Moreover, until security can become primarily an Iraqi, not a Coalition, responsibility, Iraqi sovereignty will be limited, no matter how successful the difficult political process may be in other respects. Furthermore, building an Iraqi security sector geared to success in the broad sense will entail not just creating professionally trained, well-equipped, technically competent institutions, but instilling a new ethos of leadership, discipline, integrity, and respect for legal norms, as well as instituting a system of legal and consititutional control for the security institutions of the new state that will both ensure responsiveness to the constitution and effectiveness in providing security. Iraq's history, its internal tensions, the trauma of a half century of dictatorship and a wrenching experience of occupation and insurrection make meeting these challenges a formidable task.

The final version of this chapter has been completed in mid-June 2004 at a time of serious challenge both to Coalition authority and to the prospects for Iraqi agreement on basic political issues. By the time it appears in print, much will have happened, for good or ill, and there are certainly many reasons for concern. The June 2004 transition, however, marks an important milestone in the process – the formal end to the occupation and the establishment, with UN as well as Coalition sanction, of a broad-based interim government. The latest, and, in some respects, most serious, upsurge in violence in the spring of 2004, illustrates that the potential for failure exists.

However, it is far too early to assume that disaster, or an endless quagmire, is inevitable. The author's experience both from working in Iraq and a more peripheral involvement since returning in November 2003 remains that, for all the great uncertainties and risks, there is real reason for optimism. The fall of Saddam has been deeply welcomed – even by most Sunnis and all but universally by other groups – and there is genuine gratitude to the US and other Coalition forces for liberation, despite widespread and growing impatience with the occupation. Most Iraqis recognise, however grudgingly, that continued Coalition efforts will be needed to maintain and improve security well after the formal restoration of sovereignty. Moreover, the overwhelming bulk of Iraqis, as measured by polling data as well as by comments of most leaders, recognise that they have an opportunity – which may prove fleeting – to create a decent government for their nation.

The plans, and to an extent other societies in transition can only envy, the resources, are in place. Some difficult lessons have been learned – or should be. A new, more broadly based international framework for support to Iraq's transition is emerging. An interim government, more broadly based than the Governing Council, has come to power. Under international pressure, the formal restoration of sovereignty has been buttressed by real authority, limited more by the interim nature of the government than retention of prerogative by the former occupiers.

The progress on all fronts is real, but not yet irreversible, much less satisfactory, and there is much more to do, in the face of serious challenges. Overall, however, this is a struggle that can and must be won. The enemy's goals are political not military – to intimidate the Iraqis who seek change, to destroy the population's confidence in the competence of the new Iraqi authorities and their Coalition supporters and in the prospects of reform in conditions of freedom and security, to aggravate internal tensions to the point of civil war, and to exhaust the patience of the American and other external supporters of the process. Accordingly, the key requirement is resolve – to bear the costs in money, political and military effort, and, most painful, human life necessary to overcome the forces that seek to prevent success. Iraqis will have to bear the main burden, but the international community has a critical contribution to make.

PART IV

CONCLUSIONS

Chapter 11

Understanding Security Sector Reform and Reconstruction

Alan Bryden

Overview

This volume assesses the complex dynamics of security sector reform (SSR) in key regions around the globe.[1] It also looks at the particular challenges, in specific cases, of post-conflict reconstruction of the security sector. Contributions from academics and practitioners have elaborated on both the conceptual underpinnings and the practical realities of security sector reform and reconstruction. As developed in the Introduction, it is important that definitional issues regarding the SSR concept and the particularities of security sector reconstruction are clearly laid out and commonly understood. However, it is telling that while some authors in this book focus mainly on the military components of security sector reform and reconstruction, others, embracing a 'human security' framework, push the scope of the SSR concept beyond its traditional security parameters to embrace, for example, human development. Moreover, a number of key issues, as discussed below, are germane whether looking at SSR in regional terms or at specific cases of post-conflict reconstruction of the security sector.

The gap between the SSR concept and implementation of security sector reform and reconstruction on the ground is a recurring theme. Brzoska and Heinemann-Grüder (Chapter 6) situate security sector reform and reconstruction within the wider agenda of post-conflict peace building in situations where the international community plays a prominent role. In light of an increasingly significant and sometimes controversial involvement in post-conflict transitions, the authors stress the often competing and untested approaches of different states, international organisations and other actors. Empirical analysis of past and current interventions is essential for better future practice. Consequently, dominant themes, policy dilemmas and tentative priorities are proposed for post-conflict reform and reconstruction. Basing interventions on realistic needs assessments relevant to the local context, focusing initially on the provision of physical security, providing sustainable internal structures as well as external political and financial commitment, while recognizing the importance of local ownership of reform and reconstruction efforts, emerge as central policy prescriptions.

The Euro-Atlantic Region

A number of chapters discern the emergence of regional security sectors as actual or potential engines for SSR. Law (Chapter 2) points out that the Euro-Atlantic has the longest history of multilateral practice and the greatest concentration of actors involved in SSR of any region around the globe. This represents a wealth of experience that has not been consistently applied within or beyond the region. On the national level, many post-communist transition states within the Euro-Atlantic have made little concrete progress in the field of SSR despite, in some cases, over a decade of effort. More widely, although most threats to national security can also be seen to have an international dimension, policy responses are fragmented at the national level while the architecture for dealing with such threats at the regional level remains under-developed within the Euro-Atlantic region. Multilateral-level resources for activities such as peace support operations (PSOs) and consequence management in the face of asymmetric threats including terrorism and international organised crime are inadequate, while communication and decision-making mechanisms between Euro-Atlantic states and institutions remain weak. However, these shortcomings also represent an opportunity for Euro-Atlantic security structures. Progress in the development of a Euro-Atlantic security sector remains essential if SSR at home and the projection of stability abroad are to be realised.

Within the Euro-Atlantic region, the results of SSR in Central and Eastern Europe (CEE) are considered by Donnelly (Chapter 3) and reconstruction in the Western Balkans by Caparini (Chapter 7). The importance is stressed of linking SSR to societal reform, post-Cold War changes in the nature of conflict, technological and information revolutions. Set in this context, it is argued that the experiences of CEE states, albeit contrasting due to local circumstances, have been strikingly similar. One common thread is the positive impact in encouraging reform of incentivising CEE states to join the multilateral Euro-Atlantic institutions.[2] However, common features of the reform processes themselves include reluctance within the security sector to reduce bloated force structures coupled with a lack of expertise at the executive level to understand and manage change.[3] An endemic lack of resources, compounded by the absence of effective budgeting and planning capabilities, has resulted in declining standards of performance, behaviour and public image. These problems have been exacerbated by external assistance for SSR that has proposed 'Western' models that have not reflected the particularities of CEE, at a time when those same approaches are being reconsidered at source in the light of changing strategic priorities. In most cases these problems remain today. A combination of fostering a 'strategic community' of SSR experts at the national level, developing a realistic and up to date threat assessment, creating the necessary political will and providing 'smart' external assistance are the necessary prerequisites to progress. However, these factors largely remain aspirations rather than realities in the sub-region.

According to Caparini (Chapter 7), the transition process in the Western Balkans is distinguished from the rest of CEE by the enduring legacy of armed conflict, ethnic cleansing and ethnicisation of the security sector. Security sector reconstruction has to be linked to post-conflict stabilisation in a context where national and local authorities in many parts of the sub-region have ceded responsibility for security to international actors. The goal of transferring ownership back from the international community is tempered by the risk of renewed conflict which could very easily spread beyond national borders, thus requiring a regional approach to reform and reconstruction efforts. As mentioned above, conditional offers of integration within the European Union (EU) and North Atlantic Treaty Organisation (NATO) provide spurs to reform and the consultation agreement between the two organisations on security and stability in the Western Balkans represents an important step in the direction of the 'joined up' approach advocated by Law (Chapter 2). However, the inherent weakness of security (not just military) institutions and their oversight mechanisms, a negative public profile and deep-rooted problems of inter-ethnic violence and organised criminality slow progress and raise serious questions about the sustainability of reform and reconstruction efforts.

West Africa

The need for regional approaches to SSR is also apparent in West Africa.[4] In the context of national security sectors that have historically been sources of insecurity, a loss of the state monopoly on the use of force, and the cross-border nature of many West African security threats, SSR can only be successful if state, regional and international efforts are mutually reinforcing. Ebo (Chapter 4) describes the seeds of a sub-regional security architecture in the Economic Community of West African States (ECOWAS) Mechanism for Conflict Prevention, Management and Resolution, Peacekeeping and Security (the ECOWAS Mechanism). Improving the sub-regional framework is essential to engendering political will at the national level as well as to fostering a holistic rather than regime-centred approach to security. Such a transformative agenda, linking security, governance and development, requires that institutional reform be mirrored by societal change if SSR is to become embedded. Linked to this is the dilemma of balancing external support for SSR with local 'ownership'. Key areas on the SSR agenda to be targeted include justice and police reform, parliamentary capacity building (the ECOWAS parliament represents a key entry point),[5] training for armed and security forces[6] including democratic oversight issues, expanding the knowledge pool on SSR within the sub-region, and closer donor coordination on SSR interventions. Enhancing capacity at the sub-regional level through ECOWAS, in particular with implementation of the ECOWAS Mechanism, would result in a well-needed boost to SSR at the national level in West Africa.

Fayemi (Chapter 8) concurs with Ebo both that regional responses are needed to address cross-border threats in West Africa and that meaningful change within the security sector requires a transformative reform agenda. Security sector reconstruction to date in West Africa has, by contrast, been *ad hoc*, a by product of other reforms or conducted by stealth, thus limiting the possibility of shifting power relations and cementing institutional change. Post-conflict reconstruction of the security sector in Sierra Leone and Liberia offer an opportunity to test the limitations of institutional design of post-conflict reconstruction of the security sector. A key priority in the post-conflict context is that initial efforts focus on the basic security needs of the citizen as a precondition for broader development assistance. Understanding the links between peace and nation building, as well as security sector reconstruction and improving governance and democratization, is essential. However, current donor responses seem more geared towards ensuring an absence of war than dealing with broader issues of capacity-building and sustainability. Sierra Leone and Liberia offer an opportunity for comprehensive security sector reconstruction but lasting results can only be predicated on resolving issues of ownership, political will (both of donors and within the countries themselves), resources and sustainability.

The Middle East

The regional dynamics described above, which have resulted in a perceptible moving together of the Euro-Atlantic and West African security sectors, are not applicable in the Arab Middle East. As Luethold (Chapter 5) notes, with the exception of Iraq and Afghanistan, SSR has not to date played a role in the broader Middle East reform debate. An evolving strategic environment may, however, prove the most significant driver for reform within the region. A growing shift in the threat perception of Arab states towards the importance of home-grown security threats may result in the double-edged sword of an increased onus on reform matched by increased repression of opposition and minority groups. Moreover, a shared threat perception does not equate to regional cooperation – as evinced by the very minor role of the Gulf Cooperation Council (GCC) in defence and security matters. Security issues also remain taboo in Arab parliaments; even when there are institutional frameworks for oversight they are under-funded and under-used. However, there is an awareness among Arab governments, fuelled by social and economic pressures, that traditional means of securing political control – through patronage and other regime-centred policies – are deleterious to the effectiveness of security sector organs.[7] In addition to these internal pressures, the US and Europe in particular have proposed and supported reform initiatives in order to address the 'freedom deficit'[8] in the Arab world. The perception in the Arab world that such initiatives are a vehicle for the imposition of Western ideals is a counterpoint to the dominant role of the US military from a pure security perspective in the region. It remains to be seen how far this combination of external conditions, internal pressures and the changing strategic environment will allow for an opening up of the debates on SSR and good governance while facilitating increased regional cooperation in the security sphere.

Security sector reconstruction in Iraq and Afghanistan are very specific cases. Slocombe (Chapter 10), like Fayemi (Chapter 8), stresses the importance of achieving a level of basic physical security if other reconstruction goals are to be met, requiring a balancing act between long-term aspirations and near-term realities. In this regard, a key objective for the new Iraqi government is to define the threats and therefore the national security objectives that will shape the role of their armed and security forces. These forces require a change in ethos and culture, as well as organisation, in order to be representative of the nation rather than sectarian or regime interests. Both for reasons of effectiveness and to cement civilian, democratic oversight, the contribution of the international community must be carefully balanced by the imperatives of local ownership. Although the international community remains divided and the ongoing security situation represents a serious threat to stability, it is also important that Iraq possesses levels of resources and international political commitment that compare very favourably with other countries undergoing post-conflict reconstruction.

A basic security threshold is palpably absent in Afghanistan. There is a critical nexus between guerilla insurgency in parts of the country and a criminalised economy within which warlords can simultaneously be government ministers. Sedra (Chapter 9) points out that government institutions, as well as armed and security forces, have no sense of 'nation', reflecting a lack of consensus, participation and coordination. The lack of indigenous capacity to make and implement policy is reflected by an inconsistency of donor interventions that calls into question the models being applied and denudes the process of local ownership. The absence of a thorough needs assessment for reconstruction in Afghanistan is a very specific but telling omission. The lack of progress (as well as resources), combined with a perceived shift in emphasis to Iraq, raises questions as to the commitment of the international community, in particular the US, to reconstruction and development rather than regime change in Afghanistan. For sustainable progress in the reconstruction of the Afghan security sector, key issues of policy, resources and planning need to be addressed. International intervention must balance the acute capacity deficit in the country with the need to create and empower a viable, democratically governed Afghan security sector. A reorientation of the current status quo is commensurately difficult and essential.

Having considered the contributions on both regional dimensions of SSR and cases of post-conflict reconstruction of the security sector, it may be useful to look at some of the common threads that run through this volume and their potential implications for the theory and practice of security sector reform and reconstruction.

Security Sector Reform in a Regional Context

A number of authors contributing to the debate on SSR at national, regional and international levels make use of Buzan's concept of the 'regional security complex'.[9] Cawthra and Luckham point out that harmonising reforms across countries constituting a security complex can result in important confidence and security building measures.[10] Greene argues from a policy perspective that it is important for those involved in SSR assistance to take account of the similar histories, cultures, political and developmental priorities of regional security complexes.[11]

Law's (Chapter 2) identification of an emerging Euro-Atlantic security sector reflects the particular historical and political path of a region which, according to Wallace, is characterized by 'the creation of a relatively stable institutional network for intergovernmental bargaining for the accommodation of shared interests' coupled with 'the existence of common traditions, history, culture and political values, to which political leaders and institution builders can appeal for support'.[12] Fayemi (Chapter 8) describes how the end of the Cold War and the retreat of the superpowers from Africa encouraged the strengthening of regional actors. However, in part, ECOWAS was compelled to address conflicts – Liberia in 1990 is the most extreme example – in the absence of intervention from the UN or other bodies. The Arab Middle East offers a qualitatively different type of security complex. As Luethold (Chapter 5) points out, there is limited security cooperation emerging from within the region but the US military is a dominant force and has to be considered as an integral part of the regional security sector.

Experience from all the regions discussed in this volume confirm that the erosion of the state monopoly on the use of force, the limitations of externally driven SSR and transnational threats – such as organised crime, trafficking, drugs smuggling and small arms proliferation – require regional and international responses. As Luckham notes, 'since conflict and insecurity themselves have been regionalised and globalised, regional and global collective security mechanisms should be strengthened to counteract them'.[13] The security of Kosovo affects the Western Balkans more broadly as a source of regional instability. Similarly, although the conflicts in Sierra Leone and Liberia retain national dimensions, the cross-border interventions of various actors, the illicit flow of goods, weapons (and soldiers) created what Fayemi (Chapter 8) terms 'a regional political economy of war' requiring regional solutions.

Caparini (Chapter 7) points out that the sub-regional nature of maintaining peace and security in the Western Balkans has also had the effect of placing a *de facto* conditionality on progress towards membership of Euro-Atlantic institutions predicated not just on your own behaviour but that of your neighbours. Peer pressure may become an increasingly important factor in the shoring up of regional security. In the case of the ECOWAS Mechanism, Cawthra and Luckham emphasise that 'whether the mechanism will function as it should, will depend in part on whether West African governments can exert effective peer pressures upon recalcitrant member states to abide by standards of democratic governance and non-interference in their neighbours' conflicts.'[14] This will require additional political will from a critical mass of reforming states at the national level – only four states have currently ratified the mechanism – which Ebo (Chapter 4) acknowledges is still lacking in the West African sub-region.

Regional mechanisms and institutions offer significant advantages in facilitating links between SSR and wider conflict prevention, security and peace-building while enabling capacity-building among local constituencies and grounding key norms within regional frameworks. However, from a programming perspective each case must still be considered *sui generis*. Caution should be exercised to avoid generalisations that paper over very specific local contexts, and to ensure that regional approaches are complementary to national, thematic and sectoral approaches to SSR.[15] The complexities of coordinating SSR at the regional level should not be underestimated – particularly given that the regions most in need of reform have the weakest regional organisations – but the potential benefits of such cooperation cannot be overstated.

The Post-Conflict Reconstruction Context

A number of issues highlighted in this volume are particular to SSR interventions in the wake of armed conflict. Collectively, they suggest a need for 'transformation' that goes well beyond the concept of 'reform' as used in relation to transition states.[16] The immediate requirement of ensuring basic individual security and thereby reducing public insecurity is a logical constant. Set beside this is the long term need for comprehensive, multidimensional peace-building activities. While none of the contributors consider the post-conflict context to represent a *tabula rasa* for reform and reconstruction, different accents have been placed on the opportunities and constraints highlighted in the different cases.

Ebo and Fayemi (Chapters 4 & 8) suggest that the prospects for security sector transformation are enhanced by the near collapse of state structures, contrasting extensive reform in Sierra Leone and Liberia with 'stealth reform' in various other West African states. Brzoska and Heinemann-Grüder (Chapter 6) sound the cautionary note that the ability of external actors to implement reform programmes will be shaped by the reaction of domestic actors. Opportunities for reform must be set against the danger of what Fayemi (Chapter 8) terms 'unfettered donor interventions' in the aftermath of conflict which, as discussed below, may be at the expense of local ownership. The other side to this coin is that as much damage may be done by withdrawing external support prior to the embedding of sustainable, locally owned security sector institutions and oversight mechanisms. Replacing exit strategies with engagement strategies[17] involves a long-term process which must be reflected in the political will and resources committed by the international community.

A key dilemma for external actors is the mismatch between the policy goal of trying to facilitate locally designed and implemented programmes with the absence in the post-conflict period of any indigenous capacity to set or manage policy. Brzoska and Heinemann-Grüder (Chapter 6) reaffirm the importance of sequencing SSR within a broader framework of reconstruction and democratisation. Yet their recommendation that this should flow from a restatement of national security policy may jar with the 'ownership' principle given the 'policy vacuum'[18] in the early post-conflict stages. Sedra (Chapter 9) describes the difficulty of finding qualified personnel to work in the new Afghan government ministries while Fayemi (Chapter 8) emphasises the lack of functioning security or civil institutions capable of designing or implementing change in Sierra Leone and Liberia. This raises the concern that stabilizing the peace will be unsustainable in the longer term without a wider governance framework that addresses issues of political will, leadership and participation.

Transitional justice and questions of impunity are very important during the post-conflict phase. Brzoska and Heinemann-Grüder (Chapter 6) argue that blanket amnesties may be counter-productive. Although important for demilitarisation and the reintegration of former combatants, amnesties should be clearly defined in order to avoid stimulating insurgents or undermining the democratic credentials of reformed security agencies. The Lomé Peace Agreement (Sierra Leone) included a general amnesty provision for offenders – prompting the UN to withdraw its backing for the agreement – while the Accra Peace Agreement (Liberia) did not, providing for a more holistic approach to reconstruction. Popular will to remember and learn from the past is shown by a continued groundswell of support for the truth and reconciliation processes currently underway in both countries. In the Western Balkans the inability to arrest high profile indicted war criminals such as Radovan Karadzic and Ratko Mladic has increased tensions both within the region and between national authorities and the international community. In Iraq, the first and most important test case in this area will be the outcome of the trial of Saddam Hussein. The conduct and outcome of this case will set the tone for further trials of members of the old regime. In each of these cases, there is a sensitive balance to be struck between seeking justice and keeping a lid on the security situation.

Local Ownership of Security Sector Reform and Reconstruction

The central involvement of indigenous actors with the capacity to function effectively is highlighted throughout this volume as a *sine qua non* of effective security sector reform and reconstruction. Although increasingly recognised in the policy papers of the international donor community,[19] there is an evident gap between policy and practice, which highlights the need for a better understanding of how external interventions and domestic political cultures can be brought closer together.

Problems of ownership are particularly acute in the post-conflict context. Brzoska and Heinemann-Grüder (Chapter 6) discuss the paradox of external actors having the ability to implement change but in ways that may be inconsistent with principles of popular sovereignty and accountability. In the Western Balkans, Caparini (Chapter 7) notes, the sustainability of externally driven reform efforts is called into question by the likelihood that a withdrawal of the international security presence would result in a resurgence of violence, reinforcing the premise that SSR cannot outpace political and institutional reform. Caparini's characterisation of the dilemma between 'effective security sector reform and democratic security sector reform' is well illustrated in the Western Balkans where reform has been externally imposed and domestic political process sidestepped.

A subset of this issue is the foundering of ostensibly viable external efforts through being perceived as 'Western'. Sedra (Chapter 9) describes how the Afghan National Army (ANA) is undermined by the perception that it is a tool of the US. On a different level, Caparini's (Chapter 7) example of Western-trained army officers in Albania being sacked and Donnelly's (Chapter 3) claim that, as late as the Summer of 2000, officers from some CEE countries who were sent abroad for training returned home to dismissal, demotion or rustication, are troubling. These examples raise serious questions for those Western states and institutions that sponsor or provide such training. The residual level of such practices can only be clarified through thorough stakeholder analysis, starting with the recipients of this training.

A common characteristic of armed and security forces in transition and post-conflict states is an understandably negative public profile which, to be addressed, requires societal as well as institutional re-positioning. Broad-based participation in security sector reform and reconstruction is flagged up throughout the cases as an important criterion for success in surmounting the historical legacies of recently reformed security sector institutions. Facilitating consultation and discussion fora could therefore be an important way for the international community, particularly in post-conflict states, to engender 'buy in' and encourage ownership by different levels of society in the reform processes.

The involvement of civil society in security sector reform and reconstruction is intended to reduce polarisations between security institutions, newly elected political authorities and the populace. This is important both for bridge-building between these constituencies and as a tool for transparency in a sector that has traditionally been characterised by secrecy. Moreover, given that both the concept and practice of SSR have been heavily donor-driven, civil society participation can help to address this imbalance.[20] However, again, set against the backdrop of a lack of resources and viable entry points for these actors, there seems to be a gap between the principle of a participative approach and the current status quo. Hutchful describes how 'African civil society organisations are often disinterested in this area or have a weak capacity to play these roles....the problem is magnified by the relative rarity of African research institutes specializing in security issues.'[21] This coincides with Ebo's (Chapter 4) recommendation to expand the space for public (and parliamentary) debate on SSR issues while also recalling the caveat that civil society organisations are not always representative or accountable to society.[22]

Beyond Africa, the cases discussed in this volume emphasise the importance of civil society involvement in reform and reconstruction. In this regard, Slocombe's (Chapter 10) point is well taken that the military and security services had already dominated the Iraqi political system and operated outside the established political framework long before Saddam came to power. The consequent need for a societal rather than just an institutional culture shift if the principles of democratic oversight are to become embedded is echoed by Luethold (Chapter 5). He points out that a negative public perception of the security sector is widespread in the Arab Middle East. Many states in this region do not even have defence ministries with decision-making conducted directly between elites and the armed and security forces.

The nature of foundational documents such as peace agreements can have a long-term impact on the possibilities for effective security sector reform and reconstruction through regulating relations among former warring factions and establishing institutional frameworks. Such negotiations may create a 'breathing space' for reform but, as discussed below, can also freeze conflicts and confirm asymmetries[23] or simply allow parties to the conflict to regroup and replenish.[24]

The Dayton Peace Agreement has institutionalised ethnic division in Bosnia and Herzegovina and created a huge drain on resources through its creation of parallel security sectors. In Kosovo, it is the absence of any clear legal status that defines an area maintained under an international protectorate but still riven by threats to public security, inter-ethnic violence and the increasing isolation of ethnic enclaves. In Afghanistan, the Bonn political process, reinforced by coalition support for the National Alliance, favoured a narrow, ethnic-based faction in establishing the new government. This imbalance, exploited by the now decentralised Taliban movement through positioning itself as a force for Pashtun nationalism, has exacerbated the instability around the country. On the credit side, the signing of the Kabul Declaration, a pledge of non-interference by the country's direct neighbours, represents an important step forward in reducing fears in the public mind of hostile interventions by regional powers.

Fayemi (Chapter 8) notes that the peace agreements in Sierra Leone and Liberia show a significant degree of learning from previous conflicts in terms of their comprehensiveness. Particularly important in the case of the Accra Accords was the inclusion of civil society and diverse political parties as well as the positive role of ECOWAS as guarantor of the process. Involvement of a credible regional actor added legitimacy to the process and was an important step away from problematic foreign-brokered models.

External Approaches to Security Sector Reform and Reconstruction

Intrinsically linked to questions of ownership is the issue of donor approaches to security sector reform and reconstruction. The cases discussed in this volume highlight external interventions that have frequently lacked coordination or been shaped by domestic experiences which do not correspond to a given local context. From a programming perspective, this practice contradicts the accepted policy wisdom that 'interventionists must unite in the planning and implementation of external assistance, in a way that produces an end product conducive to good governance within the broader definition of security'.[25]

A lack of policy coherence by international actors is not confined to either the reform or reconstruction contexts. In the Euro-Atlantic region, reform and reconstruction has been a work in progress for over a decade. The risk of 'reform fatigue'[26] in transition states is evident when interventions lack proper planning, place unrealistic demands on national structures, are under-resourced and, consequently, revised, postponed or cancelled. In states whose security is propped up by the international community, the danger is of creating '*de facto* multilateralist states' where state collapse and international supervision are mutually reinforcing.[27]

The US role in the Arab Middle East is characterised by duality. The US is an essential provider of regional security but is also viewed, in both public and political circles, with a mixture of distrust, fear and hatred. Concerns over the parachuting of Western ideals and practices, a perceived uncritical support for Israel and a negative view of the intervention in Iraq have fuelled this perception. US efforts towards political reform in the Middle East through the Middle East Partnership Initiative (MEPI) and President Bush's suggestion for the G8 to facilitate democratic transition in the region have been rejected by Arab governments both because they introduce the unwelcome notion of the 'greater' Middle East and more broadly through fear that they represent a Trojan horse for Western ideals and values. On the supply side, attempts at engagement by the US and Europe have been weakened by a lack of coordination or integration among stakeholders. Luethold (Chapter 5) also questions whether Western governments would be prepared to accept political reform in the region that could bring to power groups which are overtly hostile to the West.

In Afghanistan, the fall of the Taliban and the international community's very visible commitment to reconstruct the country offered unprecedented hope for a secure and stable state. The rationale behind the approach adopted was to allot specific responsibilities to given donors for different pillars of the SSR process. In reality, Sedra (Chapter 9) describes an implementation process that has been undermined by duplication, lack of donor and inter-ministerial coordination, a unilateralist approach by external actors to the Afghan government and a fundamental underestimation of the necessary resources. Taking one specific example, Sedra's description of the two externally sponsored initiatives on demilitarisation of ex-combatants in Afghanistan not coordinating their activities due to methodological differences seems a frightening example of fiddling while Rome burns.

It remains unclear whether an international actor can successfully marry the roles of security provider and agent of security sector reform and reconstruction. Afghanistan and Iraq currently fall into a category where neither security nor development goals are being met. As Sedra (Chapter 9) points out, an inherent contradiction is illustrated by the two conflicting dimensions of US strategy in Afghanistan. The US military's war against the Taliban and other spoiler groups has been predicated on alliances with regional powerbrokers that have provided the services of their militia forces in exchange for cash. However, this has empowered some of the very same warlords who have fostered the drug trade as well as other forms of criminality and proved most antithetical to meaningful centralised government. In Iraq, similar issues pertain to the various militia groupings, although Slocombe (Chapter 10) suggests that the planned transformation of these bodies into regionally-based security organisations, if falling under legitimate national and regional political authority, could actually provide a counterweight to any abuses of central authority.

Conclusion

In conclusion, if the overall reckoning from the contributions to this volume, both retrospectively and looking forward, is more negative than positive, then this can also be read as a sign that the theory and practice of SSR, and the particular challenges of security sector reconstruction in post-conflict states, may be converging in understanding good (and bad) practice. There would certainly seem to be a link between the contested nature of the SSR concept and the uneven application of SSR strategies in the policy realm. In Europe the architecture is in place but better coordination is required in the conceptualisation and implementation of SSR. Within West Africa an emerging sub-regional security framework requires significant additional political will at the national level in order to contribute more deeply to sub-regional security while in the Middle East it is a positive sign that a debate on SSR and security sector governance issues is emerging at all.

It is naïve to imagine that conceptually sound, practically achievable, consensus-based and regionally-coordinated solutions will be found to the type of challenges described in this volume. Although not a central focus of this book, how the international community's response(s) to international terrorism in the aftermath of 11 September 2001 (9/11) have coloured the international development agenda is a pervasive issue. National as well as international security issues remain very sensitive and it is therefore important that shortcomings are highlighted and analysed. The contributors to this volume have provided general and more specific policy recommendations which should serve as entry points for further work. The empirical evidence that is starting to emerge offers real opportunities for the application of lessons learned and the development of better practice in the implementation of reform and reconstruction efforts. The stakes at play, and the consequent need for effective reform and reconstruction interventions, is perhaps the clearest message to emerge from the contributions to this volume.

Notes

[1] The regions and country case studies considered in this volume have been selected because they correspond to the priority geographical areas for the work programme of the Geneva Centre for the Democratic Control of Armed Forces (DCAF).

[2] For a detailed discussion of this issue see Caparini, M. 'Security Sector Reform and NATO and EU Enlargement', in Hänggi, H. and Winkler, T. (eds.) *Challenges of Security Sector Governance* (LIT: Münster, 2003), pp. 55-84.

[3] For a discussion based on first hand experience of defence reform in the region see Karkoszka, A. 'Defence Reforms for Democracy in Eastern Europe from 1989-2002', in Bryden, A. and Fluri, P. (eds.) *Security Sector Reform: Institutions, Society and Good Governance* (Nomos: Baden-Baden, 2003), pp. 47-65

[4] DCAF is currently conducting a major research project focusing on West Africa from the perspective of security sector governance, including sixteen country case studies by authors from the sub-region. Bryden, A., N'Diaye, B. & Olonisakin, F. *The Challenges of Security Sector Governance in West Africa* (LIT: Münster) will be published in spring 2005.

[5] The ECOWAS parliament and DCAF have initiated a project to develop an ECOWAS version of the DCAF-IPU *Handbook on Parliamentary Oversight of the Security Sector: Principles, Mechanisms and Practices.* This represents the first step in a long term, programmatic DCAF commitment to parliamentary capacity building in West Africa. For an overview of DCAF's work in Africa see: <http://www.dcaf.ch/awg/Factsheet.pdf>

[6] In this area, the opening of the Kofi Annan International Peacekeeper Training Centre (KAIPTC), in January 2004, represents an important development. The Centre, backed by significant international support, is geared to provide education, training and research on peace operations in Africa. See <http://www.kaiptc.org>

[7] Reporting on discussions at a recent international workshop organised by DCAF on 'the Challenges of Security Sector Governance in the Middle East', an article in the Daily Star, one of the most widely distributed online and print journals in the Arab world noted 'our

military-security establishments have not experienced the same sort of analysis, policy reforms and practical transformations that have already started to be felt in sectors such as
the economy, education, technology, water management, and even parliamentarianism
and politics....if such assessment and transformation are done in an orderly, responsible
manner, everyone benefits, including the military, which can carry out its important tasks
more efficiently and with greater support from its citizenry'. For the complete version of
this article see:
<http://www.dailystar.com.lb/article.asp?edition_ID=10&article_ID=6215&categ_id=5>

[8]   Karawan, Ibrahim, A. 'Security Sector Reform and Retrenchment in the Middle East'; in
        Hänggi, H., Winkler, T. *Challenges*, p. 247.

[9]   According to Buzan 'a security complex involves a group of states whose primary secu-
        rity concerns link together sufficiently closely that their national securities cannot realisti-
        cally be considered apart from one another'. Quoted in Baylis, J. 'International and
        Global Security', in Baylis, J. and Smith, S. *The Globalization of World Politics* (Oxford
        University Press, 2001), p.260. Writing from a neo-realist perspective, Buzan saw the end
        of the Cold War as creating a decentralised international security system that divided the
        world into regional security complexes characterised by 'patterns of amity and enmity that
        are substantially confined within some geographic area'. Buzan, B. *People, States and
        Fear* (Harvester 1991), p. 190.

[10]   Cawthra, G. and Luckham, R. *Governing Insecurity* (Zed, 2003), p. 325.

[11]   Greene, O. 'Security Sector Reform, Conflict Prevention and Regional Perspectives';
        Journal of Security Sector Management Volume 1, No. 1, (March 2003), p. 7.

[12]   Wallace, W. 'Rescue or retreat? The nation state in Western Europe'; *Political Studies* 42,
        1994, p. 20.

[13]   Cawthra, G., Luckham, R. *Governing*, p. 25.

[14]   Cawthra, G., Luckham, R. *Governing*, p. 319.

[15]   Greene, O. *Security*, pp. 8-9.

[16]   For a compelling discussion on security sector transformation see Cooper, N. and Pugh,
        M. 'Security-Sector Transformation in Post-Conflict Societies'; *The Conflict, Security
        and Development Group*, Working papers Number 5, (February 2002). Available at:
        <http://csdg.kcl.ac.uk/Publications/assets/PDF%20files/Working%20paper%20number%
        205.pdf>

[17]   Cooper, N., Pugh, M. *Security*, p. 58.

[18]   Hendrickson, D. 'A Review of Security Sector Reform'; *The Conflict, Security and De-
        velopment Group*, Working papers Number 1 (1999). Available at:
        <http://csdg.kcl.ac.uk/Publications/assets/PDF%20files/Working%20paper%20number%
        201.pdf >.

[19]   For example: DfID, Foreign & Commonwealth Office and the Ministry of Defence, *Secu-
        rity Sector Reform Policy Brief*, (2003), p. 6; GTZ, *Security Sector Reform in Developing
        Countries*, (2000), p.33. Document available at <http://www.gtz.de/security-
        sector/download/GTZ_SSR_English.pdf>; UNDP, *Justice and Security Sector Reform.
        BCPR's Programmatic Approach*, (2002), pp. 13-14; OECD-DAC, *Security System Re-
        form and Governance. Policy and Good Practice*, (2004), p. 18. Document available at
        <http://www.oecd.org/dataoecd/8/39/31785288.pdf>.

[20]   These points have been drawn from Hutchful, E. 'A Civil Society Perspective', in Lala, A. and Fitz-Gerald, A.M. (eds.) *Providing Security for People: Security Sector Reform in Africa* (GFN-SSR, 2003), pp. 35-38.

[21]   Hutchful, E. *Civil*, p. 38.

[22]   For a useful overview of the darker side of civil society activities see 'Sins of the Secular Missionaries', *The Economist* (29 January 2000).

[23]   Cawthra, G., Luckham, R. *Governing*, p. 321.

[24]   Cooper, N., Pugh, M. *Security*, p. 10.

[25]   Fitz-Gerald, A.M., 'Linkages between Security Sector Reform and Peacekeeping Intelligence'; *Journal of Security Sector Management* Volume 1, No. 1, (March 2003), p. 2.

[26]   Karkoszka, in Bryden, A., & Fluri, P. *Security*, p. 318.

[27]   Cawthra, G., Luckham, R. *Governing*, p. 325.

List of Contributors

Alan BRYDEN is Coordinator of the Think Tank at the Geneva Centre for the Democratic Control of Armed Forces (DCAF).

Dr Michael BRZOSKA is Head of the Research Department at the Bonn International Centre for Conversion (BICC).

Marina CAPARINI is Senior Fellow at the Geneva Centre for the Democratic Control of Armed Forces (DCAF).

Chris DONNELLY is Senior Fellow at the Defence Academy of the United Kingdom.

Dr Adedeji EBO is Senior Fellow at the Geneva Centre for the Democratic Control of Armed Forces (DCAF).

Dr J. 'Kayode FAYEMI is Director at the Centre for Democracy and Development (Nigeria).

Dr Heiner HÄNGGI is Assistant Director and Head of Think Tank at the Geneva Centre for the Democratic Control of Armed Forces (DCAF).

Dr Andreas HEINEMANN-GRÜDER is Senior Research Associate at the Bonn International Centre for Conversion (BICC).

David LAW is Senior Fellow at the Geneva Centre for the Democratic Control of Armed Forces (DCAF).

Arnold LUETHOLD is Senior Fellow at the Geneva Centre for the Democratic Control of Armed Forces (DCAF).

Mark SEDRA is Research Associate at the Bonn International Centre for Conversion (BICC).

Walter B. SLOCOMBE is a member of Caplin & Drysdale, Attorneys, Washington, D.C.; former Under Secretary of Defense for Policy, US Department of Defense (1994-2001).

ABOUT DCAF

The Geneva Centre for the Democratic Control of Armed Forces (DCAF) was established in October 2000 on the initiative of the Swiss government. The Centre's mission is to encourage and support States and non-State governed institutions in their efforts to strengthen democratic and civilian oversight of armed and security forces, and to promote security sector reform in accordance with democratic standards. To implement its objectives, DCAF:

- collects information and undertakes research in order to identify problems, to gather experience from lessons learned, and to propose best practices in the field of democratic governance and reform of the security sector (which includes armed forces, police, paramilitary forces, internal security services, intelligence agencies, border guards, etc., as well as parliamentary and governmental oversight structures, and civil society groups);

- provides specific expertise and support on the ground to all interested parties, in particular governments, parliaments, international organisations, non-governmental organisations, and academic circles. Particular emphasis is placed on encouraging and supporting the principle of "self-help" and on putting the experience of countries that have already gone through transition processes at the disposal of those States which have more recently embarked on the process of reform.

The work of DCAF is primarily aimed at the Euro-Atlantic region with an emerging work programme focusing on Africa and the Middle East.

DCAF's key areas of analytical work include: standards, norms, and best practices in the field of democratic governance of the security sector; theory and practice of security sector reform (including defence reform); parliamentary and civilian oversight of armed forces, police, internal security forces, intelligence, and border guards; the legal aspect of security sector governance (including documenting relevant legislation); civil society building as a means of strengthening democratic security sector governance; security sector reform as a means of ensuring human security, sustainable development, and post-conflict reconstruction; challenges of security sector governance in regions beyond the Euro-Atlantic area, especially Africa and the Middle East; emerging issues in security sector governance (e.g. the treatment of women and children; mechanisms of civilian control of nuclear weapons, etc).

DCAF's key operational projects include: providing advice and practical assistance to governments, parliaments and international organisations in the field of security sector reform; interacting with parliamentarians and civil servants to promote accountability and effective oversight of the security sector; funding and training expert staffers in support of parliamentary oversight structures, such as parliamentary defence and security committees; assisting in drafting legislation related to defence and security; providing advice and practical guidance to governments on ways to organise professional and accountable border security structures; providing advice to governments on demobilisation and the retraining of down-sized forces; assisting governments in encouraging openness in defence budgeting, procurement, and planning.

DCAF is an international foundation under Swiss law. DCAF's Foundation Council is made up of 46 governments including Switzerland, 41 other Euro-Atlantic States, 3 African States, and the Canton of Geneva.[*] DCAF's International Advisory Board is composed of a group of over 70 experts in the various fields of DCAF's activity. DCAF's staff includes some 60 employees representing about 30 different nationalities.

The Swiss Federal Department of Defence, Civil Protection, and Sports and the Federal Department of Foreign Affairs are the largest contributors to DCAF's budget.

Detailed information on the Centre can be found at: www.dcaf.ch.

---

[*] Albania, Armenia, Austria, Azerbaijan, Belarus, Belgium, Bosnia and Herzegovina, Bulgaria, Canada, Côte d'Ivoire, Croatia, Czech Republic, Denmark, Estonia, Finland, France, Georgia, Germany, Greece, Hungary, Ireland, Italy, Latvia, Lithuania, Luxembourg, Macedonia, Moldova, Netherlands, Nigeria, Norway, Poland, Portugal, Romania, Russia, Serbia and Montenegro, Slovak Republic, Slovenia, South Africa, Spain, Sweden, Switzerland, Turkey, Ukraine, United Kingdom, United States of America, and the Canton of Geneva.

Geneva Centre for the Democratic Control of Armed Forces (DCAF)

Heiner Hänggi; Theodor H. Winkler (Eds.)
Challenges of Security Sector Governance

The war in Iraq in spring 2003 was a further indication of the 'resecuritisation' of international relations triggered by the terrorist attacks of September 11, 2001. However, the new (or renewed) primacy of security will be of a rather different nature as compared to the Cold War period. The underlying assumption of the essays in this volume is that security issues will increasingly be approached from a governance perspective and that, in this context, the internal dimension of security governance – security sector governance – is an issue whose rapidly growing importance has not yet been duly recognised.

2003, 312 S., 23,90 €, br., ISBN 3-8258-7158-4

LIT Verlag Münster – Berlin – Hamburg – London – Wien
Grevener Str./Fresnostr. 2 48159 Münster
Tel.: 0251 – 62 032 22 – Fax: 0251 – 23 19 72
e-Mail: vertrieb@lit-verlag.de – http://www.lit-verlag.de

Marina Caparini; Otwin Marenin (Eds.)
Transforming Police in Central and Eastern Europe
Process and Progress

The issue of police reform in countries in transition from state
socialism toward more democratic forms of governance has risen
to practical prominence in recent years. The collapse of the Soviet
Union initiated fundamental changes in aspirations, ideologies and
governing practices among former members of the socialist camp.
Reforming policing systems which had served primarily to protect
the party-states from their opponents into systems which serve and
protect civic society has come to be seen as an essential prerequisite
and concomitant of the democratisation process in transitional
countries. The chapters in this book describe what has happened to
the policing systems in 14 countries in Central and eastern Europe;
what reforms in ideology, organisation, policies and practices have
been undertaken; what has changed in the way policing is done;
and assessment of whether the policing system has moved closer
toward democratic policing. In combining descriptions of reforms and
assessments of whether reforms have moved policing systems toward
more democratic forms, the book provides a comparative overview of
what has been achieved since 1989 and what has been learned so far
about how to reform policing systems along democratic lines. Such
lessons offer insights for further reform in transitional countries and
for Western democracies as well, and we hope will stimulate more
theoretical discussions of the nature and dynamics of policing systems,
state-society relations, and the role of processes of democratisation of
policing systems.

2004, 376 S., 29,90 €, br., ISBN 3-8258-7485-0

LIT Verlag Münster – Berlin – Hamburg – London – Wien
Grevener Str./Fresnostr. 2 48159 Münster
Tel.: 0251 – 62 032 22 – Fax: 0251 – 23 19 72
e-Mail: vertrieb@lit-verlag.de – http://www.lit-verlag.de